FROM BAGGAGE
TO LUGGAGE

Unpacking the things that weigh you down

Mark Nixon

More Peace Press

ISBN: 978-1-7377267-0-8

Cover design by: Jonathan Silverberg
Edited by: Gary Smailes
Printed in the United States of America

To Steve McAllister

my first of many wonderful mentors

and

To my wife Carla

whose great support made this book possible

and

To the thousands of people who shared

their fear, pain and mistaken perspectives with me,

in these pages I have attempted to describe

what you experienced and how you recovered.

CONTENTS

PART 1 - WHAT IS BAGGAGE?

1. TWO LIVES DERAILED BY BAGGAGE

The ravine swing was a popular pastime in the neighborhood. James and Jessica both loved the swing and would sometimes ride it together. However, that all ended when the rope broke and both of them got hurt. James broke his leg and Jessica injured her back. Unfortunately, their parents were not well equipped to care for and support their children with their traumatic injuries and recovery. James' mother was a nervous person who was often lost in her own thoughts and worries. James' father owned a small business and worked long hours. Jessica's parents were even less equipped to support their bed-ridden daughter. Jessica's mother was not very nurturing and she would often say, "my mother never coddled me and I turned out OK, so I don't see any reason to spoil you." Her husband worked in a factory many miles away, so he was rarely home to interact with the kids.

With little help to understand that what they experienced was a freak accident and they can overcome their injuries, life for both James and Jessica took on a new course of avoidance, self-criticism, negative consequences and bad luck. As a result, James and Jessica each viewed the accident as the event that ruined their lives.

While James' broken leg healed poorly and gave him a slight limp, he could not run distances without pain. He was now teased about being a slow poke and a whiner if he mentioned the pain in his leg. Jessica was also not so fortunate, her back sustained some nerve damage that caused pain when she would move too quick or play too hard. Due to these near constant reminders both were less likely to play with others because they could not keep up or avoid the pain. Between the lengthy recovery and lingering symptoms, James lost his exuberance for play and the outdoors and became fearful and insecure about his leg and his inability to run and play sports. Jessica's once bubbly personality was now replaced for the gloomy personality like her mom and she began a new habit criticizing herself for being too delicate, dumb and clumsy to do basic chores or play.

James began to hate recess and P.E. at school since nobody wanted him on their team, so he would opt to walk or read instead. While he continued to be a fan of sports, he avoided playing any for most of his life.

Jessica lost most of her friends since she could not or would not play like the others. She began thinking to herself that she was stupid, dumb or too lazy to play. She did learn to sew like her mom and do well in school, but she never saw herself as accomplished at either one.

Eventually, James and Jessica went to different schools and lost touch. James' passion for sports continued to grow by following teams and players and reading about their lives. After college Jack landed a job with a good company and continued to avoid most things physical and if it wasn't for his interest in sports he may not have ever married. He met a young woman that was also a sports fan and they eventually married and started a family. They shared their joint passion watching their son playing sports. Jack rarely felt the pain in his leg anymore, but the habit of avoiding physical activity was now baked in and even he had forgotten why. Jessica graduated from college and became a chemical engineer. However, no matter how well she performed, she would view it as a failure. She met someone special through a co-worker and was soon married and eventually had daughter. Sadly, she was soon less excited about her marriage and her daughter's arrival than sewing. The solitude of sewing was the one thing she enjoyed most.

2. BAGGAGE VERSUS LUGGAGE

Good things that happened to us in the past are often thought of as fond memories. Bad things that happened to us are what I call **baggage**. Baggage weighs us down, keeps us from enjoying ourselves, motivates us to do things we would rather not do and haunts us like a bad movie. While we can't change the past, we can put it into a more productive perspective, so it no longer has a destructive hold on us.

We are always recording what is happening to us both consciously and unconsciously. Our stored past experiences have a lot to do with the way we experience our days. If our memories are predominately happy, encouraging and pleasant then both our view of our past and our tendency to approach our day and the future will tend to be positive. The opposite is true if our memories are predominately unhappy, discouraging and unpleasant. In this situation our view of our past and our tendency to approach our day and the future will be negatively influenced.

Many of us are burdened by our past. Regardless of what we have achieved, we find ourselves unable to shake certain negative impressions and feelings. However, there is hope. No matter what you have done or what has happened to you. There is hope for you! No matter how many consequences you have experienced and are still experiencing, things can improve. So, if you are in the habit of telling yourself that things will never get better. I am here to tell you that there is hope for these things to change.

How do I know?

I have lived it and I have seen it in countless others. I have experienced the change from awful consequences. I have been able to turn my life into one of great assets, where my past does not haunt me.

At various times in my life I too have carried a great amount of baggage. In my pre-teen and early teenage years, I had serious drug and delinquency problems, as a young adult I experienced two failed marriages, and years later one of my adult children took his own life when he was just thirty. I have been haunted by each of these events and at times it has nearly suffocated me with agony, fear, pain, and shame. Many of us have been there and felt the great weight and experienced the great obstacles it presents. It is not necessary for it to continue because things can improve greatly. If you tell yourself this is not possible for you, you are deceiving yourself.

In each of the debilitating experiences of my life I ended up taking the lemons and making lemonade, but I had help. Without help I would simply have stayed a basket case wrapped in bitterness, fear, anger and guilt. Instead I am healthy, happy, successful and grateful to be who I am.

I would not wish the painful events of my life on anyone, but I know from experience they in of themselves do not destroy the option for an amazing life going forward. The only way they can have that much power is if we do not put these events in their proper perspective. Doing so, often means getting a little uncomfortable. We must stick to the facts of our situations rather than a version we would rather tell our friends, family and ourselves.

In my life, at each set back, I was told by various mentors that to recover I would have to keep an open mind and be willing to try new ideas to possibly ease the pain and heartache that was crushing me.

Do yourself a favor and stop listening to the voices that say there is no hope. They are not true. It is very likely that you are simply buried under an overwhelming load of baggage collected over the span of your lifetime. Let me help you begin, restart or continue the journey of unpacking your baggage and regaining your life.

Baggage

When my oldest two boys were very young and we were all sitting at the dinner table eating dessert my oldest asked, "Momma' why do we always have cherry pie?"

I just figured it was my wife's favorite and that was the answer I expected.

"It is your father's favorite," she replied.

"No it isn't," I added. "My favorite is apple."

Cherry is fine and I enjoyed every time it was served, but I probably never ate so much cherry pie as I did in those early years. This was not a big deal, but this mistaken impression could have been about anything.

Have you ever noticed how easy it is to get things wrong?

Many of us tend to forget that we get corrected everyday about something we thought was a fact and it turns out we were entirely wrong. If we are talking about the location of the scissors or our spouse's favorite pie it is not very important, but when it is about whether our parents loved us or if a close friend maliciously betrayed us then the results can be disastrous. Imagine that the memory you most dread didn't quite happen the way you think. It happens all the time.

Yet when we get the impression of something that is very upsetting, it is very easy to not put a lot of energy into fact checking, much less go talk to those who can tell us the real story or at least a more accurate one. Most of us are not that motivated to inquire politely when we're already reeling with hurt, anger or fear.

We often get the wrong idea about something and occasionally it is about something really significant. Every time it is about something significant and we do not independently verify the facts, we set ourselves on a path of creating heartache. We can end up harboring bad feelings and change the course of our entire life over a mistaken impression. Unfortunately, this happens to all of us and for some of us it happens a lot.

We are all instinctive learners. If we experience something and it turns out the way we like, then we typically are motivated to take note and repeat the perceived actions that brought about the desired result. If the outcome is unpleasant then we are typically motivated to avoid the perceived actions that brought about the result.

Whether we are conscious of it or not we are constantly assessing the results of our actions and making judgments about whether to repeat or avoid them in the future. Unfortunately, we don't always make the correct observations about what brought about the results or our experiences. Therefore, armed with bad data, we make incorrect conclusions about what it takes to avoid things that are unpleasant and to repeat those things that are pleasant.

Take, for instance, a young adult car driver who may unintentionally run a stop sign or red light and nothing happens. No close call and thus the shortsighted conclusion this driver could make is that you really don't have to stop at stop signs and red lights. Nothing happens to me whether I pay attention to them or not. Of course, if a driver with those results actually applies this conclusion as a lesson learned then sooner or later somebody is going to be seriously hurt.

Most of us can read this story and easily see the flawed conclusion this car driver came to accept. However, we all make conclusions about the reactions and results we get every day. The accuracy rate of our conclusions is significantly based upon our perceptions of the circumstances. This can happen because we were not paying close attention when the events occurred, or we might not like to admit we were doing what we were doing at the time, or it may be possible we did not understand what occurred and we simply guessed what occurred based upon our observations.

Consider how this affects young children. By the very fact that a young person has limited experience in the world and with relationships they can often lack the understanding of the events that most adults would easily understand. So, a young person can come up with even wilder conclusions about the events they experience.

If they encounter a violent event while on a merry go round they may conclude that playing on the merry go round was the cause and the way to avoid violence is to stay away from merry go rounds. Whether the violent event was an accident for another child, getting hurt or even an unrelated event like a bomb going off nearby. Any of these high impact experiences can set the stage for the conclusion that playing on the merry go round made this happen.

If this child describes this to another person, especially a parent, then often the parent will help them put the event they experienced into their proper perspective. "Yes, you were on the merry go round when the event occurred, but one had little to do with the other and there is little to no reason to avoid the merry go round." If the child never speaks of the event and their conclusion, or if they do and the ones around them never help them put the events they experienced into their proper perspective, then it is likely that the conclusion can be a lifelong lesson learned. More importantly, the child may not be aware of this conclusion and simply absorb it into their everyday view of the world.

Adults can just as easily get things wrong and come to incorrect conclusions and if they never speak of these conclusions. If they do and the ones around them do not help them put the events into their proper perspective, then the experience and their conclusions have the potential to become lifelong lessons learned.

If we never learn to consider other perspectives other than those we personally experience, then we set ourselves up for a life full of inaccurate lessons. If we get into the habit of spending all of our time with people who think and perceive things the way we do, then we can also adopt many inaccurate lessons.

This is how people can become convinced that people from other countries are all ignorant, college is only for smart people, or that going to a hospital is a death sentence.

Intelligent, admired and successful people come up with in-accurate conclusions all the time. If they never talk about them or only share them with people that agree with the inaccur-ate conclusion, then flawed life lessons are established. We all do this to some extent, because we can't catch everything and make sure we put it into its proper perspective. Yet, we can begin to turn the tide of ill-conceived conclusions and life les-sons around one-by- one.

Sometimes it is not entirely our fault. Unless we were raised around adults who taught us to not jump to conclusions and to verify the facts before making any significant decisions or judgments, then we may be creating a great deal of pain and unhappiness for ourselves by simply doing what we were taught.

We all have some amount of baggage: some have more, some have less. The more baggage we have, then the more burdens we have that keep us from having a peaceful and productive life. I didn't say, "The more we have the more burden we feel and that keeps us from having a peaceful and productive life", because not all of us allow ourselves to consciously experience our emotions. Some have given up on letting themselves feel their emotions so they do not have to feel the unpleasant ones. However, one of the costly results of this method of coping is that you also shut yourself off from the pleasant emotions as well.

This is a very common way of coping. It is not a very construct-ive or healthy method, but to the person doing it can provide a sense of relief. Unfortunately, too many of us use this as a long-term method of coping.

Below is a list of common results of baggage:

- Resentment of childhood friends, family, co-workers, public figures or God
- Persistent fear of past troubles reoccurring
- Regularly reliving the pain of past disappoint-ments, losses and heartaches

- Blaming most troubles on others or institutions
- Repeating significant mistakes again and again
- Resentment of authority
- Inability to be close to family or friends
- Neglecting health issues
- Judgment of people, places and things on trace amounts of data
- Not willing to acknowledge clear problems
- Not willing to seek help even when problems are acknowledged
- Excessive behavior (sexually, thrill seeking, addictions, abuse towards others)
- Consumed with fear, rage, hate, conspiracies, etc., to the exclusion of loved ones
- Poor self-image (body, intellect, professionally, personally)
- Little or no self-love
- Constantly perceiving a crisis exists and responding to it.

Any of the above are enough to derail us. When we have multiple behaviors in the list it gets even more complicated. If a person has them all, there is a lot of work to be done, but it can be resolved.

If we have made a lifestyle of behaving in this baggage creating and collecting way, then a turnaround will have to include a change in our lifestyle to get different results. There is a saying often attributed to Albert Einstein, "the definition of insanity is doing the same thing over and over expecting different results". Different results require different actions on our part. If you are allowing old memories to limit, haunt, or discourage you then you deserve better.

While at first the meaning for both baggage and luggage appear to be the same, they are not. This appearance likely accounts for these terms being used interchangeably.

The distinction is that **luggage** refers to the containers in which we pack our travel belongings. **Baggage** refers to the total of our personal travel belongings that we carry with us. This distinction is probably why baggage picked up the additional meaning we often hear about a person's negative past. We are all traveling through this life and yet some do it much less burdened than others. This book will describe how we adopt the practice of accumulating baggage and rarely take the time or go to the trouble to unpack. We will also identify steps we can all take to shed that mountain of baggage and to refrain from needlessly accumulating anymore.

bag·gage noun
    1. personal belongings packed in suitcases for traveling; luggage.
    2. past experiences or long-held ideas regarded as burdens and impediments:
       · the emotional baggage I'm hauling around
       · the party jettisoned its traditional ideological baggage

lug·gage noun
    1. suitcases or other bags in which to pack personal belongings for traveling.

One thing that is common with the two terms is that they are both involved with traveling. Depending upon your upbringing you may have taken trips as a family or have been sent on trips to visit family or just for pleasure. As we grow older we also may travel for work in addition to vacations. Visiting family, especially when we get older may be pleasurable or maybe much more like work or worse.

Traveling can also have a much different association for us if we rarely traveled and only did so when something unpleasant occurred. Families without the tradition of traveling or the means to travel often only strike out from home when forced to by having to move or visiting ill or grieving family.

While any travel is often exciting for children. The memory of traveling typically focuses on any event we at the time experienced as significant. These could range from enjoying the open road, the smells, the shared experience of traveling or it might focus on a punishment, a disappointment, or being exposed to others who are ill, sad or mean to us.

From a very young age we are traveling whether we ever leave town or not because we are traveling through the time of our life. Much like vacationers who collect souvenirs from the locations visited, we also collect souvenirs from the various events we experience during the course of the day.

Simple types of souvenir commonly used many years ago were travel stickers that could be applied to either luggage or the windows of a car. These stickers often reflected a location such as a city, state or park or even a type of recreation that might be well known. The State stickers often showed the shape of the State and where key cities and attractions were located, but it might also show the state bird or motto. Parks would show off their well-known features. These stickers were like badges showing anyone who saw them where you have been. The more stickers you displayed on your car window or luggage, the more well-traveled you were.

So, in some cases the memories from our travels were about the destination and other times it was more about how we felt about it when we were there. The same goes for our experiences when we are simply traveling through life.

We may have significant memories about a location or event, but most often we are most impacted by how much emotion we felt during the experience. The more intense the emotional experience the greater the likelihood it will become a long-term memory. Great positive memories experienced with intense pleasant emotions often produce pleasant or fond memories for a lifetime. The negative and very challenging memories along with intense unpleasant emotions can make up those experiences that can still haunt us as adults whether we consciously remember the details or not.

When those very intense negative events are experienced and we do not have a good grasp of the facts, if not corrected we can spend a lifetime of avoiding things that are unrelated to what happened and why we had such a strong emotional response. Whatever your memories and/or the nature of your experiences they can be improved upon. This might sound impossible since we typically think of the past as being the past and that we can't un-ring a bell. Yet, despite what you believe or have been told we can unpack this baggage of incomplete and inaccurate memories and the emotions we felt along with them, and put them in to their proper perspective. Once unpacked, our luggage can be stored away and we are free to go about our lives less burdened and with a greater sense of peace.

Baggage Dynamics:
We all have a backlog.
We are all constantly acquiring new baggage.
We experience our baggage in distinct areas of our lives.
We have a natural tendency to solidify the burden of our baggage by expecting things to be bad and looking for things to be bad. When we find it, we use it as reinforcement that our baggage is a part of our wise philosophy.
Most of us have been recording memories our whole life. There are some conditions, which impede our ability to make memories, and then there are others who can remember every single day and what they experienced. Most of us however, selectively remember a sampling of events, smells, sights, sounds, emotions as well as what we were thinking at the time. These memories now impact on our relationships with the people, places and things around us. These may include our family, friends, strangers, co-workers, employees, employers, clients, clubs, associations, support groups, or even something spiritual.
This recording has been running all our lives yet what makes us remember certain things and not others?
Theories now exist based upon research that we tend to learn/remember things about experiences when emotions run high.

So, it would stand to reason those moments of great excitement as well as moments of great upset would be more likely to be remembered or more significant in our storage banks of experiences.

When things happen around us that are unpleasant but are familiar we often can temper our reaction due to the fact that we have experienced this before. Yet when we experience events for the first time we can even as adults be surprised or even shocked by the event.

Experience comes with time, yet children have long periods in their younger life when everything has a much better chance of being a new experience. Adults often relish the chance to expose a young person to a new discovery. Yet when the experience is painful and unfamiliar for a very young person, it is not fully understood and they are forced to reconcile the experience through the lens of a very young and inexperienced mind. As a result, it is no wonder that so many issues can stem from our childhood years.

A young child being in a position to try an adult activity they are unable to accomplish has probably amused us all. Wearing adult shoes, reaching far above their height, climbing out on a limb and not being able to get down, or eating too much of a good thing. So, while these are probably not going to be significant, just imagine the impact of a yelling parent that is three to five times your size and weight. Then if you are physically harmed as well, the potential for not understanding the situation is high and having to process the event from the inexperienced perspective of a very young child can lead to harmful memories. It might be your conclusion they are mad because you said, "hi". So maybe not speaking seems like a good practice. Maybe someone leaves and you either come to the unfortunate conclusion or are carelessly told you are the cause and now you have the weight of this great loss on your young shoulders.

Some examples of events we might easily misunderstand as a young child: parents fighting, getting hurt on a swing set, getting rejected on the playground, having to move away, land-lords or creditors coming to the door demanding money, a parent's illness or injury, a parent's mental illness or addiction, Mom and Dad separating or divorce or a family member dying. So even by the time we have become a teenager we have been recording for over a dozen years. Saving all the more extreme experiences and drawing conclusions and lessons from many of them and some of them will be incorrect. This is the back-log we carry with us even from a very young age. Imagine how long an adult has been recording and how many potential things they have wrong.

So, the likelihood that we have misinterpreted things is pretty high. We all have experienced this when recounting a story in front of our parents or a sibling and finding out that we have recalled the facts incorrectly. These misunderstandings can be about anything some of which are of little consequence or they can be quite significant. When they are important they can have a lasting effect that unless revisited and set straight can lead us down the path of being grossly misinformed and pos-sibly misled by our memories. It is not uncommon to be very sure about something, that turns out to be not true. Some-times we are fortunate to have reliable witnesses we can call on for straightening out these past events, but for some of us often there is no one we can call on or we choose to not ask.

Understanding what happened, or what possibly happened, is not as important as to coming to accept how we walk away from the experience.

Let's assume that after an encounter with a person in author-ity we felt rejected and ostracized. After the meeting we may replay the events repeatedly in our head planning to make sure to avoid any future rejections. It really doesn't matter if we were rejected originally or not. It may have been that during the original meeting the person had been preoccupied and we took their standoffish nature as a rejection. We still have that impression that this is what occurred.

While the facts are great to have if they are retrievable, but many times they are not available. Yet this does not have to stand in the way of us developing a better understanding of these significant events in our lives.

This especially comes into play when we think we must speak with someone in order to resolve an issue we have bothering us. When these people die, the opportunities for a conversation are gone. However, this does not mean we can't come to terms with the issues we have. There is no obstacle that cannot be overcome when it comes to dealing with past issues in our lives except when we are not willing to revisit it.

All baggage can be converted into luggage. While past events can't be erased from our memories they can be put into their proper perspective so that they no longer consume us or control how we act and feel today.

3. LOST BAGGAGE

Most of us learn of ways to insulate ourselves from the things that cause us pain. This can be a result of many repeated incidents, a single event or even something we observed that happened to someone else. We all have painful memories of opportunities lost, failed relationships, tragedy, poor treatment from others or unmet expectations.

These methods we use often mask the painful memories from our consciousness or at least shift our focus so we don't have to relive those unpleasant memories. Most of us want to avoid feeling uncomfortable and we can be quite inventive, sometimes very unconsciously to protect ourselves. Yet, these methods of coping, while they may give us the impression of improving or masking our past baggage. Like the leftovers hidden from view in the refrigerator from a glance it may look clean, but upon closer inspection we can tell something is not right. The following are some of the more common methods of coping we use to try and forget the unpleasant things that have happened to us.

Can't

One the most common ways we mask painful things from our view is by convincing ourselves that we are unable to remember or revisit them to resolve them. How we describe things to ourselves and others can both reflect and mold how we think about things. For instance, if we are in a discussion and someone asks us about a very unpleasant topic and fairly common response is, "I can't talk about that."

Most of the time when we say we can't or cannot speak of something we do not mean it literally. What we typically mean is that we will not discuss it. However, by using the term can't or cannot we have made it sound like we are incapable of revisiting this painful topic. If we tell ourselves, we can't do something long enough we will begin to believe. It is rarely the case where we cannot discuss a topic, but we will not discuss as a matter of choice. It is this choice that is often masks our baggage, even from ourselves.

While there are definitely times when the word can't is correct

- I can't lift this by myself.
- I can't reach the top shelf.
- I can't see through the fog.

There are many other times when it is very misleading to ourselves and others.

- I can't think - We really can think, but we are having trouble concentrating.
- I can't stop - I can stop for a while, but I pick it back up again.
- I can't live without you - I do not want to live without you.
- I can't drive fifty-five - I do not want to or I am not willing to drive only fifty-five.
- I can't get any satisfaction - I have not been able to get the satisfaction I want.

While the above are fairly harmless and it is likely that most people will know what you mean. Many of us have gotten rather confused in the more mysterious areas of our lives because we have repeated these, "I can't" words over and over to ourselves.

- I can't trust.
- I can't love.
- I can't believe.

In these cases, we usually have something else that goes beyond these statements based upon our experience. Nonetheless, the statements are not true.

I can't trust - We are capable of trust, but we may choose not to because we have experienced a bad breech of our trust and we are not comfortable with taking that risk again. That is fine, but we are making a choice to not trust. Trust is in fact a decision that we can all make despite our past experience. We may choose to try to trust someone or something again even though we know it is a very risky choice.

We may have gotten ourselves in the habit of saying I can't trust this person out of very strong conviction to not be hurt again. Yet, saying it this way "I can't trust", eventually causes us to believe that we are incapable of trust in general, when that is simply not the case. This may be a much harder position to defend or admit to, so to make our position sound stronger we often will use the " I can't trust" to get ourselves off the hook. I can't so therefore I do not have to try or consider the possibility. Which may get some well-meaning person trying to encourage us to trust again off our back. We also know that we like the results of trusting others when it goes well. We all do. The unfortunate thing is that what we put our trust in, will often fall short of our expectations. Sometimes we trust others to do too much, more than they are capable or want to do. But now that we have convinced ourselves that we can't trust then we isolate ourselves from the possible option of trusting again. We make it even worse for ourselves when we free associate with the end of our sentences. What often starts off as:

- I will never trust that person again (Accurate, if we happen to start this way)
- I can't trust that person (The defensive inaccurate version)
- I can't trust anyone (Defensive and free associating)
- I can't trust anything, any person, place or thing (Defensive and paranoid).

We can talk ourselves into anything if we repeat something to ourselves often enough.

Have you ever had a song get stuck in your head? Sure, you have. It may bring back a great memory or feeling and the desire to hold onto that experience and motivates us to keep it alive by repeating it over and over.

Sadly, we can get motivation from our desire to protect ourselves as well. After trusting someone and it not working out it is very understandable that we may be convinced immediately afterwards that we do not want to repeat that mistake again. And to keep ourselves from making that mistake again we may choose to repeat it over and over to ourselves. Maybe out of resolve or maybe out of anger or many other motivations. The point is that we can become convinced of anything if we hear it enough. Even if it is from ourselves.

You might say to yourself, well that is crazy I don't talk to myself. Wrong, we all talk to ourselves. Maybe not out loud, although most of us do this as well. But we all talk to ourselves silently in our head. Most of the time our self-talk is filled with observations, plans, desires, commentary, considerations on what to say to others or processing what others have said to us, but sometimes we go on a path of repeating something to ourselves over and over. Often these repeated statements we would rarely repeat out loud because they would embarrass us or we know they would draw correction from others. Yet, if kept unspoken we often will allow ourselves to repeat them over and over.

When this self-talk becomes repetitive and it is incorrect it can have a very destructive affect upon our perspective. In the case of trust, we can withdraw ourselves into such a risk adverse posture that we are not willing to trust anyone because we have convinced ourselves that we can't. Now fast forward a few weeks, months and maybe years and now this broken record and the choice of not trusting has developed into a hardened lifestyle that yields the results of someone who does not trust anyone or anything.

People who are not trusting of others typically do not make close friends and may not practice good social skills even if they used to at one time in the past. This is especially common when someone has a big shock and they perceive it as a great breech of their trust, such as the loss of a job or the betrayal of a confidence by a friend or family member. These things happen for a variety of reasons and they are rarely malicious. Yet, if we respond as if this is a very personal breech of our trust then we can easily fall into the trap of not trusting for a while. If this posture is coupled with describing to others and to ourselves that we can't trust then soon we will believe it. Worse yet, if we make this perspective more general then this can be the cause of our withdrawal from everyone and everything.

Ever know anyone who just never recovered from a big loss? The loss is real and needs to be grieved and put in its proper perspective. If it is allowed to fester in an inaccurate direction, then the results can be disastrous.

Well-meaning friends and family who try to encourage us when we have gotten this way to get out and do things, reconnect with old friends will eventually stop trying when all we have to say is that we can't. Sometimes we can even convince them. "Yes, it is a shame they just think they can't trust anymore. It is so sad". Sad indeed.

The careless use of the term, "can't", can mask the true nature of our problems. It is rare that we can't trust someone or something, it is that we choose not to. And once we choose not to over and over to the point it becomes our standard reaction to everyone and everything, we have shut ourselves off from everyone and everything and we are puzzled how we got here. We wish we could change, but sadly we have convinced ourselves that we <u>can't</u>.

Denial

Denial is another one of the ways we can mask our baggage from ourselves. It is very easy to underestimate the power of denial. It is one of those coping mechanisms that is also very destructive, since it cuts us off from the reality of our situation or condition. Until we are conscious of a problem there is nothing to address. Likewise, if we choose to be unaware that any problem exists we let ourselves off the hook of having a problem to address.

Sometimes an issue about our situation or our condition is so painful we cannot imagine how it could be true. When someone suddenly dies we often hear loved ones say, "There must be some mistake. My baby can't be dead. He was just fine a little while ago."

Denial can keep us from consciously acknowledging sudden traumas and persistent repeated trauma. These traumas can also be minor, but some reason we don't want to acknowledge the possibility. They can range from the slightest discomfort to the most painful. Some common statements of denial are:

- I have plenty of time to do that assignment.
- I didn't hear anything.
- My dad doesn't mean those things he says, he has a hard time at work.
- My child wouldn't talk back to his teacher.
- My mother loves me just as much as my sister, she just doesn't have enough time for all of us.
- If I were just a better son my mother would not drink.
- As long as I don't tell anyone what my Uncle does to me at night it will be OK.
- My son is just a spirited child; he does not belong in jail. He wouldn't have done that.
- I know my child and he wouldn't lie, you must be confusing him with someone else.
- He really doesn't mean it. If I didn't make him mad he wouldn't beat me.
- I don't think he will really hurt me; I am his wife.
- I know he is just out with the guys; I just wish he would come home before the kids go to bed.
- If I can just get her cleaned up and into bed where she can sleep it off things will be better tomorrow.
- I can stop using anytime, I just don't want to.

Denial is nothing more than a lie. A lie that we tell ourselves to make us feel better because the reality of the situation is not comfortable or too painful for us to acknowledge.

Sometimes we can be familiar with the topic or the facts surrounding a denial, but we can be blinded by our emotional attachment to someone or something. A doctor might fail to acknowledge symptoms in themselves or loved ones. A psychologist might be blind to a serious mental illness of a family member. A spouse might refuse to consider that adultery might be taking place in their marriage. A boy might think it is cool to be mean to his girlfriend. And anyone can believe that the risks they are taking will not result in predictable consequences. This is how people get sick, get speeding tickets, get caught cheating, get pregnant, get arrested and get shunned by their friends and family.

We all are capable of denial and probably engage in it a little on a regular basis. Where denial can cause the most harm is when we allow ourselves to believe that only we know the real facts about anything. Once we discount everyone else in the world, we set ourselves up to deny anything that displeases us. For some of us there are many things that displease us, but acting like they do not exist is not a healthy practice and disconnects us from reality.

When we choose to not hear the input from others we soon lose a firm grip on reality. We all are capable of being swayed. It doesn't matter if you are someone who wins all the arguments you are in, or have an IQ that is off the charts, or that you are older or more experienced. It just does not matter. We are all capable of being wrong. Worse yet we are capable of discounting new information when the new facts before us do not meet our view of the world. This is sometimes called Paradigm Paralysis where we are so used to one way of thinking that we refuse to consider any other possibility.

We can experience this with the certainty that our desired political candidate will win the election. Scientists experience this when certain possibilities are considered not possible, so therefore any indication to the contrary tends to be ignored or dismissed. This was the case for the unknown cause of the stomach ulcer.

For decades the medical community believed that ulcers were caused by stress, spicy foods, and too much acid in the digestive system. Even when cited by two Australian scientists that a bacterium was the cause of ulcers the results were denied because it was widely believed that the acidic environment of the digestive system was too hostile to support any type of organism. Yet continued research supported the finding that a particular bacterium was in fact the cause and the two researchers, Barry Marshall and Robin Warren showed that the bacterium Helicobacter pylori (H. pylori) is the cause of most peptic ulcers and they were awarded the Nobel Prize in Physiology of Medicine in 2005. If the entire world's elite medical scientists can be susceptible to denying new information, so can we.

When we deny facts about our condition or situation we are putting ourselves at a significant disadvantage. When we feel heat with our fingers we pull our fingers back, when we see the word 'poison' we make sure to handle with care, when we see a cliff's edge we take greater care to not fall. However, when it comes to matters of our perceptions of others behavior and the nature of our relationship with them, we can slip into the dangerous practice of self-deception.

If I can simply frame my perception of the situation so I do not have to consider an unpleasant thought being a reality, then why not? Yet to slip into this practice we cut ourselves off from the very warning signs that are present and can alert us that something is wrong.

- I have plenty of time to do that assignment. - Actually, it is due tomorrow and its 8am.
- I didn't hear anything. - I didn't like what I heard, but as disappointing and hurtful it is. They did say it.
- My dad doesn't mean those things he says, he has a hard time at work. - My Dad says mean things to me.

- My child wouldn't talk back to his teacher. I would like to think my child would not talk back to an adult.
- My mother loves me just as much as my sister, she just doesn't have enough time for all of us. - My mother appears to favor my sister over me, I should tell her my feelings are hurt.
- If I were just a better son my mother would not drink. Mom drinks too much.
- As long as I don't tell anyone what my uncle does to me at night it will be OK. - I want to tell someone my uncle is hurting me to make him stop, but I am afraid.
- My son is just a spirited child, he does not belong in jail. He wouldn't have done that. - I am so embarrassed that my child has these behavioral problems.
- I know my child and he wouldn't lie, you must be confusing him with someone else. - I am surprised at this news I would like to talk to my child and get to the bottom of this behavior.
- He really doesn't mean it. If I didn't make him mad he wouldn't hit me. - My husband has been hitting me and I need to leave until it is clear there is no further danger to me or my children.
- I don't think he will really hurt me, I am his wife. - He has hurt me before and I am not getting the impression anything has changed.
- I know he is just out with the guys; I just wish he would come home before the kids go to bed. - I am hurt and embarrassed that he is more interested in his friends than his own family. This is not right.
- If I can just get her cleaned up and into bed where she can sleep it off, things will be better tomorrow. - I am embarrassed that she is passed out on the floor, but if I clean her up again what consequences

is she experiencing? I think I will let her wake up on the floor and go get myself some sleep.

- I can stop using anytime, I just don't want to. - I would like to think I can stop anytime, but I am here once again embarrassed at what I said and what I did because I was so intoxicated. Maybe I need help.

When we refuse to deny the facts of our condition or situation we open the door to addressing the things that need addressing in our lives.

Anger/Depression

Anger is another effective way of masking our baggage. While the previous method's attempt to claim inability or deny its existence, anger covers over that which pains or terrifies us often placing the blame on others. All of us are capable of anger, but no doubt we have all met examples of people who fall on both ends of the spectrum. While some are frequently angry there are those seeming peaceful souls, who are rarely observed being angry about anything. Anger is one of those mystifying emotions that seems to be very comfortable for some and absolutely taboo for others.

And yet like any emotion anger is not in itself good or bad. For instance, if you are a person who has rarely displayed any anger at all, you probably know you do get mad, but it rarely gets to where you need to act on it like some do with the extreme yelling, contorted facial expressions and regrettable statements. However, those who never get angry likely fall into one of two categories 1) you either feel little to nothing and this includes anger or 2) you probably tend to feel depressed instead of anger when you are frustrated.

All of these responses are learned responses and they separate us from what is really bothering us. Anger or its bottled-up twin, depression, are what some have described as secondary emotions. These are emotions that are real and very powerful, but they are literally in existence because another emotion was experienced first. The classic example of a child who has gotten their feelings hurt and is crying around a parent. When this parent does not take an empathetic path of response, but rather a critical one asking, "What are you crying for?", (often spoken with a voice of frustration) "I don't want to see anymore tears!", "Stop crying right now!", (often spoken with great agitation), "I told you that is nothing to cry about, Stop crying now!". They are upset and crying and the adult who they look to for guidance is telling them that they shouldn't be crying and are instead modeling an agitated if not angry behavior.

This is the common type of exchange that can teach many of us to be angry when we experience emotional pain or fear. Fear can also be reacted to in a similar dismissive way and we are often taught that reacting in anger is OK, but hurt or fear is not OK to express. We probably don't remember these kinds of exchanges, but some might. However, most of us have observed them either in ourselves as adults towards our children or in others responding to their children. It is easy to do, yet it teaches a lesson that is very effective in hiding the real emotions that someone is experiencing. Hence, anger can be a very effective behavior that masks the issues that in part make up our baggage.

Not all anger is bad to express. For those who never express anger, allowing ourselves to get angry is a healthy first step to breaking the habit of depressive thinking and other destructive behaviors when frustrated. Most of us are still angry about something. We may not like to admit it, but most of us have a certain memory that revives angry feelings in us. Perhaps we don't remember what happened to us, but we can have certain hot button triggers that easily can set us off. What the initial experience and emotions were may be difficult to identify, but these are not only a common symptom, which I refer to as baggage, but it is also a very effective technique to push ourselves and others away from that is really bothering us.

A scary episode with a clown may be at the root of an unusual dislike of the circus and even cotton candy. The topic of clowns and carnivals might mysteriously cause this person to erupt in anger only to draw attention away from the fear of clowns being discovered. It is often a very unconscious knee jerk experience for the person being angry as well as a surprise for all those around them.

Anger can also feed on itself and rekindle other hurts and fears that have a history of angry responses. This is the likely case when a small irritating thing occurs and a person gets extremely angry. This can happen to any of us. We are surprised by a painful experience and we blow up as if the experience was much more extreme.

For instance, a couple who have been dating a short time when talking might mistakenly call the other by the name of an old girlfriend or boyfriend. Misspeaking is not uncommon, but if the listener has had past experiences of betrayal then this could easily remind them of the painful past experience. This often prompts a strong fearful or pained response, but is often expressed as irritation or anger when the spoken wrong name was simply a mistake.

Past unresolved experiences are often the strongest contributors to these off the chart outbursts. Their response can also be quite the opposite. We are still very angry, but we elect to say nothing, possibly become very passive. This is when we can speculate that no one knows what we are going through or what it is like to be wronged like we have been wronged. As long as we can stay depressed or angry we do not have to think about why. While we might not like being angry or depressed, it is something we are familiar and comfortable with in us. Having to explore embarrassing and possibly painful memories that may be behind our anger it is rarely comfortable and is usually avoided.

The very nature of depression keeps things away. Things including people, opportunities, enjoyment and certainly interest in exploring the cause of what is weighing upon us. While there can be many reasons for a person's depression It ultimately serves as an insulator. A fairly common contributor to depression is anger turned inward. While some may start with conscious irritation with ourselves over something, others may never consciously remember ever being angry.

When we have been rebuked when hurt, crying or angry we may learn to turn inwards, instead of allowing ourselves a cathartic outburst, expression of frustration or release. Never getting a release, never being allowed a release and then later never allowing yourself a release only further intensifies the isolation one can feel from everything and everyone one around us.

Feeling depressed can cause us on one end of the spectrum to not want to talk about how we feel and it also makes it easy for us in the worst of cases to consider ending our life as a means to relieve the pain. However, for many feeling depressed can look like this:

- Not being willing to smile or laugh.
- Not being willing to be positive about anything.
- Not being willing to listen to comedy shows or comedians.
- Not being willing to clean your house or maintain personal hygiene.
- Not being willing to enjoy hobbies that you once enjoyed.
- Not being willing to go to parties or to the movies.
- Not being willing to celebrate our own birthday.
- Not being willing to buy ourselves clothes.
- Not being willing to go to the doctor.
- Not being willing to use the phone.
- Not being willing to go out.

Any of the above does not necessarily mean you are depressed, but the isolating and self-neglecting behavior is a fairly good indicator that depression is present in our lives.

While depression is a very serious matter that can put us at great risk, it often is also a secondary reaction to other issues. When we get depressed we are more fragile than at other times. Most of us normally have a safety net of logic about what is good for us in order to maintain our well-being. However, when we are depressed this logic is less present. When it gets to the point it is barely present to not existent and something else upsetting occurs the results can be disastrous. So not only is depression another way we can hide our baggage from ourselves it is also a very dangerous place to allow ourselves to visit or live without professional help. If you have been feeling depressed for an extended period of time like for months or even years, please seek professional help immediately. Untreated depression is the number one cause for suicide.

Some of the greatest tyrants and bullies of this world have been angry or depressed much of their lives and have developed a pattern of behavior that takes it out on others. This can be experienced in a very limited way where we might use sarcasm, utter an unkind word or on the other end of the spectrum where we use a position of great means or influence to inflict harm on others. The truth is the same for both. There is unfinished business in our past and that is our baggage. The sooner we can set aside the anger and depressive behavior long enough to be honest with ourselves, the sooner we can make progress.

Numb – Not Feeling at All

Another way we mask our baggage from ourselves is by choosing to not feel anything at all. Some are much more effective at this than others. Some actually have managed to turn the switch or faucet off and literally have no conscious sensation of feeling. Now other people can see it, but the person with the switch in the off position will calmly deny feeling anything and believe they are telling the truth.

While people often refer to people like this as being tough or hard they have simply learned a way to turn the conscious experience off. It doesn't mean they have no emotions, but it does give them the relief from the roller coaster of the highs and lows. Over the years, as we get hurt and we dislike the results of letting our feelings known we naturally look for ways to stuff these unpredictable and unpleasant emotions down deep where they never have to be felt again. It seems like a good strategy. It felt bad to feel them, so don't let yourself feel them. This of course can make dealing with behavior problems of any kind a real challenge since so many issues are emotion based. However, if a switch can be turned off it can, with patience, be turned back on. Many people can't use this approach. No matter how much they want to escape their emotions they still feel them much more intensely than they ever care to admit.

One of the ways people turn off their emotions is to simply get busy. Throwing ourselves into school, our work, our family obligations, making our spouse or children happy, trying to fix everything, constantly working on projects, an obsessive focus on hobbies, sports, politics, sex or even religion, can be bad for us. Anything focused on an extreme has the effect of squeezing out the time to pay attention to the rest of our life. For example, when working too much I can limit my exposure to triggers I may experience being around my family. I can even mentally be focused on work when with my family so they still can have only a limited impact on triggering unpleasant emotions in me.

While some hyper focused pursuits can yield some helpful results such as, school, work, or religion they still are hollow accomplishments since the rest of our lives are often left in shambles. A person with a Ph.D. may have some great credentials to cite, but may have little investment in relationships or family to build upon. Likewise, a career that benefits from an over the top number of hours for many years can yield great success, but have little else accomplished in their lives. The same can go for religion, which may sound a bit counter intuitive especially for those who are still striving to be more spiritually focused.

Here a key concept to illustrate a better-balanced approach is application. If you study religious works, devote yourself to study, prayer, ministry and don't leave room for relationships and family, then this too can become another way to keep ourselves too busy to feel our emotions. Now for some, family may be so destructive that spending time with them is not a healthy thing, but generally for most of us having some investment in these relationships is a healthy thing.

If an intense investment in following sports or politics is your approach, the net effect is much the same. Watching and following events can, if over indulged, leave little time for family and the building of relationships. Not that these interests are bad in of themselves. People can certainly be devoted sports fans and make plenty of time for the rest of their lives. The same can go for those who are very politically active. However, when these activities are why there is little or no time for family or friends then this activity is likely keeping you from having to feel or deal with your emotions then it is a problem.

Another common method of shutting off our emotions is simply to eat more than we need. Whether it is a large bag of chips, a box of cookies, a dozen doughnuts, a gallon of ice cream or a dozen hamburgers. While simply eating does not shut off our emotions, the distraction of the taste and act coupled with watching television or playing video games can crowd out any emotions we are tempted to feel. We can eat till our bodies are overwhelmed with food and then start the process all over again. If this works for us, then the likelihood of a food addiction is very high. Denial of this being a problem is easy to justify since we all have to eat.

A more dangerous method to squash our emotions is the use of pain killers, tranquilizers, amphetamines or any kind of legal drug, including alcohol, that can alter the way we feel. It doesn't matter if it comes from a valid prescription, the corner store, or our refrigerator. If what you put in your mouth changes the way you feel, then you will likely use it to avoid feeling unpleasant emotions. This is especially hard for those of us who can get this effect from sugar, caffeine, tobacco. However, if your drug of choice is alcohol or tobacco and lots of it, there is a better chance this will cause you more problems that just shutting you off from your emotions.

Of course, prescription drugs that give us a euphoric or numbing sensation are extremely tempting when we are in emotional pain. Since we have a good excuse to take them (they were prescribed for this or that) we can easily justify to ourselves this is helping me. The only problem is that we can become addicted even to drugs that are not physically addictive if they produce a numbing effect that we desire on a regular or constant basis. Just because a doctor prescribes something to us doesn't mean it can't be abused.

Finally, illegal drugs can also accomplish for many what alcohol or prescription drugs can. Over time drugs can and often do lose their desired effect that once attracted its users. But, by this point the addiction of whatever type has gotten way too strong a grip on us to merely walk away and no longer use it. Some can, but they are very few. Mind changing chemicals of any type are very seductive in that they can change the way we feel with little or no effort on our part. Thus, the messiness of being emotionally upset can be vanquished with a few drinks, a smoke or a dose. This is the reason most addicts and alcoholics, once they sober up, find that they are very emotionally immature, since they have not had to deal with their emotions for a very long time. They simply drugged them out of their consciousness. So once the practice of numbing is stopped then we have to learn how to deal with the emotions we all have.

If our baggage is unpleasant enough to us, we will do almost anything to keep from having to face it. If you can't even see your baggage, then you certainly can't do anything to unpack it.

Keeping ourselves clueless about our baggage is a very misguided approach of attempting to solve the problem. If we can talk ourselves out of it being a problem, deny it, rage to assign blame and keep people at bay, be too busy for it, overreact, or over medicate, we can convince ourselves our problems come from somewhere other than ourselves. Yet, when problems consistently follow us around we are usually the common denominator that needs investigating. If we had little to no baggage then we wouldn't need any of these techniques for insulating us from what we know and how we think, feel, and believe about ourselves and the world we live. To us who have employed one or more of these methods, our baggage may be very well be lost to us, but there are clues that others can often see. Fortunately, this can be corrected. We can learn to dismantle the smoke screen and to begin putting these past events into their proper perspective.

4. BAGGAGE CONSEQUENCES

We rarely think about our quality of life. unless we are confronted with someone else who has a condition that lowers theirs. Even then we typically think of it in the areas of physical ailments or extreme mental impairment that has rendered someone nearly unconscious. Someone who is closer to the end of their life with declining health, cognitive ability and limited movement we might say to ourselves, "I do not want to go out like that! Or we might see a person in a wheelchair or struggling to walk with crutches and think that, "we just couldn't live that way". Actually, there is quite a bit more that impacts our quality of life than physical mobility or perfect health. While we may try to convince ourselves that the things we do not have are not important to us, there are some things that are at the core of our existence that many of us tend to gloss over in favor of more tangible things.

Many of these things are limited by our baggage. There are crippling results from having a huge amount of baggage. Most of us have at least a little and even it creates behavior in us that can be severely limiting. Being physically fit and mentally sharp are very valuable, but it pales in comparison to our ability to have meaningful relationships with others, to have friends and loved ones that we can be open and honest with. Our ability to accomplish goals and objectives as a result of our labor yields us a great source of pride and contribution, to have fun whether it be in play, laughter or reading, and most important is to have peace of mind. All of these things are important yet many of us are perfectly willing to trade it in for that extra loyal companion I call baggage. We may not think of it that way, but there are many things we are willing to give up to be comfortable. We may prefer to suffer through the lingering death of relationships but withhold our true thoughts and feelings. We may allow our unwillingness to interact with others cordially to impede our ability to earn a living and provide for ourselves and others. Or we may be the exact opposite, we may focus too much on work, rules and responsibilities that we make little time for recreation. Or we may choose to quietly or not so quietly, suffer with worry, regret, judgment, self-righteous and indignant anger over the actions of others when we could be enjoying what life has to offer us.

While we might have the tendency to think of a low quality of life as one that is mentally or physically impaired these are not the kinds of things people cite as regrets when they are near the end of their lives. What they regret are usually the choices they made where they allowed things to get in the way of really living their lives more fully, honestly, keeping in touch with others, balancing work and time with others better and simply focused on having a life instead of concerning themselves on our mistakes or what others should be doing. So, what are the consequences of allowing our baggage to accumulate and weigh us down? We stop having much of a life or at least nowhere near the life we could have. Let's look at a few key areas of our lives that typically get impacted by our baggage.

Baggage Consequences in our Relationships

Our relationships with others are highly influenced by the baggage we carry. Especially baggage we have about relationships and how we think they should be. Our ability to interact with our acquaintances, co-workers, family, friends and lovers, can all be impacted by the baggage we carry.

Acquaintances

Our ability to cultivate new relationships can also be significantly impacted by our relational baggage. Before we meet anyone, they are a stranger to us. Our baggage can have significant impact on our ability to make a desirable first impression that strikes other people that we are someone they might like to get to know better. Upon the first meeting people are no longer strangers, but they are not yet friends. This in between status can be described as acquaintances.

Acquaintances are equivalent to knowing each other's names and maybe even spending time with each other as a part of group activities, but there is usually not any attachment or regard developed. While this type of relationship may not seem very important, it may be the most important since all non-family relationships start off as acquaintances. If the relational baggage we have keeps us from even being able to make acquaintances successfully, then the chance for friendships is not very likely.

Coworkers

Who we work for and work with and our ability to get along with them can be vital to our ability to earn a living. If we have developed baggage that is responsible for us having difficulties with these relationships, it can hurt sales, hurt our ability to function well as a part of a team. It may even affect our performance significantly, to the point that we are either rated poorly, do not advance or end up without a job. If our baggage prompts us to isolate from our teammates, or get along poorly with our supervisors or managers, or worse yet let our performance slide our baggage can have a devastating effect upon our ability to support our families and ourselves.

Friends

Having friends is something that most of us have had at some level, but if we have had painful experiences with friends we may elect to not invest in this area anymore. Worse yet, we may have had unsuccessful and painful experiences with just acquaintances, so we may have never gotten close to anyone. Again, we have our baggage to blame.

Friends are who we typically spend time with when we are not with family, but there are many of us who have allowed themselves to avoid friendships. Relational baggage is often the culprit here as well, however most relationships have a season.

Sometimes the friendship is long term and others are short term. Some end because of distance or the change in circumstance in our respective lives. Whatever the circumstances if we allow relational baggage to pile up enough we may find ourselves without any friends.

Family

A common casualty of relational baggage is that we no longer speak to a member of our family. Worse yet sometimes we have ended up in situations where we are not on speaking terms with any member of our family. While those in these instances often have very good reasons for such a choice, this kind of isolation from family is a tough way to journey through life. In extreme cases where our family members are all gone or too difficult to interact with we have the option to adopt a new family sometimes by joining in on an existing family or simply picking from very good friends to be your adopted family.

However, when we are isolated from our family by choice, either theirs, ours or both, this is a painful situation. Now we may have family members that are not that special to us and they are not anywhere as significant as the ones who mean a lot to us, but any circumstance that creates a separation from a family member is unfortunate.

This can be especially painful for parents who no longer have contact with their children. It is a natural part of growing up to have conflict with the people who raised you. The transition years from when you need constant and near complete direction and protection to the time when you have to navigate the world on your own can for some be especially rocky. Whether it was this transition or other events, having issues that kept these relationships from being active can potentially be very disturbing for all involved.

Siblings are another relationship, which can be disrupted by baggage in a way that disconnects us from those who we journeyed through our younger years together. Often these relationships can be especially meaningful when there are family events and issues to attend to, but often these relationships can be nonexistent if we have allowed enough relational baggage to build up.

Lovers

Romantic relationships can be the most challenging in our lives if we manage to have one at all. Often the culmination of all our relational baggage comes into play as we meet, become acquaintances, become friends and eventually become romantically involved with someone. Due to the intimate nature of these relationships they are very prone to get derailed.

One of the ways we can allow our baggage to derail this delicate process is if we skip immediately to physical intimacy. Barely knowing each other and deciding to jump straight to the most intimate exchange possible is like jumping out of plane without a chute. You get all the exhilaration, but typically it isn't going to end well. So instead of building a sustainable relationship we elect to have multiple exhilarating shorter ones. When the challenges come, we only have the physical intimacy to keep us together. No matter how you try to spin it, physical intimacy is not a problem-solving skill. If we manage to build a good friendship that eventually includes intimacy in other crucial areas like mentally, emotionally, socially, and spiritually, then when there are challenges we have a rich set of connections to help address them. When the relationship is mutual among these non-physical areas, we can work together or reconnect when we have allowed aspects of our relationship to become broken.

Additionally, it is pretty rare that any two people are raised in the same type of family where the relational baggage collected is the same. Therefore, in the high stakes world of romantic relationships we encounter hundreds if not thousands of odd little pieces of baggage that either motivates us or repulses us away from what is best to build and maintain the relationship. No wonder so many never marry or fail to stay married.

So, when it comes to relationships baggage can derail them all to some extent or another and really make a mess of things. And yet our natural tendency is to hang onto our baggage because it is what we have always done, it protects us from getting hurt or looking stupid or we think it is the smart thing to do. We know because we have been here before and besides it just feels comfortable. And that is a problem when being off course feels comfortable.

Baggage Consequences in our Work

Baggage can significantly impact our ability to perform at work. Issues we have with job requirements, policies, and personnel can all have a negative impact on our performance at work. Often these issues come from previous work experience, but they can also be from our pre-working years.

One of the most common examples of baggage that can create problems in nearly every work situation is the resentment of authority. When an authority figure of any kind has the role of giving us work direction or the enforcement our compliance we may react to this relationship poorly. If the poor response occurs on a regular basis, then it is likely there are authority issues present.

The word resentment comes from the Latin words "re" and "sentire". Sentire means "to feel" and re means "again". Therefore, resentment refers to the instances when we repeatedly experience anger.

During our teenage years it is not uncommon to struggle with authority figures in our lives. For some this transition never is completed and the struggle continues into adulthood. Yet when we accept a job, we agree to perform work in return for compensation. Usually, there are elements of every job we don't care for and maybe even disagree with. Most employers do not have a policy of allowing their employees to opt out of having to do things they disagree with for any reason. As a result, if we refuse to comply or refuse to comply fully we are subject to consequences that could include docking of our pay, lost advancement opportunities, a lowered performance rating which could impact future pay increases or we could lose our job altogether.

It is not uncommon for an entire culture of resentment to be present in some workplaces where the rank and file resent management. It can also occur within departments or divisions within a company when there is interdependency and conflict. Thus, Manufacturing may resent Sales and Sales may resent Service. It also can commonly occur among separate company employees when their respective firms are joined together in a partnership, joint venture, merger or even occur when prime and subcontractors are in conflict.

While conflict is a natural part of doing business with others, resentment of authority is not. While it may be tolerated in certain circles, eventually those individuals, who are bent out of shape on a regular basis are often passed over for preferred assignments and passed over for promotions because attitudes are just not suitable to work with others. People who make a regular habit of expressing their anger openly or by allowing their work performance to be impacted are often viewed by their management and others as high maintenance and may be referred to as a part of the 20%, which require 80% of the energy.

Another type of baggage that can impact work is the perspective we have about work. If we grew up with role models who were constantly lamenting how their employers were taking advantage of them and how they were out to get them then we may very well share that frame of reference. If the ways we observed our roles models dealing with their employers was clear to us or if we became sympathetic, then we likely would adopt those same attitudes about employers. The employers we have later on may be very different, but we may default to the same attitudes if we have allowed that kind of baggage to go unprocessed. This can apply to changes in work assignments, transfers, policy changes and others. This is not to say that bad things don't happen, but if we are constantly seeing bad things happening and those around us are not and this happens time and time again then it is likely there is baggage impacting your ability to successfully work with or for others.

A common refrain of those who have trouble working for others is, "I need to be in business for myself, so I won't have anyone telling me what to do". Yet all businesses have customers, if not employees, suppliers and regulatory agencies that have to be worked with to conduct business. So, the only business where you don't have to deal with others is on a deserted island where you are your only customer.

Baggage Consequences in our Recreation

Some of us have developed such a practice of avoidance that we no longer have recreational activities. When it has become extreme, we only work, sleep, required daily living activities and do the absolute minimum of social duties. I once heard a woman describe her life after losing her only child in a custody battle. For the next seventeen years she only worked, slept and did the bare minimum to live. No outings, no vacations, no family visits, just the bare minimum.

Baggage whether it is from a traumatic loss or emotional pain can have a devastating effect upon the choices we make to treat ourselves to enjoyment. When we have limited resources, severe constraints upon our time or health issues we can also be significantly at a loss on what options are available for entertainment and leisure. Sometimes we grow up in an environment where there was no recreation modeled for us. Play for some may have been considered a luxury for people with money, food and a place to stay.

When we have a bad experience, we can over associate the pain or displeasure with the entire experience and as a result cut ourselves off from another part of the world. For instance, let's say as a young child we get in a car and we are mesmerized that it is a bright shiny red car. While riding in the car we are eating a sandwich and drinking a soda. Then out of the blue we are catapulted from our seat into the back of the front seat hard. The soda bottle collides with our mouth and breaks a tooth. Our arm gets caught between our body and the front seat and is broken. And on top of it all the peanut butter from your sandwich gets in our eyes and makes it very hard to see for what seems like quite a while.

Now any accident can be a shock, but the subtle long-term effects can stick with us for a lifetime. We might now have no interest in red cars. When driving in cars we no longer dare to drink or eat. As a matter of fact, we may not like peanut butter anymore at all. Now the color of the car had no contribution to the incident. And the eating and drinking had only secondary contribution to the injuries. Yet all could easily be associated with the traumatic experience and once and for all cast from our list of preferences.

Probably the ultimate joy killer is the guilt of surviving. On top of the loss there is the added trap of thinking it is not OK to have any enjoyment because of this recent loss. When someone near and or dear to us dies we can easily take the perspective that we were remiss in taking some action that could have prevented the death. This can be a very powerful notion for young children and for people who lose someone very close regardless of age. If we happen to be involved in an accident or tragedy where one or more people lose their life suddenly for any reason we can experience this survivor's guilt even about people we never knew, but we just happened to be standing near when the event occurred.

Two other types of loss that can cast a very dark net of survivor's guilt and that is for the survivors of suicide and the deaths of young children. For parents, either one of these can be especially difficult. Mix any of the previous scenarios together and the impact is multiplied. Whether we were close or not these types of losses have their own category of guilt and sadness associated with them.

Between the guilt, the sadness and the ideas that we should not or do not deserve to enjoy ourselves, have fun, joke, laugh, play or the ultimate slight, forget the departed, we can easily squeeze out nearly any remnant of a life under the weight of this type of baggage. While no amount of work will undo these tragic events, the impact can be significantly reduced without dishonoring anyone.

Baggage Consequences for our Peace of Mind

The baggage we carry shows itself in many unfortunate ways. It often motivates us to do what do not want to do, pass up on opportunities we would like to engage in, refrain from speaking, or speaking carelessly, we may refuse to engage in relationships or throw ourselves into them so quickly that all hopes of long-term commitments are out of the question. Things often go poorly at work, with others and sources of fun are getting more and more limited if they even exist at all. It is as if we are boxed in like an animal.

On top of the things that we remember that are painful there are the things we do over and over that we cannot explain; silly, sad, and destructive things that often cause us and the people around even more pain. We have plenty of choices, but we are often unsure which ones to take. We have many options and yet it appears we have very few. It is as if we have made many poor choices and don't remember making most of them. As a result, we find ourselves constantly finding scapegoats for our troubles. Our boss or our family, they don't get it. They do not know how hard it is to be us. You find yourself either thinking or saying out loud, "Don't even get me started on the neighbors and the local, state and national government". Pressures from money, lack of time to do what we would like, see who we would like, be where we would like to be, etc. If everything was just the way it was supposed be. If everyone would just do what they are supposed to do then everything would be OK. Or least it would be better, a lot better.

The swirl of unease, anger, guilt, choices, poor results, memories of past events literally haunt us with regret, more anger, and more disappointment. We may or may not make a practice of showing it, but a life of unfinished business carries a heavy load of skeletons in the closet. They may not be felonies and then they may be or maybe we are simply not sure and that worries us as well. Many things we have vowed to never tell anyone and thankfully we rarely remember often carry enough misperception to help draw all kinds of inaccurate perspectives.

When the majority of the things we think about and are reminded of are ones of displeasure, unease, anger, frustration, conflict, irritation, indignation, outrage, disgust, worry, and anxiety, there is little room left for peace of mind. You may even be a religious or spiritual person and still have a great struggle keeping your thoughts from things that bring you great discomfort. This constant drone of unpleasantness, stress and irritation has little in common with feeling good. When we are in this unpleasant state there is the great likelihood that more poor choices will be made. Things will be said, actions will be taken and more consequences will be added to the pile.

When we have no more room to process what is coming in our lives because our heads are full, we are on our last nerve, we are tired, we are stressed already and our bodies are breaking under the pressure, we are constantly one more thought away from another spiral. Your spiral may be despair, and deeper depression or it may be over the top drinking, yelling, running stop signs, breaking things, inappropriate or risky sex, speeding, hurting people or animals, or committing crimes. We do a lot of crazy things when we have no peace and no capacity to absorb and deal with the everyday pressures of life. Unless we have a totally stress-free future and amnesia to blot out all the things from our past we are going to have stress. Peace of mind is a perspective where we are able to experience calm, quiet, and be serene amidst our present, past and future all at once. Most of us have way too much baggage to get even close.

The consequences of baggage are a system that is overloaded.

On top of the everyday issues that a normal life entails we carry with us a history that makes it hard if impossible to have successful relationships, to succeed at work, have fun or to have any peace. The consequence of baggage is misery. We may not be miserable all the time, but it is commonplace for us who are carrying a great load of baggage with us day in and day out. Despite our impression or the reality that the things that haunt us are real, it is possible to reduce their grip on us and often eliminate the grip most of the time. Even for those of us with chronic baggage of family history, cultural history, racial history or a history of horrific acts, this baggage can be lessened and, in many instances, eliminated with the right kind of action and time. But first we need to have a better understanding of how we got here in the first place. This is the first step of putting our baggage in its proper perspective.

PART 2 - HOW WE ACQUIRE BAGGAGE?

5. HOW WE EXPERIENCE LIFE

Considering how we experience our lives can help us understand how we are impacted by the events that occur around us. Most of my life I have considered that I experience events either mentally, emotionally, physically or spiritually. More recently I have realized that I also have a dimension that is equally significant in many ways and that is socially.

Each of these areas can have a great deal of variation from one person to the next and as we live our lives each of these areas are continuously experiencing new input. From birth we are experiencing our environment and soaking it all up like a sponge. We will not become conscious of any memories until we are a toddler and most of us have very few memories from this period. However, this does not mean we are not experiencing the events around us, recording these experiences, and being affected by them. Within each of these areas there are aspects that we are born into. Experiences that occur around us and then there are those that we choose. Granted, the selection begins modestly earlier in life, but we are choosing nonetheless and these choices, plus the base characteristics of each area we start off with, all play a role in how we experience our lives and what baggage we acquire.

For instance, mentally most of us are born with a near average I.Q., but we may have one that is lower or higher and that will impact how we make use of the information we are exposed to. Plus, the amount and types of information we are exposed to during the earlier years of our lives can have a tremendous impact on our frame of reference. The more we are exposed to early, at an age appropriate level, allows us to better navigate the world.

Emotionally, we may have been reassured and held on a regular basis or we could have a much different emotional frame of reference, if we were exposed to frequent frightening experiences and reassured very little. Physically, we may have been born with smaller and weaker frame or a larger and stronger frame. We may be naturally graceful or we may have fewer fine motor skills and coordination. We may have grown up in a religious home where kindness and integrity were constantly present or in a religious home where cruelty and deceit were the more prominent examples. Then again, little or nothing may have been modeled when it came to spiritual matters in your early life.

Finally, our exposure to others also can vary quite a bit. We may have been raised in an environment where there were many friends and family who were close by and visiting on a regular basis or you may have grown up in a home where the only visitors were landlords, bill collectors and the authorities. If you were born into the dominant race in your part of the world, then you will have experienced more privilege than other races and ethnic groups. If you were born into a minority group in your part of the world then you may have learned at early age the world can be unfair and at times very cruel.

In each of these areas, what we are born with or into or what we are exposed to early on in our lives establishes a base level of input and experience that forms our initial frame of reference against which we will compare everything else. If we grow up in a quiet home and visit at a friend's house where the parents frequently communicate with louder voices, we might conclude that they don't like each other or that they are mad.

As a young person we have little to no choice on the things we are exposed to early on. However, with every exposure we are adding to this base reference of information and experiences. Likewise, very early on we begin being selective about what we take to heart and what we discard. This is truer in some areas than others in a large part due to the previous experiences we have already had. The same young person who is exposed to a teacher with a very loud voice might be frightened as the child from a quiet home while the kids with louder parents, friends or relatives will perceive the loud teacher as someone who speaks normally.

Then on top of each of these base levels of experience and information in each one of the areas: mentally emotionally, physically, socially and spiritually, we begin a lifetime of choices and resulting exposure to positive and negative experiences and information. While for many of us this averages out fairly evenly over the weeks, months and years, there are those of us who end up in situations where there is a strong skew towards one or the other.

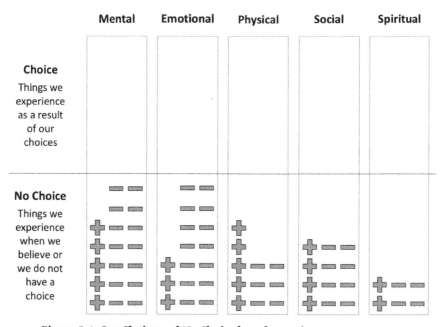

Figure 5-1 Our Choice and No Choice based experiences

When it is predominately positive then we are much better off. However, when these experiences are predominately negative then our frame of reference for some or all of these areas begins to be tainted. A person with a more positive frame of reference will generally have a more positive outlook and attitude towards life and in general have more positive results.

However, the person with the more negative frame of reference will generally have a more negative outlook and attitude towards life. Since our frame of reference is the basis upon which we judge all we encounter this can have a significant impact upon our lives. When the input has been more negative in early life we have a greater tendency to acquire more and more baggage that loads us down and keeps us from having the best results that life has to offer.

Imagine we are a sponge, a sponge with five separate sections. Each section is tuned to absorb certain kinds of experiences and information. However, like a real sponge our sponges have a limited capacity to absorb new information based upon the amount of information and experiences we have experienced in the past. Mentally, emotionally, physically, socially, and spiritually we begin absorbing experiences at a very tender and impressionable age, an age too early for us to even recall typically.

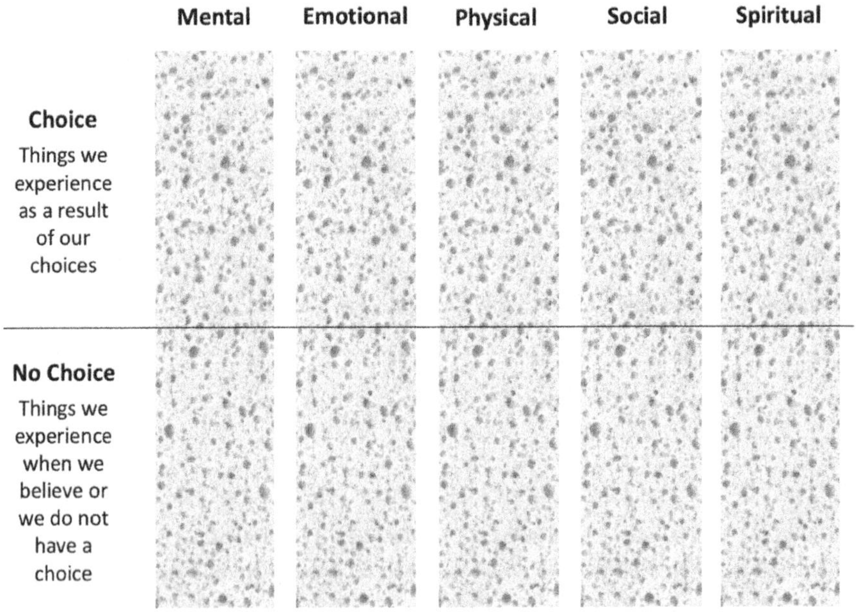

	Mental	Emotional	Physical	Social	Spiritual
Choice Things we experience as a result of our choices					
No Choice Things we experience when we believe or we do not have a choice					

Figure 5-2 Our choice and no choice sponges

As a result, it is probably safe to say that in these very early years we have no capability to understand what happened to us much less to be able to put the experiences and information in their proper perspective. So many things are misconstrued and any conclusions are often based upon incomplete or misleading information. While this might not sound like a very good start it is not a problem when the parents or caretakers managing our lives at that point are observant, attentive, loving, patient, nurturing and able to provide age appropriate care, interpretation, and teaching as we experience things in those early years. It is safe to say that we are like very dry sponges when we are born and continue to absorb experiences and information at a tremendous rate indiscriminately.

However, once the sponge becomes saturated unless its contents are squeezed out it has little room to absorb anything new. So earlier on when we had the least possible ability to put things in their proper perspective we soak up everything thrown at us. Now that we have more potential to actually understand what is happening today we tend to have less capacity to take it in. Some of the ways we exclude new information are we dismiss, deny, ignore and refute which could help us to finally put things in their proper perspective. All because we do not know how to wring out our sponge and make room for a better set of perspectives, experiences and information.

While we will get to how to wring ourselves out, first we are going to explore how and what kinds of information and experiences we typically take in.

We are incredible beings with the ability to learn from our mistakes, however if we have previous experiences that disrupt our ability to perceive the world around us accurately, then our perception of the facts becomes distorted. Very early in life when we are paying attention, given our limited understanding of the world, we may end up making distorted observations and learning distorted lessons.

For instance, the person who grows up around parents who often rage about even the most trivial of offenses may learn that speaking up is punishable even when asked for a response. As a result, the distorted lesson may be to never speak up even when asked to. Other lessons learned could be that this is how parents raise their children and or this is how a man treats a woman and how a woman treats a man. Thus, unconsciously a person can actually grow up instinctively being quiet and selecting abusive mates while very naturally being attracted to them.

Not everybody will draw the same lessons from the same set of experiences, but the dynamics are the same. When we are soaking in these experiences if we are unable to put the events into their proper perspective then we will likely come up with a variety of distorted lessons that can become hardened rules. Whether we are conscious of these lessons learned or not they are there and they are the lenses through which we view and experience the world around us. It is as if these sponges are like the lenses of a telescope through which we always use since our past lessons learned are always with us.

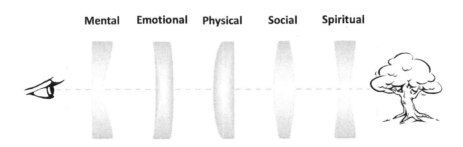

Figure 5-3 An undistorted view of the world

While the lenses in a real telescope are clean, polished, sealed against dirt, and aligned to magnify the image clearly for us to see, in our case, our baggage impacts the quality and accuracy of the lenses and our view of the events unfolding around us.

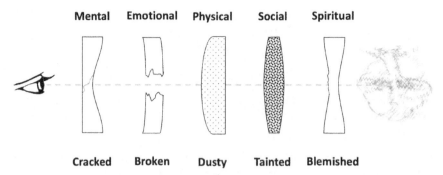

Figure 5-4 How our baggage influences our view of the world

If our mental lens is cracked, then it distorts what we see when we experience the things around us. This can cause us to miss or misread information that can help us. It also may cause us to have preferences or attractions to things that are clearly harmful or dangerous for us.

If our emotional lens is broken then our view is not corrected we will place too little or too much importance on our emotions associated with the people, places or things around us.

If our Physical lens is dusty or dirty then this dims all we experience to the point we may not be able to perceive helpful information or mere existence of experiences like when people complement us or awareness that our actions are causing others harm.

If our Social lens becomes colored or tainted by our baggage, then we may consider all future opportunities to simply be more of the same unpleasant experiences and thus they should be judged accordingly or avoided at all costs.

If our Spiritual lens is full of blemishes as a result of our baggage, then the view is full of missing or convoluted details created by these blemishes. This can happen as a result of spiritual experiences that are not age appropriate or associated with inappropriate behavior.

All of these baggage sourced defects can influence each of the lenses through which we see the world around us. This results in our perceptions being distorted, uncorrected, dim, tainted and incomplete. Thus, we continue to experience the world around us in a highly different way than those around us that are carrying little or different baggage.

This is how really intelligent people can think either they or everybody else are dumb, how perfectly sane people can think they are crazy, irresponsible people can think everyone is supposed to clean up after them.

From the time we are able to pay attention, to well into our adult years, we can be in a position to not be able to put the events we experience into their proper perspective. When this happens, we draw some pretty wild conclusions. Unfortunately, these wild conclusions often become ingrained in us as lessons learned that we use to navigate the world for the rest of our lives.

We now know from research that we remember experiences better when adrenalin levels are elevated. This allows us to better record and recall our memories of significant events so we can retain critical survival lessons. The rush of great fear, pain or anger can be that emotional and physiological reaction to imprint a very poor interpretation of the events just experienced. This is a byproduct of how we are wired to survive and this is how it can play out in our everyday lives. Next, we will explore how our experiences in these five areas are unique and become of a part of us.

How We Experience Life – Mentally

Every time we are introduced to new information, we compare it to what we already know. If it is like or closely related to something we are already familiar with, then we associate the information and consider it as understood. For instance, if we hear a person say the dog was excited when she saw us. We might think of our own dog and how she can wag her tail and playfully come up to us and want to play. However, if our only previous experiences with dogs are the large barking dogs we pass on the way to school, then we might think about a dog when they are barking aggressively and lunging at a fence trying to chase us away. While very different, both of these are ways of relating to the same event mentally. However, if we have not had any personal experience with dogs then we attempt to relate the idea of an excited dog to how we act or how we have seen other people or animals act when they are excited. This new information may prompt us to ask more questions. As long as we have the option to ask more questions we can gather enough information to create a more complete new concept and image of an excited dog. Yet if we are not at liberty to ask questions we will walk away with little understanding of what the excited dog looked like.

As a young child we can go through this process many times a day. The parents, teachers and others around us as a child are the ones who help expose us and help us understand what has occurred. When conversation is invited and allowed to explore our curiosity then most of these concepts and images will be formed with greater accuracy. Yet if the ones around us are not open to answering questions we are left to come up with our own interpretation of the events. When this occurs, the interpretation is usually less accurate.

While a person may have an average or above average I.Q. they may still have below average comprehension skills and process new information more slowly than others. As a result, they may not be able to follow the story being told because they are still busy trying to comprehend the concept of the excited dog. We all experience this process when we are exposed to events and information. We are exposed to something and we immediately try to understand it based upon what we already know. This body of previous impressions is often referred to as our 'frame of reference'. If our frame of reference is comprehensive, then we are able to understand most of what we are exposed to and continue experiencing the event. When our frame of reference is less complete, then we constantly have to spend time to attempt to understand the new information. In the meantime, we may miss some other new information while we are not paying attention.

As a result, multiple people can be exposed to the same events and interpret them in very different ways based on their previous experience and skills. So, a loud voice might bring up the memory of things getting broken and a parent, relative or family friend responding with a loud voice. Or it might trigger the memory of a landlord demanding the rent or a police officer shouting orders to stay on the sidewalk at an intersection. Observing the reaction of others to the loud voice may cause us to adopt the same reaction. If our parents engaged loud speakers calmly or confidently, then we probably think of this as normal. However, if our parents react to loud speakers with avoidance, then we are likely to learn that we should do the same.

As we become conscious of what we do know, we immediately begin using this base level information to build upon, in the process increasing our understanding of the world. We all have a unique set of initial experiences and these have been further refined with either a modest or very robust set of subsequent experiences. If we are unfamiliar with excited dogs at an early age and there is no one around to explain that the dog is glad to see you and wants to get to know you and play, we may just retreat in fear. If this is never cleared up, then we can grow up afraid of all excited dogs. Out of that fear we may choose to avoid dogs altogether.

If we take into consideration all the different paths a person may travel in the gathering of information and apply it to the key topics we are exposed to it becomes easier to understand how we all can come to see ourselves and the people and the world around us differently.

This process applies to:

- How we choose to think about people, places and things.
- How we choose to think about ourselves.
- How we choose to think about our life.
- How we choose to determine if something is fac-

tual.

- How we choose to determine if something is wise or unwise.
- How we choose to identify if something is right or wrong.
- How we chose what we will and will not do.

You will notice I wrote, "How we choose to" at the beginning of each of those statements. Just because we have been exposed to looking at something a particular way doesn't mean it can't be changed. Constant refinement is appropriate because few if any of us ever collect all the information there is to know about a particular topic. It is possible that a person has decided that they understand a topic and there is no new information to be collected. This position is rarely correct, but it is easy to come to this conclusion. I understand this topic therefore there is no more information required. So, when a person adopts this perspective they stop learning, refining or correcting their view of things and possibly even themselves. We can be with ourselves our whole life and still not know everything there is to know about us.

So, we might think to ourselves we can't be around that dog, but actually we can. We might think to ourselves we can't deal with that loud person, but actually we can.

Little by little we develop this collection of memories that lead us to the conclusion of what we can and cannot do. When these things that we think we can't do may or may not be a matter of safety, right, wrong or wisdom, but may have more to do with our misunderstanding of the facts. To us our experience is our collection of facts, but yet our experiences are riddled with incomplete, misleading incorrect and misunderstood information. When this occurs in the areas that concern how we think about ourselves and others it can be what I call *baggage*.

These things stand in our way of having a much more enjoyable life and we often don't even know it. A person might later in life find that they are very comforted by the companionship and affection from a dog even though they grew up afraid of dogs.

The mental recording is on all the time by default unless we turn it off. When we turn our attention from the present and all the things going on with us and around us and choose to think about the future or the past, we no longer are recording memories. We are either replaying old memories, fantasizing how we would have preferred things to have occurred or we are fantasizing about how the future might unfold. Any of these actions disconnects us from the present and the making of memories of actual experiences.

Replaying old events is just that, a choice to re-experience an old experience rather than to have an actual new one. While this may be desirable in the case of pleasant memories and for the purpose of processing extremely painful events; however, it can become a very destructive practice to choose on a regular basis. The past can be a very tempting competition to our present since we are already familiar with it. And like in cartoons we can be stronger, smarter, try new responses and get the outcome we prefer until we come back to reality.

Everybody loses a few minutes every day reflecting on the past. When it is done constructively to extract a lesson for present day guidance it can be very valuable. However, when we are replaying events over and over hour after hour, day after day, week after week for months and possibly for years, we are robbing ourselves of having a life. We don't develop fond memories of the hours, days or weeks we spend living in the past. No, that time is lost forever. You have to be living in the present to experience life and make memories. Sadly, baggage often draws us back in to the past and robs us of our present.

Likewise, the choice of thinking about the future and how it might play out while in of itself sounds like good planning or a positive visualization technique, but when we opt to fantasize about the future it can become another very destructive habit if it is preferred to choosing to experience the life we have in the present. When we fail to develop ways to have pleasant experiences in our real and present life, then reliving the past or fantasizing about the future can become very attractive. The catch is when we do this on a regular basis, we have no idea what we are missing. Sometimes it is a few words of someone's sentence because we have floated off, or it may be their entire point, or worse yet it might be a stop sign or the plea for help from a loved one. How much we allow ourselves to be disconnected from the here and now can cause significant repercussions for us and the loved ones around us.

While we all have a little mental baggage, those of us who have held onto ours throughout our life carry an especially heavy burden. Some of us have managed to drown out the baggage with a disciplined focus on positive and pleasant memories, but once a hardship occurs we are especially prone to allow the baggage to once again dominate our thoughts. Destructive and negative thinking that we had managed to arrest for years or even decades, can return with unforeseen traumas such as the death of a loved one, a serious illness, a significant betrayal, the loss of employment, or the fall from grace of a friend or family member, a greatly admired mentor, spiritual leader, employer, civic leader or any group or entity that once had your respect and admiration.

Mental Baggage can weigh us down to the point that it is hard to see the possibility of a better day. And yet it can be resolved. There is no miracle pill or medication, but it is possible to rid ourselves of most of our mental baggage, much in the same way we can squeeze a sponge and expel the gunk and filth that has been absorbed. If it has been a long time since we were open-minded and teachable to consider new information, a simple squeeze might not be enough for our mental sponge to address the baggage in us. Sometimes the only way we can accomplish a deep purge of these hard to expel burdens is to microwave or boil them like we would a common kitchen sponge. The point is that old baggage sometimes takes time to expel, but it can be done. Even small releases of our mental burdens can bring significant relief. No baggage is too great to be lessened and may very well be eliminated even if the facts we hold onto remain. It does not have to always be the way it has been and there are ways to lighten the load you have been suffering. If you are still skeptical, try to keep an open mind. Much of our baggage may employ a certain close-mindedness to ward off ever getting better. Often this is part of the reason why it can have such a hold on us. If you want to be relieved of mental baggage, consider seriously the idea that it is a possibility that new information can help us gain a more appropriate perspective. Now let's continue to review other ways we experience life.

How We Experience Life – Emotionally

If you are a person who allows themselves to be conscious of their emotions, then you may experience the time connection when certain emotions are felt along with certain details. For instance, you can as an adult visit a carnival and smell a particular food commonly served, such as funnel cake, and feel irritated or angry. Now nothing might have happened in the present time to trigger that emotion other than your memory that as a child you were never allowed to have funnel cake when visiting carnivals. You were angry about it as a young child and now it bubbles up to the surface once again when you are confronted with sight and smells of funnel cake at the carnival. You may not act on this emotion, but you will be much more prone to act on the irritation or anger if something in your present world also irritates you. So, if the person you are with teases you about something, you might find you have not only the current day irritation from the teasing, but also all the anger originally experienced by the recently triggered memory. All this together can often result in an angry reaction towards your friend who merely teased you. Most of us have many of the past experiences, just waiting to be triggered.

So, we are recording and reliving many of our emotional memories on a regular basis. When emotions are remembered they can also reinforce the original experience's impact upon us. When pleasant emotions are remembered we often refer to them as a pleasant or fond memory. If unpleasant emotions are remembered and we are motivated to act in a way that is more to do with the past then the present, this is baggage. If the unpleasant original experience involved being angry and we chose to remember and re-experience this memory and emotion again and again we may develop what is called resentment. If the original emotion was fear and we chose to remember and re-experience this memory and emotion again and again we may develop what is often called a phobia.

So how we experience our emotions today: not at all, somewhat moderated or very uncontrolled, is a result of how we are able and have chosen consciously or unconsciously to cope with them.

Emotions can be confusing. Psychologists disagree on how many emotions there are or what to call them. Yet there is little disagreement that emotions are very different from thoughts, despite the common practice by many of us to confuse the two. Here lies the important distinction, we physically feel our emotions and we think our thoughts. Now that may sound overly simplistic, but we all have heard someone say, "I feel like (someone) or (something)" such as, "I feel like Superman" (an expression of characteristics) or, "I feel like a pizza", (an expression of desire). However, you will never see on a chart that lists emotions, "Superman" or, "pizza". However, most of us have gotten into the habit of speaking and thinking this way. As a result, we can confuse ourselves and others by referring to things we are comparing ourselves to and or desire. All are very common expressions, but they are not emotions. More common emotions are joy and sadness, not Superman and pizza.

Figure 5-5 Two emoticons and two objects

There are some who appear to manage their emotions well while many others seem to be very disturbed much of the time. Yet both of these groups of individuals can be very troubled. One set has chosen to manage their emotions by not consciously feeling them and proceeding through life in a very controlled manner. While the other set appears to be riding their emotions like they were a team of wild animals, raw, explosive and very unpredictable.

If you are not conscious of your emotions you probably at some point in your past decided that feeling your emotions was too painful or messy. This is a common coping mechanism. Young boys are often chastised for being afraid and young girls are often chastised for being hurt. When both are upset with their respective feelings and are crying, it is common for a frustrated parent to demand that they stop crying and carelessly say, "there is no reason to be afraid, so stop crying", or, "there is no reason for you to be hurt, so stop crying". When it continues the parent or adult can follow up with, "if you do not stop crying right now I will give you something to really cry about". Where it goes from there can be very unfortunate, but the point is that the child can learn from an experience like this and decide that I am not going to let on how I feel anymore because it gets me into trouble. This along with subsequent experiences that lead you to the same conclusion can reinforce the merits of turning off the faucet if you will of our emotions. So, we bury or mask our emotions from certain people, all others and often times from ourselves as well. If we only bury them from ourselves, we can appear very emotional to others but we are oblivious to their existence. If we manage to bury them successfully from both ourselves and others, then we can appear very together and controlled while deep below we are still churning with emotions from today and every day before it. This last approach often leads to periodic emotional blow-ups, when we finally can't take it anymore. However, there are those few who have managed to never blow up or let it out in any way. Despite how these approaches differ all are influenced by the emotions stewing inside of them.

Despite the positive and negative perceptions that are easily related to emotions, they are not inherently good or bad. They are just emotions. We may like them or not like them, but they are just feelings. While they can be an indication about what we are thinking, they are often unpredictable and a very poor guide to wise behavior. And while we might already know this when we experience the flood of an emotion it can influence us to do some rather unfortunate things. Yet, it is very common for many of us to use our emotions as a guide for our actions.

When asked why we didn't attend a certain event, we often will remark "we didn't feel like it". Or why we suddenly took that trip, bought that car or got married, we will say, "it just felt right". While these statements are more about what we were thinking or judgements, it does provide a clue to our hyper focus on our emotions and our efforts to acknowledge them and understand them. However, emotions are little more than a physiological reaction to what we are experiencing or thinking. If we are thinking and experiencing only what is going on right now at this moment, then an emotional reaction will be about this current moment. However, if we are also consciously or even unconsciously reminded of past experiences while experiencing the present, then we can be easily drawn into focusing on that past event or set of events. This is why we can get really angry about little things, overly excited about small things or mentally and emotionally tortured when we are reminded of really painful events like the death of loved ones.

Since we all have a past full of emotionally charged events then the likelihood that we have emotional baggage is certain. Yet the possibility to defuse those unpleasant emotional filled memories is also certain. As we age we are no longer in the dark like we were when we had those experiences. As a result, heartaches, tragedies, traumas, losses, torture, humiliations, discrimination, abandonment, betrayals, murders, suicides, amputations, and the loss of all bodily functions or freedoms can be overcome. Many have done it and there can be a day when this is your story as well.

How We Experience Life - Physically

One of the ways we should all be most familiar in how we experience life is through our five traditional senses of sight, hearing, taste, smell and touch. There are other senses that detect stimuli beyond the traditional five such as: pain, temperature, balance and acceleration to name a few. The things we see, touch, hear, taste and smell all give us a glimpse of the world we live in from one day to the next.

While these senses are common to most of us, we all don't have equal capability in each of these areas. Some of us are born without one or more of these senses and others just have more or less capability within each of these senses. Most of us are used to the hearing tests given in school and occasionally we have taken eye tests. Both give us feedback on how well we are able to hear and see. It is much less common for us to be tested for our ability to touch, taste and smell. While relatively few of us have no ability with these three senses, there are many conditions that can impact our abilities to touch, taste and smell.

Whatever our capabilities with these senses when we are born, there is always the possibility of variation due to our health, diet and, in some cases, our emotional health. We have all had a cold and have it disrupt our ability to smell, usually because our sinuses were all clogged up. While all of our senses are very important to us we probably notice changes in our sight and hearing the most often while variations in our sense of touch, taste or smell may be overlooked especially if they are temporary. Illnesses, stress, depression or exposure to a medicine or other chemicals can be the cause of temporary impairment of the senses.

Given that, the abilities we start off with will change over time. Sometimes due to temporary conditions and sometimes due to more permanent events such as injuries. Our bodies also may improve over time if we are careful with how we treat our bodies with diet, exercise and how well we keep ourselves from injury. Impairment aside, all of our senses are merely receptors of external stimuli, which give us bits and pieces of information about the world we encounter. While we may be convinced, about what we just saw or heard or smelled. the truth is that we can all be mistaken and at times easily misled by a variety of factors. This is probably most apparent when two persons stand side-by-side and observe the same event and recall it differently. One will say the boy was riding a blue bike and the other will claim it was green. One will say the boy's hair was red and the other will recall that it was brown.

Law enforcement runs into these issues all the time and have to take special care when asking witnesses questions, preparing suspect photos and line ups because not only can people's memories be flaky, they can also be easily misled. A collection of photos of suspects can be leading if some of the photos are in color versus black and white or if some of the individuals are dressed in jailhouse clothing versus street clothing. Likewise, social research has found evidence that the things we have seen in the past or recently can impact how we perceive events in the present. As well we can be influenced by leading questions and assumptions. All of these conditions have been found to contaminate memory. Unfortunately, crimes do not have to be involved for our perception of what we see, hear, etc. and our memories of these perceptions to become contaminated. Many things can contaminate a perception from data collected from our senses and especially our memory of the data collected. As a result, our memories of what our senses captured, upon which we base significant aspects of our lives can easily be incorrect.

It is common for us to have a firm impression about the ways of the world through experiences we have had in the past. We experience something and we made conclusions based upon our perceptions we assign as the facts. And yet we have all experienced a time when we were certain something was true only to find out was not. Our physical world while it seems so solid and certain can easily be misperceived. This can be important when we start working on our baggage since the essence of our baggage may be built upon things we have believed to be the facts of our world or our past and it may turn out they never happened.

Every hunting season an excited hunter kills livestock mistaken for legal game. We too can misinterpret what we see, hear, smell, feel, or taste. So, if we focus on a fearful past event where we have certain sights, sounds, aromas, sensations, or tastes then we can be prone to re-experience those stimuli even when they are not present. In the same way the brain can fill in color of images for those sights we only see with peripheral vision (the visual receptors in our eyes that detect peripheral vision do not detect color) we can see things clearly that are not there if we are strongly anticipating a sighting.

If we have those sensations that seem to reoccur on a regular basis and they cause you great distress this is physical baggage. Like all baggage it may not ever be forgotten, but it can be reset in a way that it no longer has the hold on us like it does today. These things can be brought into the light and seen for what they are with a much clearer and more mature perspective. It is possible that a changed perspective on the past and on the present can change what we tend to experience in our environment.

How We Experience Life - Socially
Our earliest interactions are often with our parents or some other caregiver. How those interactions proceed are thought to have an effect on how we form relationships for the rest of our lives. Two key experiences established early on in our interaction with others are attachment and safety. Since we come into this world with no social skills we are taught by those taking care of us. If our parents or caregivers are engaging, sensitive and kind, we will likely establish a strong attachment with them and have a sense of safety. However, if they are aloof, insensitive and unkind, then our take away will be one more of isolation and hyper vigilance. Most of us experience something somewhere in between these two extremes with either the tendency to seek connection with others or to avoid it. When our primary role models are unpleasant or unavailable to us we may look elsewhere for guidance. The recipe for baggage is optimized when a person has little attachment and or does not feel safe to share what unpleasant event they have experienced. Without the input of someone to help put the unpleasant experience into its proper perspective the resulting lesson learned will likely be based on very few facts.

If our parents or caretakers suffer from mental illness and exhibit behavior like extreme mood swings, violence, intoxication, paranoia or delusions, the child can be thrust into the role of the adult to ensure meals are prepared, everyone gets to bed and wakes up on time to go to work or school. This situation often robs the child of having childhood and lures them into a role of extreme responsibility. While from the surface these children may appear high functioning, they are often incapable of normal relationships where they are not in control of the people they love.

We not only experience how we are treated, but we observe how our role models treat each other and our siblings, if there are any. As we age and we are exposed to how our role models treat others including relatives, neighbors, landlords, police officers, cashiers, teachers, nurses, doctors, clergy, employers and sometimes even employees. Since our role models are our guides we are significantly influenced by how they demonstrate how these people should be treated. This often is also refined with how our role models interact with people of different classes, race, culture, wealth, class, sex, appearance, or attitude. Even if these people are never observed, various sentiments can be overheard when topics are discussed or movies and television shows are made available. If the content is not age appropriate, then social norms can easily be misunderstood.

Our first opportunities to explore social interaction are usually with siblings, relatives and playmates. If there are none available, then we may not get this opportunity until we are in school. Unless we have visited other homes, the classroom may be the first experience we have with role models with different rules that are enforced. Sometimes the classroom may be the first time we experience consistency and age appropriate information and this may extend to greater attachment and a greater sense of safety. Often the social norms are close between the home and school, but when they differ dramatically, we may struggle to reconcile the two. In cases of immaturity or mental illness on the part of our role models we may be directed to be the go between to resolve any conflicts. Since we are not typically equipped to do so, the results can be painful, disastrous and rarely understood. These opportunities for baggage may or may not be remembered. Our interactions with classmates can go well if we have already learned how to get along well with siblings and playmates. However, if school is our first opportunity at significant social interaction then it can make our early years a bit rocky. It can be further complicated if the guidance from home is counter to that of the school. The greater the conflict, the more delayed our social skills can be along with developing more social baggage. Participation in sports is usually a great introduction in team environments where shared goals are pursued and achieved. If the coaching or the parents inject an overly intense focus on success or individual achievement it can be counterproductive and may also create baggage for the child. Youth development programs like scouting and religious youth groups can be a helpful supplement to the social and mental health development of its participants with programs designed around adventure, survival, character building, moral development, spiritual development, peer development and support. As long as the leaders are mature and age appropriate they can become great additional or alternative role models. Working also introduces a new social exchange of work for compensation. This can be effectively introduced within the family if defined well. However, it typically is still a shift when we become an employee in exchange for money or services. Without guidance and encouragement this experience can be rocky, but extremely satisfying to independently earn separate from family. Early work experiences help us to adapt to this new set of social skills.

As we get older and more freedom is allowed opportunities for more social interaction increase and usually gain in importance. The opportunities for play dates, gift exchanges, neighborhood games, parties, sleep overs, dances, trips, etc. all intensify the opportunities for social interaction and the emergence of attraction, popularity and rejection. This is accelerated significantly with access to social media at any age, but too early and much access can be overwhelming increasing opportunities to acquire more baggage. Once peers eclipse our childhood role models, we may no longer trust anyone or we may dethrone role models we once trusted for a peer that may have a much-reduced ability or desire to help us put disturbing experiences into their proper perspective.

When we leave our home either for school or work there is a significant shift in our interactions with our family since we no longer live with them. If we are still under their support we are still obligated to them for whatever are the terms for us in return for their continued support. This obligation may be clear and well communicated or it may be neither and a constant source of conflict. Once we are on our own completely, the independence is often a great builder of our self-esteem.

What we observed between either our parents or caretakers about their romantic relationships establishes our more significant example of how these relationships are conducted. Whether we liked or agreed with the behavior of either party the example set is often the most familiar as adults. Since this example was experienced at such a young age we often have relationship baggage before we have one ourselves. This baggage can cause us to be attracted to what was modeled for us even when we dislike and reject what we observed when we were growing up. A similar effect can happen when we become parents. While we may dislike and reject how we were parented, we can easily default to how we were parented since this is what was modeled for us and it is familiar.

All relationships range somewhere in intimacy for all five of the areas of mentally, emotionally, physically, social and spiritually. If we become extremely intimate in one or more areas with the other areas far behind we can end up assuming we are intimate in them all. At least to the extent that was modeled for us when growing up or to the extent we desire. This is where so much disconnect can occur between relationship types of acquaintances, situational friends, close friends and romantic partners. Our history and what was modeled for us and what we have refined in us since is often quite unique from others. As we become acquainted with someone little information or common experience is shared until mutual interest and or a situation creates the opportunity to become more acquainted. Common situations that can drive a situational friendship are living together or nearby, school, work, events for sports, hobbies, charities, or any significant shared experience. If we become more familiar over an extended period of time then most of the areas can become more intimate in more of a balanced fashion. Most of us tend to unconsciously fill in the gaps of missing information about others with assumptions drawn from people we have known in the past. This filling in with assumptions can be much more pronounced when there is a great intimacy in a single area and little known in the others. If romance quickly results in living together or marriage, then these assumptions are likely filled with our social baggage about these types of relationships. Even when someone reveals or demonstrates how they differ from our baggage-based assumptions we can still expect our assumptions to come true and get met with repeated disappointments. Worst case scenarios of social baggage are when we never had attachment modeled towards us nor experienced safety while growing up and we have continued to avoid relationships and any intimacy since it has never shown itself to be of any benefit.

How We Experience Life - Spiritually

For those who have never been exposed to religion or have been exposed and rejected it, this may seem like an out of place topic. However, spiritual experiences are common for all of us in very diverse ways. Any experience that contributes to a belief that there may be a reality we cannot see, feel or touch can be considered a spiritual one.

When we are trained to interpret these immaterial experiences, a belief is often given the opportunity to form. If we are raised in a setting with no spiritual instruction we are likely to have no opinion on such things or the belief that there is no God or anything else spirit like. Families that make a particular belief the center of their view of the world tend to produce believers with a similar perspective. Especially if the behavior modeled with the spiritual teaching is kind, supportive and respectful then a similar belief is often adopted with great personal success. Other homes that have no spiritual belief discussed tend to produce children with no particular spiritual beliefs and thus when they do eventually experience something they can't explain they tend to gravitate to whatever explanation is close by whether that is from family, friends, literature, movies, or even magazines. When a family makes a particular belief the center of their view, but they are mean-spirited, unsupportive and do not respect personal boundaries these homes produce individuals that tend to be spiritually confused, abusive or reject the spiritual ways of their family of origin. Homes can also have inconsistent models taught over the years and produce a wide range of results.

Regardless of the belief system, when taught early in life carelessly the result can be disastrous. Events where spiritual concepts are modeled or taught without being age appropriate are often very confusing and can create great challenges for a person on spiritual matters. This can especially happen in very large single belief communities. If nearly everyone a young person knows is of one major religion like Christianity, Islam, Hinduism, Buddhism or Judaism, then there is a tendency to only be aware of this one perspective. If the initial exposure is pleasant and is age appropriate and modeled by responsible adults who act appropriately, then there is a greater likelihood for the person to grow in a similar spiritual direction. However, there are always exceptions.

Often the personal spiritual experience is much less sophisticated than the public spiritual events of organized religions. Distinguishing between the two is a challenge for many even as adults, but it is especially challenging for young children. Significant events or traumas if they are carelessly explained in religious terms may add to a superficial appearance that the entire religion or any spiritual perspective becomes invalid to the recipient. Some end up rebelling against the beliefs or religion of their parents, caretakers or significant role models in part out of rebellion of authority during the struggle to transition from a young person to an adult.

Ultimately, what any person believes is a very personal thing that involves their experiences and choosing to believe in something that cannot be entirely understood or supported with material facts. Sometimes children are exposed to extreme pressure to participate in religious practices, since they are the chosen practice of the parents. This can be diversified when each parent is of a different belief or there are other significant role models that are of a variety of beliefs. The exposure to a variety of beliefs can aid in a person's selection, but there is a tendency to adopt the beliefs of the role model who appears most attractive or who appears to get the best results. Thus, a young person from a religious home that is unpleasant with set worship practices may be quick to adopt another type of faith when exposed to a different belief and they have a more pleasant or intense experience.

It is possible to encounter destructive manipulation when participating in some religious communities. Sometimes this is by design with the more extreme cults and sometimes this occurs in part due to individuals that are simply controlling people and are a part of a faith community.

For some the minor variations of a particular faith can be significant or not significant at all and nearly all faiths have subdivisions that fall within a spectrum that range from the more liberal to the more conservative perspectives.

All this variety only adds to the confusion since there is so many options and interpretations when it comes to spiritual matters. It is not uncommon that a young person's first exposure to other faiths comes when they attend school or move away from their family of origin. So, our initial spiritual training may be absent, only a few comments, to moderate instruction and modeling to very detailed instruction and modeling to a completely immersed lifestyle. From this initial collection of spiritual experiences, we often head out into the world only to find there are literally thousands of other beliefs practiced by others from no God, only one God, one God in multiple forms and also the belief in many Gods.

Since faith is the act of choosing to believe in something and in the spiritual sense it usually has to do with something greater than ourselves, it is something that can be changed or recommitted to each and every day. With new information and especially new experiences we may continue to grow in a similar direction of belief or make a change. If the new experiences are coupled with new or more positive and intense emotional experiences, then we tend to change what we believe in. This can occur by joining a friend or spouse to a different faith's form of worship service for a period of time or by simply learning about a different type of belief.

We may be very content with our beliefs and something painful occurs and we really expected our faith to keep anything like that from ever happening. In these instances, it is common to pull away from a particular belief system temporarily or to reject it entirely as a fool's path.

Regardless of your spiritual perspective, if it has been more of an actual source or perceived source of pain and confusion for you then you have spiritual baggage. This baggage may be the conflicting and confusing concepts and information you have in your mind or the existence of experiences that don't appear to fit into a single cohesive belief. It is not unusual to be a member of a faith community and still have spiritual baggage that inhibits your life.

How We Experience Life – With and Without Choices

All of these areas can contribute to the baggage in our lives. It weighs us down and motivates us to act in ways we don't even desire. It is not uncommon for us to have baggage from all of our areas of experiences, with many of them linked to each other and adding to the obstacles in our lives. Each of these areas have an initial set of experiences as we are raised by our parents, guardians, or caretakers then we add to each of these areas with additional experiences some of which are positive and some of which are negative. Since these initial experiences begin at such a young age our collective frame of reference is often skewed with all kinds of misconceptions. We all are a product of this experience.

The experiences we have at a time in our lives when we had no choice in what we were exposed to or didn't know we had a choice about what we were exposed to has a tremendous impact on us. If these experiences modeled perceptions, behaviors, physical treatment, concepts about the world we live in, and they were predominately negative, then we will tend to have a negative perspective on how the world is. If the experiences we had were predominately positive in one or more of the five areas then we will tend to have a positive perspective about these parts of our lives and the world. Most have a mix of positive and negative experiences yet many of us struggle since it is hard to make sense of it all. While the positive things that occurred were great it is those negative ones that can really grab a hold of us and can have a dominate influence over us. If this occurs, it can motivate us to repeat enough bad decisions to keep unfortunate results happening to us.

So, we have these past experiences that happened to us when we had little or no choice about what occurred then we have the rest of the time in our lives when we have had a choice about attitudes, behaviors, our boundaries, our interaction with others and about what we believe. Many of us find out, if they had not noticed already, that we even make bad choices sometimes repeatedly even when we have the freedoms to choose otherwise. Baggage motivates much of this destructive behavior and it can be stopped, but first we have to be aware of how we got to this point.

Knowing this can be somewhat of a relief since it can make a little bit of sense of how such a confusing and diverse array of memories and experiences came to be a part of who we are. While it is still just a beginning it almost always helps to know in general how we got here. And it may give you a little brighter sense of hope that things can get better by choice. The key is choosing to make better choices even when it feels uncomfortable, but the facts support the better choice.

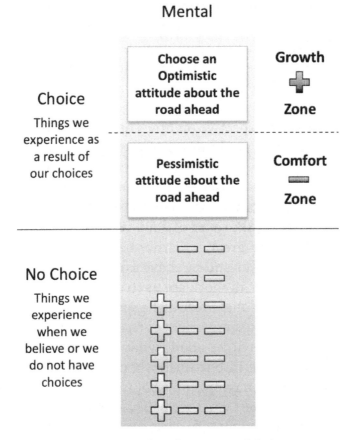

Figure 5-6 Directional impact of our future mental choices.

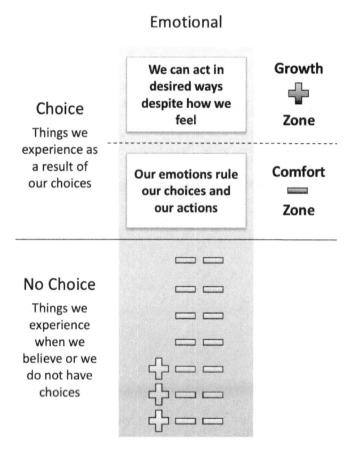

Figure 5-7 Directional impact of our future emotional choices.

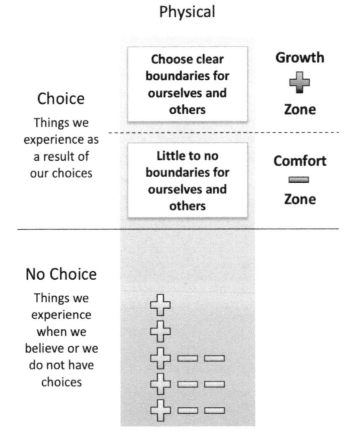

Figure 5-8 Directional impact of our future physical choices.

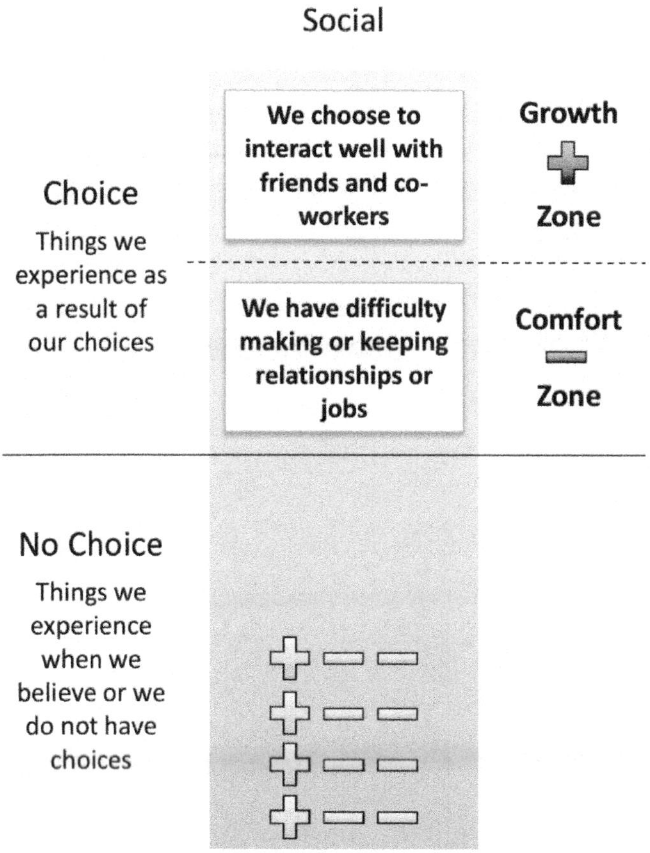

Social

Choice

Things we
experience as
a result of
our choices

We choose to
interact well with
friends and co-
workers

Growth
+
Zone

We have difficulty
making or keeping
relationships or
jobs

Comfort
—
Zone

No Choice

Things we
experience
when we
believe or we
do not have
choices

Figure 5-9 Directional impact of our future social choices.

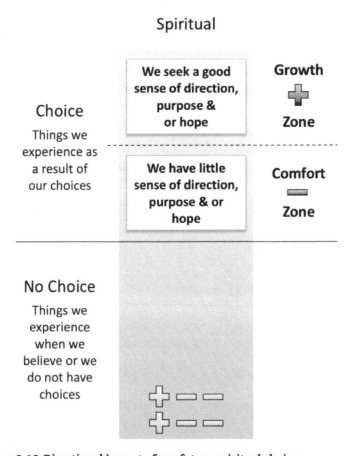

Figure 5-10 Directional impact of our future spiritual choices.

If what we experience trends predominately negative then our comfort zone for future choices will tend to trend negative as well. Our lessons learned create warnings for us to avoid past undesirable outcomes, yet when those lessons and related warnings are based upon faulty data we are led astray by our own perspective based upon our past experiences. When our perspective is negative any change in to a positive direction is going to set off alarms and be very uncomfortable. This is why change is often so uncomfortable because it is going against our lessons learned. Based upon updated and more complete data we may recognize that alternate choices will allow us to grow out of old habits. However, it is usually very uncomfortable to move from our comfort zone to what I call the growth zone.

Normally you would think that those things that initially hurt us, shamed us or scared us would be crystal clear in our memories. However, it is very common for the exact opposite to be true. Over time it is easy to forget the details, but the resulting shame, anger, depression or fear can be laying there dormant until triggered to motivate us to make poor choices over and over. While learning about the way we experience the world around us adds to our awareness of the how it occurred, it does not identify our personal baggage. Now that we have an idea of the many different ways we can experience the events in our life and the potential baggage that can come along with it, let's take a look at the more common sources of the baggage we can accumulate.

6. OUR UNCLAIMED BAGGAGE

Over one third of our planet's population travels by plane each year and over 70,000 of their bags are lost every single day. Half are lost in transfers and the next greatest percentage is simply not loaded at all. As bad as this may sound this accounts for less than 1% that are mishandled and do not arrive with the passenger at their final destination. The vast majority of these bags are eventually reunited within a few days or months. However, with our own personal baggage the percentages are nowhere nearly as impressive. Over 350 million of us suffer from depression which accounts for nearly 5% of every man, woman and child in the world.

Our personal baggage weighs us down, makes us tired, wears us out, motivates us to do very unusual things, and ultimately it makes us sick.

While it is entirely natural to want to avoid things that are painful and unpleasant, the unfortunate truth is that unless we acknowledge our painful and unpleasant aspects of our lives, they tend to impact us whether we realize it or not. The person who is drawn to abusive mates, the person who can no longer bear to be touched, or those who cannot hear disagreement without hearing criticism. While we may learn from some of our mistakes, we also learn destructive behaviors by trying to avoid repeating our painful history. Often, the more we try not to repeat painful mistakes the more we seem to be destined to repeat destructive choices and behaviors.

Not claiming our baggage sets us up to be controlled by it. Our natural instinct for survival gets short circuited and we repeatedly find ourselves making choices we regret, behaving in ways we know will yield us undesirable results, our thinking is often plagued with negative thoughts towards ourselves and

we literally can feel physically ill and alone as if there is no solution available to bring us peace.

In the same ways we experience life mentally, emotionally,
physically, socially and spiritually let's take a look at how not
claiming our baggage can affect us. In each of these areas we already have a past, a present and a future. Our past is often filled
with distorted lessons learned (the baggage of our past). Our
present is often significantly derailed by our distorted lessons
learned and our future is full of baggage collecting behavior,
because we are often viewing our new experiences through the
lens of our distorted lessons learned. Many of us tend to hang
on to old lessons learned many years ago rather than to correct
them with new information. While there may be similarities
between us and others in how this takes place most us have our
unique path and collection of the things that weigh us down.

Mental

How well we can concentrate without outside distractions,
make decisions based upon our values and priorities, and how
well we can control what we choose to think about at any given
moment can gauge our current mental state. A person who is
in a healthy state of mind can easily be very present in the
moment and appreciate the things currently occurring around
them. While we can all be distracted by noises, emergencies,
obligations, responsibilities, etc. the idea is that on demand we
can stop and appreciate the world we live in. When we literally
struggle or can't do this then more than likely you have a good
deal of mental baggage that is keeping you from enjoying your
present experiences freely.

Examples of old mental baggage are thoughts, impressions,
perceptions, or interpretations of events in our past. Many of
these memories can even be about events that do not stick out
as significant events to others. A careless phrase of criticism
between parents, to other siblings or directly to us can stick
with us in a way that it appears to be permanently etched in

our memory. It might be as simple as a childish taunt of you like, "stupid, fat, ugly, slow, weak, clumsy, silly, poor, dirty, a sissy, a crier, a liar, a momma's boy, a loser" and the list can go on and on. Children can be cruel especially when unsupervised.

Adults on the other hand who say things carelessly in front of us when we are very young can easily leave a lasting impression upon us like, "I am going to kill you, why can't you be like your Sister?, I am ashamed of you, I can't even believe you are my child, I wish you were never born, etc. Seeing them in print will make most of us cringe to think of an impressionable child and them hearing one of these statements from one of their idolized parents for the first time. These kinds of statements are said very infrequently in many homes in moments of great frustration or anger, but there are some homes where these kinds of statements are said on a regular basis.

Real events of loss, disappointment, tragedy, shame or embarrassment can easily create a significant memory that is not quite clear on the facts. A young child whose parents divorce may secretly believe they were the cause, or they may blame themselves for a house fire, or a parent's abandonment, illness, or alcoholism. Shame and embarrassment may haunt a person because of inappropriate behavior of a parent or other older person in their life that was conducted in their presence like a crime or abuse.

While no one is immune to their past often we have to take conscious steps to reconcile ourselves with it. Just distracting ourselves with something else is typically not an effective answer. Even a life devoted to the service of others has to rest and once again be alone with oneself. When we seek out pleasure, fun and things that interest us we are even more subject to our baggage. In the middle of parties, games with friends, conversations, concerts, family outings, on vacation, even during sex our past comes to mind. If we are fortunate they are pleasant thoughts and memories, but when they are unpleasant thoughts and memories it is our mental baggage that is pulling us down.

If we haven't been able to face and reconcile ourselves with our mental baggage, then we are likely to instinctively collect more baggage. Despite the weight of what we are already carrying we tend to make the same mistakes, make more bad choices, begin to believe that we are never going to be happy and free of all the anguish that we have promised we would never reveal. We agonize over the painful moments in our past and we somehow find ourselves in more painful situations again and again.

It is not that we create all of our own pain, but when we are overloaded with mental baggage we tend to be attracted to things that bring more of the same kind of pain. If we say to ourselves, we are stupid over and over, then we will tend to look for evidence to support that perspective. If we tell ourselves, we are unattractive, then we will be harsh critics of ourselves and tune our ear for criticisms and looks from others to confirm our opinion. The way we spend our time thinking creates a deceptive bias in the lens through which we view and experience our lives. No amount of advanced degrees can squash the pain felt by the nickname of "dummy". Achieving professional celebrity for our looks can't overcome the self-loathing developed out of becoming convinced early on that we are unattractive.

When we are experiencing mental anguish we also tend to dish it out not only on ourselves but others. If not the closest parties to us, we consume our time with lashing out at public persons, places or things. It makes little difference if we are right. If we are consuming ourselves with the issues of the world and neglecting our responsibilities and the loved ones around us, then we are probably influenced by our mental baggage. Being angry at the world or at least part it robs us of the beauty and wonder before us and yet if we find ourselves constantly drawn to the situations, literature or media that is consistently proposing the same painful arguments we would likely benefit from trying something different.

When we are unaware of how we think we likely have settled into repeated patterns of thought. If these thought patterns that are challenging, uplifting and inspirational we are benefitted in countless ways. For the thought patterns that are comfort seeking, disparaging and destructive we are loaded down by their negative weight in ways that can significantly limit our view of everything. While both can be self-perpetuating, the negative type of thinking can literally undermine all aspects of our lives. If we continue to be unaware of our way of thinking, then we are likely to continue down one of these two paths.

While other people, places and things may have been the sources of the way we think about things, these are our thoughts of choice. The choice may be unconscious, but they are our thoughts. Since they are our thoughts they can be redirected and most cases changed with effort. Yet the first step making any change is to claim these thoughts as ours. They may have started elsewhere, but they are our thoughts now and they are ours to deal with if we so choose. If we never get to the point where we can acknowledge and accept that our thoughts are ours, then we will never see them as something we can change. As distasteful as it may be, the benefits of accepting our own internal thought behavior is the first step to turning around out mental baggage-collecting behavior and redirecting it on a path that can result in a much better life.

Emotional

If we are predominately loved, protected and nurtured growing up then we tend to experience more pleasant emotions in response. If we are predominately ignored, endangered and deprived we tend to experience unpleasant emotions in response. We also learn to express or suppress our emotions as a result of our experience. We all can remember some pieces of our childhood, but most us will never know about those earliest of years and the details of what we experienced. If our parent or caretaker is observed raising a newborn when we are older we may gain some clues. Our early years are known to play a role in what we become as adults. Our personality, our mental health and our likelihood to express and manage our emotions are all influenced by the experiences we had early on and along the way to this very day.

Just like the mental images we see with our eyes and interpret based upon our knowledge and experience we capture emotional experiences as well. However, the difference is that a reminder of an emotional memory often causes us to re-feel the emotion of the past event. This can range from a mildly pleasant or unpleasant memory, to an extremely pleasant or unpleasant emotional memory.

Examples of old emotional baggage are overwhelming or explosive emotions that have little to nothing to do with the current moment, a much greater emotional reaction to person, place or thing than the current event calls for, opposite emotional reactions to people, places and things than are typical, or the absence of an emotional reaction to the people, places and things in our current surroundings.

Emotional baggage is probably the type of baggage that is experienced the most intensely. It can teleport us back to past emotions as if they were being experienced for the first time in the present. They may mystify, intensify, contradict, or completely stifle us where we emote nothing at all. Unfortunately, as a result, our emotional baggage can derail a perfectly nice evening, a much-anticipated vacation or potentially the rest of our life if we let it.

Now this may all sound rather off to those who have managed to not feel anything at all for many years, but we all have emotions even if we have managed to bury them. The common phrases people like this say to themselves and others are: I am not an emotional person, I don't feel anything, I don't want to feel anything, I don't have any emotions and the classic, I am a rock.

There are a number of possible ways to account for not

consciously experiencing emotions. One, you may have been significantly deprived of responses when showing your first emotive facial expressions as an infant and never developed an awareness of emotions and their connections with the events in your life. Two, you may have a mental illness that involves what is believed to be a disruption of normal brain function that deals with emotions. These first two are fairly rare, so it is much more likely that those of us who experience a life without emotions are simply choosing to not feel them. This choice may be very conscious or very unconscious. Those who have reported making this decision consciously describe a painful or disturbing emotional event where the expression or actions motivated by emotions created a very undesired result. To ensure this result was never repeated a decision was made to never let ourselves feel again. Others who have no recollection of such a choice can sometime identify when they started turning off the emotions after a difficult period in their life. The net effect is the same. Expressing our emotions brought us trouble, so we eliminated the practice from our lives or at least for the most part.

Most of us who experience what appears to be a life free of emotions occasionally still demonstrate what most of us think of as an emotional reaction such as anger, crying, depression, distress, and sadness. In addition, this failure to express emotion that really exists inside, but is simply bottled up has been associated with many physical ailments such as headaches, hypertension, nausea, irritable bowel syndrome and back pain to name a few.

When we carry a lot of emotional baggage we are time bombs just waiting to go off. We often have no idea when it will happen since we are unaware of our emotions. All we know is that someone or something really got to us and we couldn't take anymore. This is often accompanied with blame of other people, places or things for our reaction which of course we will not describe as being emotional. Somebody made me angry and we reacted like anyone would by screaming for a very long time in a very extreme manner.

The triggers that can set off someone with emotional baggage can be anything from a smell, an image, a word, phrase, language, hearing a subject, hearing a tone, hearing a type of voice or even the most innocent of touch. As a result, most days can provide a trigger for those of us with emotional baggage. We experience the trigger and away we go on an emotional roller coaster. We may recognize the trigger and we may not. Either way our life is disrupted. As a result, relationships, occupations, and responsibilities can be significantly impacted by these emotional events. Even if we are able to suppress our behavior, we often have a powerful storm of energy brewing inside of us impacting our choices, our actions and the way we think.

The way emotional baggage creates even more baggage for us is while we are suppressing and experiencing these reactions we make more poor choices. We may create additional reinforcement for trying to keep a lid on our outward expression of emotions by redoubling our promise to ourselves to not let anyone see us lose our cool. Or we may create more consequences for ourselves through impulsive behavior choices while we are acting out.

Our emotional baggage is like a time bomb that can go off at any time and the more we are exposed to the normal events and experiences of a day the more likely there will be another episode. Even if all is contained and no unintended word is spoken, our judgment in these situations is impaired. While it may be that we can have many past emotional based issues, once we begin the process of processing them we can very soon see that we are making progress. However, if we never become aware of the emotions we have experienced and we are experiencing, then this processing cannot begin.

Each emotional history is like its own time bomb ready to blow again and again. The work of identifying the trigger, the actual emotion that occurs in response and the history behind that response is all a part of the processing that can dismantle the trigger and the bomb.

Some emotional bombs we have may have many triggers. A simple example of this is when someone uses unfamiliar words or slang and we interpret a statement as an insult when it is actually a complement. As we begin to react and the person explains the meaning they intended the trigger may be defused for this one particular instance or source. The time bomb of being sensitive to comments about ourselves or certain topics may still be an issue, but at least that one person's use of that particular term is now known to not be an insult.

Claiming our emotional baggage is the practice of acknowledging our past emotional experiences and beginning to see how they are impacting our current lives. This is a process of identifying and diffusing the emotional time bombs we have collected though a lifetime. While this may sound unattainable to us, that is the baggage talking. However, the truth is that all of our emotional baggage can be either diffused or significantly reduced so we can get back to having a more enjoyable life. While it takes time to unravel a lifetime of emotional baggage, each step of progress results in decreased stress, less poor choices and consequences, all of which are well worth the effort. As a result of taking the first step of claiming that we have emotional baggage, little by little we find ourselves better able to deal with it, happier and our lives are less disrupted by our emotional past.

Physical

Our physical baggage can vary from the physical characteristics we were born with to the acquired conditions resulting from our behavior or experiences such as illness, accidents or aging. Most of us struggle with some aspect of our physical self at one time or another especially when confronted with a comparison that highlights our differences. These differences can be as basic as our height, weight, shape, type or color of hair, and the color of our skin to more sensitive differences due to birth defects, heredity, injuries, or illnesses. While many of us eventually come to terms with our unique physical characteristics, some of us never do. And even when we grow out of certain physical characteristics like being heavy or clumsy, we often have a hard time shaking the impression that we are still that heavy or clumsy little kid.

Our physical bodies are what most everybody associates with us since we have it with us wherever we go. The only exceptions to this are relationships that are all remote which most often occur in business. However, most of our interactions are with people we meet and we both can see each other before every meeting. Based upon our reactions from others we often have built up a known range of reactions to our appearance. If those reactions have been unpleasant for us, then we typically have become less and less pleased with our appearance.

Sometimes we can make alterations to our appearance, but in many cases, there are limits to what we can change. If we are shorter than most then we can't do much more that wear shoes and boots with taller heels. If the adjustments that are possible have been exhausted then we have a few choices: typically, limited change with surgery, accept the facts about our physique or to be weighed down by the negative aspects of being this way.

This choice is the same for those naturally born this way or to those who acquired new undesired physical characteristics after birth. The same applies for those of us who have noticed changes in our bodies once aging becomes more noticeable. There are numerous industries that have been created by our desire to not look our age. And while some may look down upon those who might choose to alter their bodies, dye their hair, or mask certain blemishes, these practices can be quite liberating to those who have been plagued by negative reactions to their appearance.

For the most part we are stuck with our bodies and if we are unhappy with them we can let it make our lives miserable and possibly in turn motivate ourselves to mistreat our bodies and make things even worse. When we do we often think about where we fall short physically, notice others that are more like we would prefer to be, and then we are more likely to assess our worth, attractiveness and role in life as somehow less meaningful.

Through this lens we often overlook the ones that overcome it with astonishing success, yet we can easily see most of the examples of those more fortunate from our perspective. We may be jealous, angry or highly critical of them simply because they have a physical characteristic that we want. As we devote more and more time to this we can become consumed. In that state we tend to make more poor choices that often do not treat our bodies well.

If we continue to let this baggage go unanswered without being put in its proper perspective, then it will haunt us for the rest of our lives. Yet most of us are aware of others who are like us yet not as weighed down with their less than perfect physique. We tell ourselves they had it easier with more money, a better job, family or personality, and this is just the way we are and there is no changing it. This is the lie that our physical baggage creates. While in reality it can be fixed. Maybe not in the fantasy version we have dreamed of much of our lives, but in a way that makes the physical characteristics we have been haunted by irrelevant. It takes work to put our history of judgments about ourselves into their proper perspective, but as this begins to occur this baggage about our physical selves begins to melt away.

Social

Our social baggage impacts every relationship we have or if it is severe we don't have them at all. These relationships include ones with parents, the opposite sex, the same sex, romantic ones, siblings, friends, authority figures, peers, people at work, other family members, our neighbors, people with more money or power and people with less money or power, salesmen, business proprietors, landlords, government employees, police officers, professionals, tradesmen, laborers, members of our political party/policy/position and non-members, members of our faith/religion/denomination/house of worship and non-members, acquaintances and strangers. Actually, the list is much more extensive, but you get the idea.

Our initial impression, encounter or most impacting social exchange with anyone different than us often results in a casual judgment that all the rest will be very similar. People with less are poor; people with more are rich, etc. As a result, if those events have not gone well, we tend to distrust, fear, resent, avoid, suspect malice and generally expect little or negative things from the individuals we encountered.

If this pattern continues over a good deal of time, then we can run out of people and groups of people in the world that we like. This is in limited doses and the more extreme is the result of social baggage we have allowed ourselves to acquire over time. The extent we limit or over generalize our distaste for others is often very personal and not necessarily consistent. When this becomes rampant in our lives it can destroy families, both our family of origin and any we create. We may be unable to keep many friends, jobs, hangouts, groups, etc. because they always end up ruining it for us, by falling into one of our disowned groups.

The reality of course is that we are the common denominator in all these relationships. As long as it is all or mostly everyone else's fault then our social baggage will continue to be with us. Our social baggage can cripple our ability to work with others even at a distance despite how resourceful we are.

There are many types of social relationships we have from the ones who raised us, any friends and acquaintances of ours and our family or caretakers while in our pre-school years. While these relationships may have been close and pleasant for many they are a bit more distant and at times not so pleasant. Worse case we have no caretakers or we are in the hands of many caretakers, some of which are mean and maybe abusive. Prior to a daily public schedule like daycare, pre-school or school outside of the home, we are exposed to a lot of information about how people interact with one another. If we are exposed to other families or caretaking situations we may obtain new information or merely see what appears to confirm our original impressions.

This also applies to adult relationships with each other, with us, with other family members, with the neighbors, salesmen, business proprietors, landlords, meter readers, police officers, acquaintances and strangers often based upon their appearance. Add to this that we are at this age very unprepared to perceive events in context and you have the conditions for many everyday events being misunderstood and painful events to be devastating.

A parent or caretaker's mental illness of any kind, say depression, could have resulted in a childhood devoid of love, encouragement, healthy social behavior, and simple everyday lessons about the world. The lessons taken from such a childhood could be that the world is silent, sad and painful. While a healthy parent or caretaker focused on our upbringing could result in a much better result where love and encouragement and a variety of healthy engaging social interaction are observed as a constant experience and the world is seen as a bright and inviting place to explore.

Spiritual

Our spiritual baggage often determines how much serenity or peace of mind we have. Whether or not you are a believer in something greater than mankind, most of us are pretty clear there are things mankind still has yet to learn. That gap of knowledge can be a source of torment. When it torments us we may tend to find ourselves wondering or maybe even screaming out why is there so much heartache, sickness and death in this world? When the available answers seem to fall very short it tends to gnaw at us in a variety of ways. This may motivate us positively or negatively. When it is negative we may be mainly fearful, angry, lonely, defeated, frustrated, anxious, detached, irresponsible, violent, haunted, hateful, irritated or maybe a little of all of the above. Not knowing can be quite unnerving and not knowing about things we see as important can make matters much worse. So many of us develop beliefs about what we don't know and what we can't see. While some of us create our beliefs from scratch most of us are exposed to established religions and belief traditions of our particular culture and either adopt or reject them.

How well this belief approach appears to work for us in our eyes determines if it is seen as beneficial or not. When our experiences are disappointing and we see the belief as the cause of the disappointment then disillusionment sets in about the belief. At this point many take a step back as anyone would do from a source of pain to recover and reevaluate our next moves. Usually, if the person sticks with the belief it is often because new information was received that puts the painful experience into a new perspective. If the person steps away from the belief then whatever benefits were being received are afterwards lost or diminished. These series of less than desirable results can become a part of our spiritual baggage. We may come away rejecting full participation or any participation of the original belief or we may venture elsewhere to other beliefs in search of a better one that is not so painful or disappointing. This often results in a community or place of worship change or a new philosophy adjustment.

If we are taught a very detailed version of a belief that has many rules and tenants, then we are likely to unconsciously adopt many of those rules as facts, regardless if we are practicing the belief later in life or not. While we may choose to reject the overall belief many of us fail to consciously reject the piece parts that go along with it. So, we may reject prayer as a practice, but believe if you do pray it must be done in a certain way.

Spiritual baggage may undermine a faith we once held, or it

may limit us from benefitting from one we have. It can motivate the perception that any evidence of hypocrisy is more reason to not choose to believe in some particular belief, while at the same time it may reopen a sense of betrayal that our past belief was incorrect or that we were deceived. Another reaction is that all beliefs are false once we are disappointed.

As a result, we may have changed sects or denominations of a particular religion or we may simply have changed where we gather to worship to find one that better suits our preferences. While others may make a more extreme change and adopt an entirely different religion. Then there are the interest related religions that have nothing to do with a stance in God or Gods at all such as sports, business, music, politics, exercise, science, ecology, animals, literature, art, fun, traveling, etc. Granted this seems to have strayed from what most would call a spiritual pursuit, but we all have probably met someone whose religion is not typically thought of as a religion.

What people see as things greater than themselves, that they have a great interest in, and they often participate in activities related to this interest can qualify as a religion and have spiritual significance in their life. While the God related religions typically define and promote a broad personal journey of development or improvement in life, the interest religions tend to be more limited. Spiritual baggage can cause us to be repulsed from where we have been and even keep us from ever investing in any position similar in the future.

PART 3 - IDENTIFYING OUR BAGGAGE

A Reference of Baggage Source Candidates

One of the greatest obstacles to resolving the baggage in our lives is simply not acknowledging that it exists. You can't fix what doesn't exist. In this part I have described some of the more common baggage sources in four categories of People, Events, Flawed Concepts and Negative Self-talk. These are here to help with your recognition and awareness of what sources you may have experienced. If some of the sources listed here seem like a likely candidate for you, then make note of them and consider it for a while. It may be as simple as recalling what happened and when considering the memory with the current day facts you may be able to put it into a more appropriate perspective yourself. However, many old lessons learned are more complicated than that and it may take discussing it with a trusted friend, mentor or professional to put it into a more appropriate perspective. The greater the reaction you have to reading a source description the greater the likelihood you have baggage from this source.

A word of caution, the descriptions in these following chapters may stir up unpleasant reactions for you. Some may irritate you, anger you, scare you, insult you or make you think, "I can't stand to think about this". If any of these occurs, make note of the topics that have an impact upon you for future reference. These are likely candidates for baggage sources that have been significant for you. You may very well identify some baggage that you have been carrying around with you for a very long time. If what you read becomes too overwhelming for you, I suggest you skip ahead to Part 4 on Converting our baggage into luggage. It is normal to feel discomfort when facing our baggage areas and it is best to take it in limited portions. You can always come back to the chapters in Part 3 at a later time when you are ready to explore some more potential candidates.

7. PEOPLE

From the day we are born we are 100% dependent upon others to keep us alive. Who they are, what they know, when and where this care takes place and how prepared they are to provide for us are all factors into how well they treat us. This has a very significant impact upon our lives. People in the best of circumstances make mistakes and occasionally fall short of their intentions and their typical character, knowledge and skills. However, for most of us we are in the hands of people who are capable and that care about us, but who are also facing challenges that will cause them to stumble eventually and the impact of those events often affecting us.

People are by their very nature going to make mistakes. Some mistakes are made without knowledge and some are made consciously, but rarely are we conscious of the impact a single act can have on another human being. A simple word of encouragement can be the catalyst of a lifetime of inspiration. And a single unkind act can devastate another's hopes and dreams. No matter how careful or careless, we all are the source and the recipient of these acts. The kindness and encouragement of a loving family and friends can help mold a life with an outlook that can result in great achievement and peace. While an environment of hatefulness and criticism can break a person's spirit one of many ways.

Our parents, caretakers and significant role models

Our parents, caretakers and significant role models are the ones we learn from the most in early life. And while they do not set an unbreakable mold they do help form an image and translation of the world that can be either very bright or very dark. What we were exposed to prior to having a choice in the matter is simply unavoidable. Once we become aware that we have a choice, things have the potential to change. Sometimes this change is to simply no longer value the input from those who treat us poorly, while others might engineer ways to put physical distance between themselves and the offending party. Most drastically some simply leave completely to separate themselves from the painful treatment from others.

Once we turn away from the original cast of influencers in our lives we usually encounter new ones either consciously or unconsciously. Who we encounter from this point forward tends to either counter or reinforce what we learned early on. Even people who overwhelmingly encourage, inspire and motivate us can at times disappoint us or cause us pain.

Our sensitivity to these negative experiences and our willingness to forgive them often determines whether the relationship continues to flourish or begins to be held at arm's length. A person who has developed a great tendency to shun anyone who disappoints them may end up isolating themselves from the very people who can help encourage, inspire and motivate them to great possibilities. So thus, the possibility of the self-fulfilling prophecy can begin at a very early age. If we become convinced that people cannot be trusted and that they will always hurt you then we will look for the first sign of human error that disappoints us and we confirm for ourselves that this is just another that is just like all the rest. This suspect population can be members of the opposite sex or the same sex, they can be authority figures or those who are responsible for us, a different race, creed or culture or just anyone. Sometimes only siblings or strangers have a slight chance of being trusted by someone who is so convinced others cannot be trusted.

The same applies to others we typically encounter in our lives. Unless our parents or caretakers are regularly having encounters with authority figures, teachers are usually the next significant person of influence we encounter. If the authorities often stop our parents or caretakers, we will often take on a strong set of opinions about authority figures. These can be landlords, police officers, immigration officers, child protective services, social workers, educators, business owners, people with jobs, people with money or simply anyone who appears to be an enemy of the family.

Growing up with parents or caretakers like these can help create a very distorted view of the world. So, who we are most exposed to early in life makes a significant impression upon the way we view the world. What we are exposed subsequently and how we choose to interpret these experiences determines how we emerge as young people and adults. All along the way we have choices whether we recognize them or not.

Our Teachers

Our teachers are often one of the first adults outside of our family we encounter on a regular and sustained basis. We are also exposed to a new set of rules and consequences. How these are explained, understood and experienced often has a important bearing upon how we perceive limits. If we have been used to highly inconsistent discipline we may not respond well or, if we have had a lack of discipline, we might interpret the consequences as another lashing out for no good reason other than to cause shame, pain and anguish. The teacher may be good and well meaning, but if they remind us of our abusive parents or caretakers, then most attempts at clear communication will be challenged. Unfortunately, there is no way to know if something we do or say or simply about the way we look will remind someone of an abusive person in their past.

So, by the time we arrive at school if we have had troubling experiences we can be drawn or repulsed by anyone new we encounter depending upon who they remind us. This is our experience for the rest of our lives. If we are reminded of someone and they happen to be associated with a very painful or distressing part of our past, then we will likely be teleported back to those disturbing memories when we see or hear from these new people. Most think of this as daydreaming, but I associate this term with more pleasant thoughts and memories. Rather I would call these less pleasant moments just what they are, unpleasant memories. Most of us however, conceal these moments and are often influenced by the old emotions. The problem is that this impacts how we interact with the innocent person before us. We probably can all recall times when we have acted angrier towards someone in our present day simply because they remind us of someone we are angry at from the past.

Healthcare Professionals

Experiences with physicians, nurses and dentists can be challenging since we or someone we love encounters them typically when we are ill or hurt in some way and require treatment. The more serious the issue or the more unpleasant the experience, it can result in baggage even while still receiving appropriate care. While shots can stick out for children, any visit that involves unexpected pain can leave us with an unpleasant experience. Broken bones and dislocated joints that need resetting can be painful, but the treatment usually brings relief pretty quickly. Probably, the interaction with the doctor and nurses is what can ease or magnify the trauma of the visit. Surprises and increased pain without kindness can create baggage that may be associated with that doctor or any doctor. Also, unkind support during treatment can easily make the potential for baggage to multiply. Being ostracized, scolded or threatened at a display of fear or pain can significantly increase the likelihood the patient can walk away with baggage. Carrying this baggage can lead us to put off regular checkups, tests and treatments. While it is natural to have some reluctance to getting a tooth drilled or a surgical procedure, avoiding the appointments all together is likely due to our baggage. Yet like with so many things the natural avoidance if we act on it brings more poor results. In extreme cases, healthcare professionals can be looked upon as the enemy who are out to take advantage of us and force us into treatments that not necessary. Challenging and arguing with these professionals versus obtaining a second opinion can interrupt our timely treatment and impact our health. As we age or our condition affects our communications abilities we may find that having someone accompany us can ensure we understand what our condition entails and how to properly do our part to take the prescribed treatment.

Unpleasant people

Encounters with unpleasant people often cause us to have unpleasant opinions of all kinds of things. Scary encounters with a train conductor can create an aversion for trains. A clown who scares as a young child in their attempts to surprise and entertain us may begin our dislike for clowns or even the circus. Probably our most common unpleasant memory can be receiving a shot from a doctor and from then on all doctors can make us apprehensive. Yet it is in our personal relationships where the most damage can be done. If our early experience with friends is that they cannot be trusted since they break confidences, then we will likely have trust issues. If all of these early unpleasant experiences were with members of the same sex, then we may selectively only distrust members of that sex. What makes it even more complicated is that siblings can have the same home environment and friends and have slightly different experiences and come away from them with radically different frames of reference. One may be fearful and distrustful of others while the other may be more forgiving and trusting.

As we get older, and enter the working world, we are introduced to people once again in a new environment where individuals remind us of people we have encountered before. As a result, we will have the tendency to react to these individuals like they were the ones we encountered in the past. We may be correct, but if it is based on our emotional experience rather than our knowledge of the facts then we probably are wrong and have judged another unfairly.

This can be a problem if we have had a great deal of problems with taking direction from our parents or caregivers as we have gotten closer to the transition from teenager to young adulthood. If we have been angry about the direction or orders given by our parents, then we may find ourselves having a very inappropriate and angry reaction to our supervisor. The real clue is when we react much stronger than the current event should have stimulated. When we know why, realize our over-reaction and can apologize, then little new damage is done. However, when we don't even know why we are so intense in our reaction then all we have done is create new problems for ourselves because of our baggage.

Strangers

Strangers can also build up a history with us that can influence our perceptions of the people we encounter today. If we have had a great deal of bad experiences with strangers or even just perceived bad experiences, then we can create an avoidance behavior that severely limits our options in life for new relationships.

For instance, if we assume that all people are dangerous since we have been told since we were very young that strangers are dangerous, we can continue to view strangers with a very wary eye as adults. Young children are often taught to stay away from strangers. This is a successful lesson that has saved many young children, but if later on in life few new relationships have gone well, this perspective of strangers can be a continuing challenge.

People unlike us

People unlike us is a much more common unpleasant experience for most of us. If we grow up in a working-class neighborhood, then people with money are suspect. If we grow up in a neighborhood where everyone is all one race, culture or religion then people of other races/cultures/religions are unknown to us and much more likely to be misunderstood. If we have no personal experience, but grow up getting an earful of family and friends telling us these other people are to be feared, not trusted, are thieves, lazy, etc., then we will likely be influenced by this input as we encounter these other populations in our life. Often, if we give new people a chance and get to know them we find out they are just like us with just a different background and a different frame of reference.

Just like opinions formed as a result of our own unpleasant past experiences we may pick up on and adopt the opinions of others around us without any personal knowledge to back them up. As a result, we may be prejudiced against certain types of people with no experience with them what so ever.

If our parents expressed a dislike or distrust of a certain group(s) of people we likely will share that opinion until we have a set of experiences that disproves it. The sad thing is that people often like to talk bad about people they dislike. If they are doing it with close friends in order to reason out their troubled thoughts and feelings on the matter that is one thing. However, when this line of talk is repeated and in front of children it often indoctrinates a point of view.

We can be hired or not hired because of baggage we have about other people. We can become estranged from our children when they choose to marry people that belong to the groups we have great issues with that are not backed up by facts. Friends and couples of different races, cultures and religions etc. can often be challenged by the baggage others have with race, cultures and religions, etc. And even when we can manage to stay with, "our kind", no matter how small that makes our world, we will constantly find these other people creeping into our lives.

While we may have a lesser form of bias taught to us as young children or young adults, we can develop it just as inaccurately as adults through either limited experience or through the opinions and perspective of others. As communications technologies advance this increases its chance to influence us with an overwhelming amount of other people's opinions that can also be absent of any facts.

We may with little personal inclination end up identifying ourselves with a political party or movement, or we may come to think of ourselves as very liberal or conservative, or some other large group of opinion. When people we respect or admire have an opinion we can often end up adopting that opinion with little or no facts to back it up. When the source of the opinion is entertaining and appears necessary to make sure the future of the world will not be destroyed, then the influence can be overwhelming. This has long been the case with charismatic leaders and organizations yet it may or may not be actually based in fact. So as a result, we may end up creating new baggage for ourselves since we either agree or disagree with one group's opinions or not and if we allow ourselves to agree with an over elevated sense of urgency that the opposition groups must be neutralized, we can become consumed with a new prejudice. If this new set of opinions now steers you to only have friends with the same outlook you have allowed yourself to let your world get a lot smaller and supposedly for good reason. A lot of times it is not and you have developed some new baggage for yourself.

Spouses and Children

Spouses and children are often the most meaningful relationships we experience. Many of us marry, have children and raise them to prepare them to live in the world. Others that either make other choices or are not so fortunate to find someone to share their adult life as married may have alternate options through close friends, extended family or through social work with others. Regardless of the exact circumstance you choose, sharing a romantic regard for another and sharing your life with them creates an intense exposure to another person. The same goes for parenting or intensely caring and mentoring children. This intense exposure with other people creates endless opportunities to run into your people related baggage and the more baggage we have the more these relationships are affected.

If you are certain that spouses are to be kept in the dark, then you will likely hear that the lack of closeness is an issue. If you were intensely beaten as a child you may be inclined to never say, "no", to your children and they may grow up learning few lessons about healthy limits. If you and your spouse were raised in very different homes, one where there was a great deal of criticism and another that was very loving and supportive, you may find that you have a hard time parenting from a single agreed upon approach. If your same sex parent died at an early age and you are approaching that age, you may find yourself distancing yourself from all your loved ones since you assume you will die soon as well. We all have impressions based upon our past and even when they do not agree with the facts, we are influenced by them. Some we are conscious of and many, probably most, we are unconscious of when their influence begins affecting our closer relationships. It is not uncommon to have this dilemma. It is actually very common to have baggage that misinforms us about what is going on with the present relationships we are in.

People are one of the more dynamic sources of baggage and we can as a result have many conflicting impressions about who people are, what they are intending to do, and what they are capable of. While we are very young we are intensely dependent upon people and also least prepared to understand what their actions towards us really means. This inability to put our early experiences with people into its proper perspective is often at the heart of our struggles with other people and ourselves. It isn't a matter of blame, just the facts.

Most people who leave poor impressions with others, especially children, are not intending to be malicious, but they tend to highly underestimate the impact their actions can have on a young person who is so limited in their perspective of other people. We have all had our moments with other people that have lodged themselves into our memories. From that moment on we may over react to the person standing in front of us, or more often, we may go back in time and re-experience what happened many years ago that was unpleasant.

This is baggage that we are carrying that serves no good purpose. Yet we carry it with us everywhere anyway, because we do not know how to unpack it and put it into its proper perspective.

Friends and Lovers

While some of us are fortunate to marry our lovers, this is not always the case for many. We may marry out of infatuation, lust, obligation, the desire to rescue or maybe as a strategy to get ahead, or to have a better life. However, whether we have romantic relationships or not, or marry or not, we all have some degree of romantic baggage.

The truth is whether we tell anyone or not our actions usually give us away. When we are interested, we tend to stare and or smile or respond in some over the top manner that gives us away. Others, even young children pick up on this and usually will make it known they think we like/love someone or that we are liked/loved by someone.

When this is about someone we have no interest in or creates little or no embarrassment then it is likely soon forgotten. However, when it is about someone we do like or is very attractive to us, we are especially vulnerable to the teasing from others. If this attention draws attention to our actual desire and the other person is disgusted, uninterested or responds in any way we do not perceive as a positive, we can experience this simple event as a meaningful rejection.

Remember, in elementary school we have little understanding

of the world and the way social situations can play out. If we didn't have siblings or ones that were close enough in age to spend time with us, school was maybe the first time we experienced teasing, kindness, bullying, sharing, flirting, friendship, rejection by a peer, teamwork, competition, and all the things that make up typical relationships.

All it takes for us to gather baggage is for something to not go well and we never talk about it. It never gets put into its proper perspective and we keep remembering the hurt we felt when someone we liked or might have liked didn't like us back. It may sound silly, but for those who have lived this scenario, it can stick with us for the rest of our lives. As a result, if this experience is significant enough or repeatedly occurs and is interpreted as reinforcement that we are ugly, dumb, undesirable, etc., then we can develop some very odd conclusions about the way the world works and the way it is going to be for us.

This can also, unfortunately, be reinforced by our adult role models that may also have social skill issues. If what they say appears to reinforce what we have already concluded, we may decide that we will never like anyone again or something equally destructive. We may start recoiling from all social situations, or we may start hurting others emotionally or physically to preemptively avoid any unpleasant responses. The response path we take can vary wildly, but often when we start down a path of behaving a certain way we can get very comfortable with staying on that path unless some event occurs that forces us out of our comfort zone.

As we get a bit older and the social opportunities become greater, we may once again get opportunities to like and be liked by others. If we take an extreme path of avoidance of all others, then these opportunities become less likely to the point we may never connect with anyone romantically, or even as friends. Yet most of us try again. We let our guard down even if we are guarded normally and like someone or something.

Between our experiences, our reaction to them, and the opportunities we have to meet others we might mutually enjoy, can determine a lot about who we like and don't like. We may decide that dogs are the only things one can truly trust. For others it may be books, TV characters, toys, or even fantasy. This is not to say that all book lovers are socially stunted or that all animal lovers are people who can't make friends, but it can end up being that extreme. Usually, most of us fall somewhere in the middle, where we have had bad experiences with friendships and romantic related interests of ours and it didn't go well. So we may have taken a break for a while until we were willing to try again and hope better opportunities would come along.

For some of us these influences are comical and out in the open. You may have heard someone say that they once told a classmate they liked them and this other person responded by pushing them down and they have never liked people with that hair color ever since. However, when these past events are significant to us and keep us from being open to new relationships at all or we are only open to relationships with people that are bad to us, then it is a problem. If we get into the habit of seeking out abusive or irresponsible people because that is all we know, then we will likely keep walking into friendships and relationships that are very destructive.

This is how what we experience, and what we see modeled for us at home, by the adult role models impacts our life. They impress upon us the way things are supposed to be. Now we are not helpless to these influences, but if they align or appear to align with our personal experience or misguided conclusions, then we may simply conclude that married people all break confidences, smack each other around, spend the rent money, are promiscuous and or will leave you. If we never share these stilted impressions of the world and the people within it, then we may very well continue to believe and see the world through a set of very jaded eyes that fail to see how much better things really are if you just make different choices.

8. EVENTS

Events are another key category of sources of baggage. Many of these you will recognize as potentials sources for yourself as well. While people can create baggage for us with repeated behavior, usually event sources of baggage are tied to a single type of experience. Thus, when we are reminded of a similar experience we are teleported back to the effects of that experience. Sometimes the memory is so painful that we avoid these events, avoid any reminders of these events and avoid thinking about them. In others these negative past experiences merely influence our preferences to this day.

Avoiding parties, birthdays, celebrations, places of worship, or even sex can be the result because we still are carrying the baggage of these past events. The following are a few of the more common past events that can leave such a lifelong impression on us that we continue to carry its baggage for the rest of our lives.

Birthdays

Probably the most personal event for most of us is our birthday. It may not be a day you are used to celebrating, but it is the most constant shared event that we experience. Each year on the anniversary of our birth we are a year older. While our families usually celebrate this in some way when we are younger, if we do not have a traditional family this can be a much different experience.

How our birthdays are acknowledged and how they are celebrated when we are young and throughout our life can be another significant source of baggage we can acquire. There is of course the first disappointing birthday. There is typically one for each of us. We may not remember it, but it usually comes about when either we do not get what we expected or someone didn't show up or worse yet, it was simply forgotten. This is not only a circumstance for young people. Adults also can go through similar expectations and let downs over how a birthday turns out. Did I hear from my closest family members? Did anyone at work wish me a happy birthday?

If we have baggage about our birthday it can range from not wanting to be let down again, or embarrassed or worse be reminded of our age when we have been keeping our birth date a closely guarded secret. While this might seem like a wise strategy it actually causes more pain in the long run. As we limit the individuals that are aware of our birthday, we limit the number of individuals who can make note of it and help us celebrate the event. Whatever our reasons for not sharing our birthday or asking people to not acknowledge the date, it only further isolates us from others and reduces the opportunities for others to congratulate us and show us their kindness.

We all get older every year; it is no secret to anyone you are getting older. Also, as we get older we usually have learned that having high expectations for such events is unwise and is likely to result in disappointment. With experience we often learn to lower our expectation to be more realistic and have fewer new disappointments except for the ones we thrust upon ourselves from the past. If past unpleasant birthdays are clear memories, then they likely are holding us back from being able to enjoy our present ones. Birthdays don't have to be perfect to be enjoyed and appreciated, but we have to participate.

Holidays

Probably the next most common baggage laden event are holidays. Different ones probably rise to the top in importance for each of us, but usually within your family/culture/religion/race a prominent holiday means to you that it is supposed to be a joyous time of celebration with family and friends.

Holidays often take on a life of their own, whether your family is into them or not. With all the attention they often get you can hear a lot of talk about the upcoming event. Yet when we have had either a very painful experience or a series of very painful experiences associated with a holiday then we can eventually come to dread these events. We may go through the motions and fake interest or we may have been disappointed enough that we can no longer bring ourselves to even pretend to enjoy ourselves. For some the disappointment and unpleasant memories has turned into disgust where nothing but sarcasm and criticism can come from our mouths when discussing the topic.

Finally, the ultimate rejection that some of us come to is avoidance all together. Instead of attending we simply refuse to participate. We are aggravated and maybe complain about the holiday items in the stores especially if they show up earlier than we think they should. We don't join in any kind of informal events and certainly do not show up for family gatherings. Worse yet, to avoid any other reminders when we get this far we often will isolate completely by quietly staying home and reading a book or finding some other alternative activity no matter how unwise, just to not have to be reminded of what we are choosing to not enjoy.

With the intensity a holiday season can bring, the pain and or pressure can be unbearable for some. If you are already someone who drinks alcohol or does drugs whether they are prescription or illegal, then the temptation to increase your use during this time is even greater. While the effects may appear to release the pressure or pain, the net effect is that this approach numbs us and this increases the risk of poor judgment. Being under the influence when highly aggravated or in significant depression can result in very regrettable things being said, arguments escalating to very extreme limits, violence, self-injury or suicide.

Yet participating in formal events can ease our unpleasant feeling. Yet it helps to have a well thought out plan. It is perfectly fine to celebrate or not celebrate holidays of your peers or of your family of origin. Also, as we age and are more on our own we may choose to alter the way we celebrate that is different from our family of origin. Finally, those family celebrations that involve very unpleasant individuals can be limited. If someone else is hosting the event, then you can limit your time spent exposing yourself to the unpleasant persons. When hosting celebrations, you can set the ground rules for behavior at the event and if they are not followed invite the parties to leave or choose to not invite them. Unruly family members may be missed, but the event will be more pleasant for everyone else if they are not included. If our families are much too toxic for us, we can join another family or friends instead. If we find ourselves too burdened to do anything, then your holiday baggage has gotten the better of you and unpacking it could help.

Significant Events for Others

When things happen to others we can have all kinds of reactions depending upon our relationship with them, but more importantly what those events represent to us and what memories they trigger. We probably can all relate to the discomfort of having something bad happen to someone we know. Accidents, serious illness, affairs, divorce, death of a family member and worse yet suicide. Regardless of our emotional reaction we are often tempted to consider what it would be like to have the same thing happen to us.

What would we do? How would we react?

When we are in contact with the person we often feel empathy for the person even though we might not be sure what to say no matter how close we are. We can often speak too casually and carelessly to avoid getting emotional ourselves. This can result in some fairly regrettable comments. when trying to be reassuring like, "I know how you feel", "It was for the best", "Be strong, I know I would die if this happened to me" or the real clincher, "Take comfort and know it was God's will".

Sometimes our discomfort with an unpleasant event that has happened to others is so great that we can't bring ourselves to interact with them at all. We will avoid them in the store, not call them and even avoid certain locations, gatherings and social events just to avoid having to run into this person. Unresolved feelings about past events are the common type of baggage that will cause this type of discomfort. The cost to our relationships can be devastating if we can't bring ourselves to visit hospitals, attend funerals, comfort dear friends or even have contact with friends who have lost someone all because of things in our past. Yet this happens all the time.

When good things happen to others it can be even more uncomfortable for us, but for very different reasons. Usually because we would rather those things were happening to us. We might think to ourselves that we are surprised we were passed up for the award, promotion or opportunity or we may go straight for the jugular and think or worse yet say that this person doesn't deserve this. It should have been us. Everything that we observe occurring for others is an opportunity to compare it with what has happened to us. From birthday parties, and weddings to how spouses, friends and family treat others we know. Anything is game, but the more significant events tend to stick out since we all have significant events in our past that we would have preferred to have gone better and for some of us they were extremely disappointing. If we allow ourselves to playback these disappointing events on a regular or even an occasional basis and re-experience our disappointment, hurt or anger about it again, then we are very susceptible to comparing ourselves to others when these same events turn out so much better for others.

If we know them, it can be more intense since we have more information about them and may frequently see them only to be reminded of the comparison. However, we can be irritated that movie stars and other types of celebrities and successful individuals are having a much better time than we are. No one can blame us for wanting things to go well, but it is not realistic that everything can go the way we want. If we look around us we can always find someone who has had a better experience than we have in some way or another.

The unfortunate thing is when we are sore about others having a better experience we let it get in the way of having normal relationships with them. We tend to avoid them as friends because they only remind us of the things they got to experience that we didn't get. We can also just treat them poorly and talk bad about them which often comes back to hurt us in some way. If we tend to avoid others or talk bad about them because they remind us of what we do not have, once again our baggage is controlling us.

Celebrations

Past celebrations that went poorly can be a source of baggage. The times most people would want to celebrate and even personal causes for celebration more privately can be muzzled out of a reluctance to somehow repeat a bad celebration. Most of the things we don't like often has to do with past events where things didn't go so well. If we grow up in a caustic environment where we are berated and criticized for many things we do, then celebrations can be one of those things that gets spoiled for us in general.

Some parents and siblings can be very cruel, whether they are conscious of it or not. As a young person, there are some people we can't get away from, our family, extended and sometimes the friends of family. When they aren't nurturing that is one thing, but when they are sadistic and are regularly taunting and belittling us we can end up having a pretty hard time.

We may not avoid celebrations altogether but we may mute our enthusiasm so to not draw attention to ourselves. If we don't become very excited, then there is nothing for people to make fun of or criticize. Or maybe you can let yourself go and celebrate, but only when really tired or under the influence of alcohol or drugs that reduce your inhibitions. The sad thing is this can get in the way of a lifetime of celebrations. To others we may appear like we are rarely having fun and as a result we may end up not being invited to go along because we regularly appear to be uninterested or unimpressed. We actually may be having a good time, but when our outward appearance and behavior looks very close to depressed or just neutral then people will often misread us. Some may take the time to find out how we are doing while many others will not.

So we may want to be a part of a celebration, but for some reason we don't seem to know how. Baggage can do this to us. Now being averse to all celebration is probably not as common as being turned off by more selective types of celebrations. We may loathe the idea of having a surprise party thrown for us. Yet if we are afraid of being shot down or shamed for receiving a lot of attention we may shudder at the thought of having a surprise party thrown for us and we may even make a point to let other people know to never do it.

The good news is this is all fixable. A thing that we have never been able to explain and never knew was a problem can be changed. So, our aversion to parties large or small, quiet or loud, organized or chaotic, just may be because of some past experience or set of experiences that at the time seemed like a really good idea to promise yourself you would never let yourself get in that situation again. Years go by and we forget about the promise we made ourselves, but the resolve to not partake remains. When this happens, we have a strong aversion to something and we have no idea why. It is not necessarily repressed memories as much as it is likely a crowded-out memory. We can only store so many memories and sometimes we forget the reasons why we started avoiding, hating or not preferring celebrating.

Accidents

When we are younger having accidents can be fun, embarrassing, or what seems like serious trouble. Outcomes like broken items of value, someone getting hurt by us, or wetting the bed, can stick with us if we are not guided by someone who is kind and understanding. If the reaction we receive leaves a strong negative impression, we can come away with baggage that drives all sorts of odd behavior. Coming away with the idea that we can never make a mistake, we have to be perfect, we are responsible for the well-being of others beyond our capability can drive an unrealistic expectation of responsibility and make us miserable. Accidents later in life often come with greater consequences. Drinking too much, being abusive towards others, being reckless with weapons, or risky driving, can hurt ones we love, ourselves and lead to legal trouble. However, accidents that lead to serious physical injury can have a lifelong disabling impact. When the result is a minor scar the event is typically easy to forget. However, injuries that affect our eyesight, our speech, our appearance or our ability drive, walk or work are life changing for the injured.

Loss of relationships can occur if accidents are repeated and occasionally after one instance. However, what we categorize as an accident may really be our way of not taking responsibility. As we become adults, we are constantly weighing risk factors when we share information, climb ladders, get on a roof, or we handle a potentially dangerous object around children and sometimes adults. As we advance in age and become less agile and balanced, the lack of appreciation of our increased risk of injury can lead to accidents that can be quite serious. If our vision becomes impaired, driving can become quite risky and possibly fatal for ourselves or others. Even walking can become quite risky later in life without a walker or assistance from someone else. Ultimately, we are responsible for our own actions and sometimes we calculate incorrectly and bad outcomes occur. So, accidents at 8, 18 or 80 can all be ones to create baggage. Since the variables involving potential accidents are constantly changing, we can be fooled by our old ways of mitigating risk. Hyper-vigilance is not typically necessary unless we are in a war zone or facing attackers. However, staying aware of new information and being open-minded on how to make use of new information can help us best evaluate how to avoid the more serious accidents of any type.

Illness

Illness that is pronounced and long term can also bring its own baggage. Beyond the immediate symptoms, there are the limits they can create for us in our daily lives. If the illness is congenital, then we may grow up with the limit appearing as natural to us since they have always been there. Until we encounter unkind and insensitive people we have a good chance that we will have adapted to our limitations very well. However, when an illness occurs as an older child or as an adult where there has been a clear memory of our life and abilities before, then there is the potential for even more substantial baggage. Questions of why did this happen to me? Did I do something wrong? or is God punishing me? How can there be a God if he was willing to let this happen to me? Illnesses can leave us permanently scarred, disfigured disabled and easily ostracized and challenged for the rest of our lives. While the pursuit of a cure, treatment or ability enabling surgery can often remain the constant focus in response, eventually this can also get in the way of not enjoying our life. For some the symptoms can become the reason to not engage in desired passions and relationships. This can be more tempting when the condition is progressive where new challenges or the disability increases. As it may be easy to feel sorry for ourselves, find sympathy and a lack of encouragement to adapt, the baggage of illness can be addressed. Focusing on the disability symptoms as opposed to the solution can keep us in a cycle of not trying. While many may agree that disability means we can't, upon closer inspection there is likely some things we are including that we are choosing to not try for fear of falling short. If everyone around us allows us to get away with not trying, then we need a new healthier tribe to nudge us towards growing beyond the problem towards solutions.

Then there are illnesses that can be fatal. These are often put in large categories that are not necessarily a death sentence, but need clarification of our specific situation and condition. Also, many conditions are able to be diagnosed far ahead of its ability to kill us. So, the baggage created by such an ominous prediction is probably the worse most will experience. Yet, baggage created by a fatal diagnosis does not have to cripple us. Sticking to the facts and methodically exploring options while taking care of ourselves can dramatically minimize our suffering.

Visiting healthcare facilities can carry baggage that when extreme leads us to believe those are places people go to die or the expectation to get a painful shot. Bad news and emotionally filled unpleasant experiences can drive us to avoid these places if at all possible. While there is always the possibility we can die in one, the vast majority of the time these places are the location of healing, even for repeat customers. However, any bureaucratic organization can have bad actors and mistakes occur. Extended stays, especially as a child, can carry very unpleasant isolation and restricted movement that can create baggage.

Loss

We lose things all the time, such as change, pens, thoughts, but it is the big things that really get us. Probably our earliest losses have to do with toys that are misplaced or that wear out or break. Some harder lessons come early when friends move away or we are the ones who did the moving. Classmates may not like us or include us in the sandbox, ones we are friends with change classes each year and sometimes we stayed back a year and we no longer share a lunchtime and recess with those in our previous grade level. Pets grow older and can no longer play like they used to and eventually they die. These are all the more common and minor to moderate types of losses that while upsetting and traumatic to a young child, they are still fairly easy to get over and begin developing a history with loss and learning that, while sad for a time, an enjoyable life can continue once again.

When more tragic losses occur when we are really young, we are simply not equipped and often not well guided to deal with the grief. All too common is the event of parents divorcing. What was once the family system that had been consistent as far back as we remember, is now changing to people in different homes and sometimes worse out of town, where frequent visits are not even possible. Despite reassurances from well-meaning parents it is very easy for the young children of a divorce to see themselves at least partly to blame. If the parents are very angry with each other within earshot of the children, then the parents as a team are not only lost, but so is the peace of the home. Each day we continue to live in the same house, seeing the one parent we live with or visit the previous home we are reminded of how it used to be and how sad it makes us.

Worse yet, a family member or close friend can get extremely ill or die. One day they are sick and then all the sudden we are told they are not coming back home. There are few greater losses than to have a loved one die. It is especially devastating when it is one of our parents or children. Unfortunately, like with divorce too often the older siblings and adults around us are often so grief stricken themselves that the guidance of helping a young child navigate the loss may be overlooked. If the death was self-inflicted, then young people can easily entertain the same kinds of unrealistic guilt that adults struggle with. Other extreme losses for a family like the loss of a home and the ability to maintain employment and shelter can be devastating for a young child in many ways when the more basic needs of food and shelter take precedence.

Finally, the loss of our emotional and sexual innocence through abuse is probably one of the more devastating types of loss a young child can experience. When there is regular emotional and physical abuse, the young person's frame of reference for viewing the world for the remainder of their life can be severely skewed, often in a highly self-critical and tormented fashion. When the abuse is of a sexual nature, the young person not only experiences guilt and shame, but the isolation from the secrecy, whether elected or forced, which separates the young person from any adult who could possibly protect them and guide them through this traumatic loss. Long term effects can disrupt all future enjoyment of sexual experiences by either a constant tendency towards avoidance or high-risk promiscuity.

The younger we are the less capable are we to understand what has happened and often we lack the ability to articulate what we are experiencing. When anyone experiences great loss there is grief which can take many forms from the moment we experience the event, perhaps even for the rest of our lives. Grief is the natural expression of the sadness and other feelings while we are adjusting to the loss.

There are a number of stages or responses to loss described by psychologists. Most start off with shock or denial phase followed by a concerned, bargaining or anger phase and then depression. Depression is a very normal reaction to a great loss. Yet a prolonged depression can be very dangerous since it can become a pattern of behavior that we may have trouble leaving behind. Once we begin to stop the focus on the loss and the pain it brings us, then we often experience acceptance and recovery. These phases do not necessarily occur in this order, but they often do.

What is also very common is that we experience the various phases again and again in a variety of orders. As a very young person these phases may be more or less evident, but overall, they can result in very positive behavior or very unhealthy behaviors.

While loss can be difficult at any age, we are much more likely to have lifelong behavioral impact if we experience great loss as a very young child. While this behavior can be redirected there is the temptation for those who have not experienced such loss to agree with people who claim that their poor behavior is cast in stone because of the great loss they experienced when they were very young. Adolescents can also be very vulnerable to great loss since they are already experiencing great levels of emotions as they are transitioning into adulthood. The loss of a spot on a team, a part in a play, the returned affection of someone they like, or the loss of a desired image among friends can also be great sources of adolescent and young adult grief. If allowed to go untreated or guided through the grief by friends, family or other interested parties, then the depression can lead towards a tendency to make very poor choices like resentment of authority, dropping out of school, promiscuous sexual activity, or befriending others who are even more troubled.

If we were raised in a faith-based home we were exposed to the concept that God was someone who could guide us and strengthen us in our times of loss, trouble and pain. While this type of home can be a great and supportive atmosphere sometimes it can be very unpleasant and painful. If we in the course of developing our relationship with usually the God of our family of origin and we come away hurt and disappointed, some choose to reject the relationship from that point forward. If grief and disappointment is not shared and put in its proper perspective this can become the end to the benefits of a conscious and intentional spiritual life. If participation is mandatory in a family, we can end up choosing to live a double life of outward believer and inward a non-believer.

Loss continues for all of us throughout our lives. Dating relationships end or never materialize, good friends part ways or move away, civilian and military careers are pursued and don't work out, and continued employment may or may not materialize and if it does it may be lost. The loss of income and the ability to provide stability and support for our families and ourselves can be devastating. As we reach various millstones in our lives such as getting an education, having a place of our own, a vocation, marriage, having children, exotic travel, the pursuit of other dreams we continue to experience loss. Often, in anticipation of the milestones, we have created an image of what it would be like. If somehow, we managed to hang our hope on these milestones unfolding as expected, we can experience a great deal of disappointment as they fall short of our possibly unrealistic expectations. Unrealized hopes and dreams can be treated like the last hope in life. We begin to look back upon our life and compare ourselves to others. It can be very depressing to think that we are not going to get to achieve what we had hoped for ourselves. Now our hopes and dreams may have been unrealistic, but it really doesn't matter since our mind they were our future. Hopes and dreams unfulfilled are experienced as a loss. Some more than others obviously, but they are losses.

As we tally our life's accomplishments and we find ourselves coming up more and more short, it is easy to want to assign blame. While it is very uncomfortable for us to blame ourselves, most of us find it very easy to blame others. Maybe not specifically, but if we are unhappy, it is easy to want to find who is responsible and at least call them out from afar. As we listen to community, corporate, spiritual and political leaders describe the issues of our world, we may find ourselves very easy to be convinced our troubles are in part due to certain groups or races of people or nations, certain industries or businesses, certain political parties or even God. Repeated loss that either goes un-grieved or we are still very much in the process of grieving can make us easy targets for those looking for more to join their fight built upon assigned blame. Having baggage often makes us good candidates for a fight. It may be our participation is limited to being often irritable at work, angry and yelling at our television or radio, or even having vigorous discussions in public, parties and bars. However, if we are more troubled it can easily lead to more serious altercations especially if we tend to be physical, armed with firearms or intoxicated.

Life is a wonderful and amazing thing, but it can be over in an instant if we have been letting the juices in us heat between simmer and boiling for years and we pile up risky behaviors on top of one another. While most losses we experience are not that significant in of themselves, if the grief is not allowed to occur and the loss is not accepted, the accumulation of many year of everyday losses can be more devastating than having a close friend or family member murdered.

The baggage of loss is difficult for everyone, but it can be put into its proper perspective in time. While all loss can be painful, choosing to not grieve in a productive way can be devastating to the rest of our lives and all those around us.

Tragedy

It is probably common sense to most if not all that when a person experiences or is made aware of a tragedy they are impacted. Granted it is much more significant if the tragedy happens personally, but even the knowledge of tragedy can be a very significant experience. Some experience great tragedies very early in life, while others may be well into their adult years before a significant event happens to them. Whenever they do occur there are some common aspects to them: they are shocking and disorienting, they are often quite painful, they create a demarcation point in our lives and typically we are forever changed. A tragedy can be as simple as unexpected news of something undesired, but that is of great importance to the person hearing it. Or at the other extreme a tragedy can be the horrific end of the lives of many loved ones and friends witnessed firsthand.

While most of us are spared the most intense of tragedies, the ones we do experience seem significant to us until confronted with something worse. Some of us can appreciate that there are worse things happening to others simply by hearing about them, while others must have a close friend or relative experience a tragic event before it sinks in that some may have

suffered more than we have. As a result, what might be horrific to one person may be a common experience to another.
This doesn't mean it isn't a tragedy for both, but the relative
significance will vary. Many tragedies are very public events, a
car crash, a severe weather event, a drowning, a robbery, a kid-
napping or a murder. However, there are tragedies that many
choose to keep private for a variety of reasons such as affairs,
deformities, mental or physical illness, significant debt, a relative's incarceration, a relative's undesirable employment, or
the presence of addiction in the family. Public or private, these
all can cause great distress that has lifelong effects.

The unique aspect of ones we choose to keep private is that
there is an additional amount of baggage added to the shock
and grief of the actual event or circumstance. Keeping things
secret often becomes a greater burden than the secret itself.
Keeping secrets, especially the ones that have a great deal of
significance to us, can be an all-consuming part of our lives.
Ultimately, the facade we have to create involves a very large
web of lies that are often very difficult to inventory and manage successfully. And if we do manage to keep our big secrets
from being known, the damage it does to us is immeasurable.
Beyond the fear and shame that is a constant companion for
many that have big secrets, the certainty of rejection if the
secret was made public can haunt a person into significant
psychological issues.

When tragic events are known they are often still devastating
during the time immediately after and sometimes, if not processed, it becomes an almost unbearable burden for the rest
of our lives. The prolonged shock and grief is something we
might more expect of people exposed to mass murder or the
graphic horrors of war, but it happens for everyday tragedies
as well. Losing a child, having a friend murdered, rape, adultery, serious illness, crushing debt, prolonged unemployment,
etc. all can create symptoms of Post-Traumatic Stress Disorder
or other stress related symptoms that impact our abilities
to think clearly, work, maintain relationships, be emotionally

stable, be physically healthy. While many of these reactions are normal to experience for a limited time after a tragic event, it is the prolonged impact that can turn the life altering event into a much more destructive one.

We all are impacted by the significant tragic events in our lives, but when they are successfully navigated they add to our understanding of ourselves and others. They add to our sense of perspective of loss and acceptance and they add to our ability to empathize with others who are experiencing great pain. It gives us a greater sense of the common experience that all people have.

People of faith may experience great comfort in their faith while others may experience significant doubt, if their view was that their faith should have kept them from harm. Regardless of the path we take while processing the tragedy, the outcome can always become a very significant benefit even if it still afflicts us. The reassurance that the tragic event hasn't killed us and doesn't have to disable us can often only be communicated by someone who has been through the same experience. While we might not be able to bring ourselves to reach out and be of comfort to others while we are still stinging from the recent event, sometimes our mere presence is a reassurance to all that can observe us.

One of the perspectives that is hard to ignore is that others can't imagine what it is like to go through what we have experienced. It is true that certain tragedies such as murder, suicide, addiction, catastrophic weather events, etc. qualify us for membership in a very unwanted club, but there are others out there and therein lies the hope that we can get through it.

So, if we keep our original tragic experience secret or simply how we continue to be effected by it, we often cut ourselves off from experiencing the hope that all is not lost. The truth is that there is nothing that has been experienced that has not been overcome. You may not be aware of it, but it has happened.

While the continued shock and pain of our most tragic experiences may have maintained a stranglehold upon us up until now, this does not have to continue. What most sticks out as the result of a tragedy by those who successfully navigate the event is that they have discovered a much greater appreciation of their life, the world and their future because they have new or renewed purpose in their life. It can happen, even for you.

School

Depending upon the atmosphere at home, school may be a scary place or a very welcome vacation from where we live. However, the structure and grading may be our first encounter with consistent feedback. It may also be our first significant experience with being a part of a group where we do not get as much attention. If we are used to being hovered over fairly closely then the teacher to student ratio may be quite disconcerting. While there are many other aspects to the school experience to attract us, there is typically that loss of highly personalized attention from our caregiver.

Also, the day becomes typically much more structured than at home. While the schedule is often very flexible at home, at school we find that there is a time for each type of activity and they repeat on a daily or weekly basis. This transition may be more significant for some and many of us may have trouble recalling those early days of beginning school for the first time. Yet, those experiences can play a role in how we adapt to change going forward.

The difference in structure from home to school provides us with input about how things can vary from one environment to another. Then as well as changing grades, classes and teachers we find that there is variation in the school experience. As we visit friend's homes we find that the rules and structure of the environment in their house is different from ours.

Of course, school is primarily about academic education. The amount of interest, curiosity, attitude and capability play a significant role in how well new information is learned and mastered. The better we can adapt to the curriculum, the more positive the rewards. When we struggle with the feedback and frustration of having to repeat material to meet proficiency requirements, the experience is not as pleasant. While these results are cyclical it doesn't take long for a standout memory to be established. So even the most proficient student can struggle for a short period and come away with a negative memory of failure. Whether it has to do with test scores and grades or specific activities such as speaking before a class, doing problems on the board in front of the class or not faring well in the playground during recess, usually we have some low and painful moments related to school.

If our academic experiences are mostly negative then there will be a greater likelihood you will not be inclined to pursue extra school related activities and an advanced education. Later in life this may also cause a tendency to avoid employment requiring training and continuing education. Some of these struggles may be due in part to learning styles, acquired study skills and learning disabilities. Depending upon how recent and the degree of focus on learning issues in the schools you attended you may have gone undiagnosed if you have any significant learning disability. Untreated you may have come away with the conclusion that you are either incapable of learning, stupid or intellectually disabled.

Disabilities are merely differences that require unique assistance or modification of the standard education delivery to meet you in a way you can understand it. Not addressing a disability is sometimes what occurs when there is no identification of the disability, or when there is a diagnosis, the parents refuse or fight the special education available. The bottom line is that if we have a disability and it is not addressed, then we have much less favorable results in life and may use these experiences as a reason to conclude we are less of a person or less deserving than others.

Academic results can also be impacted by competing priorities. When the needs of the family or just survival, get in the way of a complete and successful education through high school, it is possible to spend all of our lives not being able to read or read well. Illiteracy can be one of the most devastating contributors to a life of hardship. While many people who cannot read or write simple sentences can be very hard working and can accomplish a good deal in life, the likelihood that all the communications not understood will cause many opportunities to be missed.

In many cases the results from lacking these basic skills can contribute to a much higher degree of delinquency, poverty and crime. Over half of the people in U.S. prisons read below the fourth-grade level. When addressed later in life, dramatic changes can occur even among prison populations. Typically return rates for U.S. prisoners hovers in the two-thirds range and this percentage, when the inmates receive basic education services, falls to less than 25%. Learning to read and write above an elementary school level enables individuals to fill out applications, read the news and understand warning signs accurately.

The last big arena we experience in school is social. No matter how large our family of origin is there are more people at school to interact with on a daily basis. We are confronted with more opportunities to coexist, share, compete and to play with others for the majority of our days for about three fourths of every year until we conclude our education. As a result, we are given both the opportunity and requirement to interact with others.

While a lot of early education focuses upon interacting well with others, it is not unusual for us to come away from the social lessons and experiences in school with some pretty inaccurate ideas. People who experience more teasing and abuse may decide that most, or all people, are mean. While others may decide that some people just don't like people and that is why they are quiet. People that are more average may come away with the impression that the better students, richer students and the more athletic students are all snobs. And likewise the more successful students may come to view the poorer academic student as less deserving or lazy. Sometimes these impressions are entirely from the student's observation and sometimes it may be influenced by attitudes and biases shared by their parents or teachers. These attitudes, unless proved wrong with later experiences, can stay with us and shape our view of others for the rest of our lives.

If we keep an open mind later in life, we often will discover that we have many misconceptions about what people are like once we get exposed to people in different settings. Many workplaces, volunteer organizations, interest clubs and places of worship create new environments, where these narrow assumptions about others can be corrected.

So our attitudes and impressions about structure, our intellect, education, social norms and how we view ourselves are all in part formed while we are in school. If we come away with many negative experiences in these areas and do not experience or acknowledge any information to the contrary from that point forward we can end up quite burdened with some fairly inaccurate perspectives about the world and other people. It doesn't have to be permanent and more than likely you have been revising assumptions you have had about the world and others since your last time in a classroom. If you choose to be open minded, then more corrections can be made that will allow you to better navigate the world you live in and interact more successfully with the people you encounter.

Spiritual Worship

Worship is a very personal practice that may or may not have been prominent in your childhood and the remainder of your life. A lot of our experience depends upon the religious legacy of your family and community. Key baggage about spiritual matters often comes with the use of teaching techniques that are either not age appropriate or respectful of the student.

Extreme scare tactics coupled with physical threats and violence can in fact produce a lifelong impression that is not
one of choice but one based upon a terrified child's search for
safety. Since the mental and emotional record of these events
can be so intense, it is not unusual for those of us who came
from very intense and at times cruel spiritual lessons to have
a very negative or destructive perspective associated with spiritual matters. If the past experiences resulted in a very negative impression, then avoidance of all things associated with
spiritual matters is very common. When investigated many
times it is found that the people who delivered the poorly con-
structed spiritual education were also poorly prepared for the
role of a healthy spiritual mentor.

Similar baggage can also be acquired later in life when exposed
to friends, acquaintances or religious leaders who use some of
the same poorly chosen techniques. While children have less
choices about who they are exposed to for input than adults,
some adults may feel attracted to others who appear to have
it significantly more together or have a near issue free life.
This appearance can be a product of others who are very comfortable talking to others in a confrontational and compelling
manner while painting a very positive picture of the results of
their spiritual path. While this approach is not in itself a bad
thing, it can lure less worldly individuals into considering spiritual paths even when their better judgment tells them to do
otherwise. When highly skilled recruiters of various spiritual
paths are respectful and considerate the results are likely to be
positive, but when recruiter's techniques are without bound-
ary or ethics very destructive results can occur.

The idea that these spiritual beliefs cannot be proven in the
physical world with reason is often rooted in the perspective
that faith must be proven versus faith being the act of choosing to believe in the absence of facts. While some religions
are based upon the existence of multiple or many gods and
are therefore non-exclusive, the two most popular ones (Christianity and Islam) are based upon the concept of there being

only one true God. These exclusive, versus non-exclusive, beliefs coexist in the world with those who believe the existence or non-existence of God is unknowable (agnostics) versus the belief there is simply no God (atheists). Many factors especially the baggage we have acquired in our lifetime can make one or more of these options more attractive.

Within a particular spiritual belief, the leaders can be assumed to be greater than others as a result of the religious doctrine or the assumptions of the followers. While nearly all religions hold a higher standard of behavior and beliefs for their leaders only some of the lesser popular religions or sects actually formally describe their leaders as God like or uniquely favored by God. Yet the adoration of followers in enthusiastic terms can easily give outsiders the impression that the religion itself holds it leaders as gods or God-like. Followers who are not that well versed in the religion they follow and thus pass on a view that is not accurate, give most of these impressions.

The more active and mature a follower of a faith is, their behavior helps spread a better perspective about the spiritual belief they have chosen. The occasional bad behavior of leaders can be very discouraging for the participants, who actually tied their faith largely in the leader being always faithful or God-like. These types of struggles present the opportunity to gain maturity and wisdom about the everyday possibilities that occur despite what you believe in. However, for some it creates more baggage. People of all perspectives can make mistakes, have doubts, struggle with temptation, do destructive acts such as: suffer from addictions, get sick, get divorced, lie, cheat, steal, commit adultery, suicide, murder, and all other forms of destructive behavior.

Being a follower of a faith or non-faith way of life does not keep people from being human. Yet the spiritual faith paths typically provide hope, guidance and strength to its followers to resist these poor choices and to provide an improved way of life and in a few instances the promise of a very pleasant afterlife as well.

Regardless of your faith or non-faith path new disappointments in life can be attributed to our path, and change sought or we may just back away and isolate ourselves from our current faith or non-faith choice since it has appeared to have failed. If this is the last experience of an active spiritual way of life, then it may be a great candidate for unpacking.

Speaking

Speaking in public is often cited as one of our greatest fears. Most of us probably remember the dreaded book report or some other school assignment which called for us to get in front of the class to deliver our assignment. Yet the first thing we do when we are born is make noise and plenty of it. With no regard for others desire for quiet, as babies we make all kinds of noise. They cry out when in pain or discomfort, make random sounds to express desire and laugh for happiness. Little by little they are comforted and encouraged to be quiet as their parents or caretakers try to bend to the wishes of the adults around them for quiet. While some parents are more accommodating of infants and young children with the noise they make, some of us know all too well the biting responses of parents who believe that children should be seen, but not heard.

As we are learning to talk we are constantly refining our ability to speak, how to make sounds, how to put them together and often by imitating those around us. Once we form words we often assemble them in ways we have had them demonstrated for us and we develop our own voice over time with experimentation. We encounter many responses to our communication by speaking. Some experiences are successes by the pleasant results of understanding and being able to exchange requests, responses, thoughts and ideas. Then there are other experiences where things are unpleasant. Either we speak out of turn, or it is something we said or the way we said it and maybe we don't even know why we are getting such an unpleasant response, but we can easily come to the simple conclusion - I spoke and things became unpleasant. Under these circumstances, the motivation is to at the very least choose our speech more carefully. However, when we have no idea what it was about our communication that was the problem, we can come up with the unfortunate conclusion that we should not talk so much.

If when we are very young and the feedback we get when trying to communicate is unpleasant and very unclear, then some of us do conclude that it is very risky to speak freely. If this is the conclusion we make about every circumstance, then we can become very quiet individuals. We may even stay very quiet even when among friends until a great deal of reassurance is experienced. Sometimes there is never enough new experiences. Sometimes we learn that speaking freely or at least a little bit is acceptable in certain situations, with maybe certain individuals, or with certain types of individuals such as members of our own sex or maybe the opposite sex. Strangers may be less risky for us to speak to or riskier. Also, people of different races, cultures or socio-economic levels can be the risky populations for us to speak to with ease. In more extreme cases, we may not be able to make ourselves speak at all while in some selected relationships or settings we are much less at ease.

As we navigate through school and eventually the workplace, we typically will broaden our circle of acquaintances and thus the number and maybe kinds of people and situations where we are more at ease to speak. However, if we continue to perceive that it is too risky we may continue to be very quiet to avoid any unpleasantness. Now we may not consciously think this way, but it could very well be the reason. A good clue this may be the case is if you were once much more at ease as a very young child and became quieter as you got older. If you have been very reluctant to speak since a very early age, there is evidence that this can be caused by ridicule or child abuse. Abuse whether it is physical or verbal can be a very persuasive teacher. There are other possible causes that can influence us to be very reluctant to speak. If we are much more introverted than extroverted, then the interaction with others is much less appealing. Introverts prefer more solitary activities over social ones and often experience an energizing effect from activities without interaction with others while extroverts tend to be more outspoken and energized by interacting with others.

Our tendency to be introverted versus extroverted is our normal and natural state from which our speaking experiences are built upon. So, if we are naturally an introvert and we have a series of unpleasant experiences speaking with others we are likely to draw inward even more, but possibly without much discomfort since we are more at home with the more solitary life. However, if we are more of an extrovert, then a series of unpleasant experiences in response to speaking can be torture if we have to conclude it is best to not speak with others much at all.

Most of us experience some of these influencers in moderate amounts, while less of us have had minimal or much more severe series of unpleasant responses. In rarer cases, there are physical anxiety conditions that can contribute to a tendency to be shy in order to minimize the anxiety. It is also believed that there is likely some genetically based conditions that can influence a tendency to be either shyer or more aggressive; however, there has been very little study in this area.

While we may never know the full extent of our nature related influencers to our reluctance to speak with or before others, one thing we can be assured of is that history of negative responses to our speech and speaking freely can produce a reluctance to interact with others verbally.

Punishment

We have all been punished in one-way or another. Usually we have received punishment as a part of the discipline we received from our parents or caretakers. In some instances, we knew the rules, we knew the punishment and we chose to break the rules and risk the punishment anyway. Then there are those times that somehow, some way, we got punished and we didn't have it coming. As hurt as we were for being mistreated, we probably figured out that we were limited in our ability to set things straight. Occasionally, we were able to set things straight and we were vindicated. Then there were the times when we believed we were being punished for no reason at all. Hopefully, this was not that case for you. However, if it was, then you likely came away with some unfortunate views of authority.

While most of us are treated fairly much of the time, there are those instances when we are not. When this occurs and we realize what is happening we are at risk of becoming very bitter. Sometimes in this bitterness very extreme choices are made to get even, to never do those kinds of things to others and to never let anyone ever treat me this way again. When punishment is wrongfully administered on a repeated basis it is called abuse. Most parents who slip into this behavior are troubled and unfortunately take it out on their children. When it occurs for a short period of time, we can often forgive them, but we rarely forget.

Punishment can come from anywhere and unfortunately any adult or anyone who outweighs us can choose to administer punishment our way regardless of whether we had it coming or not. This is where we learn about bullies. They come in all shapes and sizes. If we are bullied enough, we may even turn to the next smaller person than us and dish it out just out of sheer frustration and rage. Bullying can motivate bullying behavior, but it doesn't have to. In reality there are few people who have the authority to administer punishment upon us without our consent. Yet every time we break a law, or break a rule, we are giving the authorities the consent to impose punishment upon us. It doesn't matter if we have been unjustly detained or punished many times in the past, if we cross the line, we are open for punishment.

Where punishment often goes terribly wrong for so many of

us is that we fail to be honest about our actions and how we at least contributed to bring actions upon ourselves. The facts are very often that we deserve much of the punishment we have received, however we also probably have received some punishment we did not deserve and that is simply the way it goes. People make mistakes and when they do others pay the price. We too have probably dished out some injustice in our lives in the past. Maybe we realized and maybe we didn't, but the likelihood is that we all have participated in the imperfect execution of holding other people accountable in our lifetime. We are all human and we all deserve to be forgiven so those of us who are still hurt can let go of the pain that comes from holding unjust punishment towards us against others. They are not worth it and most of the time they don't even know we are still fuming about it. They may not even know us. However, even if they do, it doesn't matter.

Life is too short to hold on to that kind of baggage. Abuse, of course, is a different story.

Abuse

There are many kinds of abuse that we can encounter, but when we receive it as young children the effects can be devastating for a lifetime. I think any effort to characterize one type of abuse being more harmful over another would be naive. What probably doesn't get enough attention is the possible road back to a less burdened life from a life of abuse.

Probably the saddest characteristic of abuse is its latent ability to create continued damage. While physical scars may heal, they are often still visible. Much of the same occurs with other types of abuse: sexual, emotional, mental and yes, even spiritual abuse.

Sometimes we can be abused by people who are simply ignorant or wrapped up in their own struggles, but regardless, if the abuse is unintended or intended, the results are often still the same. For the recipient the consequence is always the presence of the abusive past. For some of us it may not be remembered and for others it is a daily conscious link to our present-day experiences. While the past cannot be erased it can be reframed and put in its proper perspective with a great deal of work and time.

If you suspect that you might have been abused, you may just not remember as a means of coping. While nearly all of us have experienced some forms of abuse most encounters are brief and something we can avoid. However, the more destructive incidents of abuse are those where we do not believe we have a choice. Many times, in these situations there is no choice and sometimes it just appears that way. The net effect is still the same, sustained and repeated exposure to abuse. As result of this exposure we begin processing these experiences in a variety of ways. Extreme presence of fear, stress, agitation, illness, PTSD, panic attacks and many forms of physical medical issues can all be responses to abusive behavior.

Strangely enough, some forms of abuse are veiled as a part of a higher purpose. These scenarios typically occur later in life when we are young adults or older. It may come from friends, romantic relationships, work, social groups, and even spiritual worship communities. Cloaked in the name of the greater good, taking one for the team, this is the way love and friendships are, this is the price for money and power and finally God is telling me this is OK.

None of this is correct. Abuse is never called for or OK. The truth is that sick people, often the ones who have been abused themselves, many times naturally abuse others they encounter. So, we aren't necessarily going to recognize them and before we know it we are caught up in a relationship, where to get away from the abuse we have to give up something that has become important to us. The sad thing is that this is often used as a justification to stay in abusive situations and not only do we deserve better, if there are young children also involved they definitely deserve better, since we have little to no choice.

It doesn't help that high-profile people of all types are often envied and yet they have had to make huge sacrifices to get where they are. Not all sacrifices are worth it and allowing you to continue to be exposed to abuse is never worth it since it is so challenging to reconcile. So, if you are still in an abusive situation simply have an open mind that there may be other options for you and things could be better. Having an open mind is the first step to being able to see other choices. It is not uncommon as a part of being abused to believe there is no other choice worth having or available to us.

This is never the case.

Once you consider the possibility that you are or have been abused, learn more about it. Hopefully, you will come closer to seeing your situation more for what it really is, destructive and creating more and more baggage for yourself every day.

Some people are crippled in all ways by the abuse they have endured and are unable to work, have relationships, stay in contact with family or take care of themselves. Then there are others who are driven by it and have become what many think are wildly successful despite a persistent haunting that plagues them. The rest fall somewhere in between. We remember or don't remember, but we are affected. We have trouble with relationships, self-image, sex, self-worth, responsibility, parenting, power, money, alcohol and drugs and there is often very little if any peace.

Peace of mind and joy are once again possible, but it involves being able to put our past experiences in their proper perspective. This is usually only possible with lots of help. And while it may be embarrassing, believe me our future peace and happiness are worth a little embarrassment of others knowing what we have been living with for a lifetime.

Sex

Sex is one of those super charged experiences. However, in most cases much of our early experiences are reconciling what we thought it would be against what actually occurred. As a result, how the first occurrence goes can have a very significant impact on our outlook of sex from this point forward.

If the first experience is one that is planned, respectful, and considerate between the two parties, then there is likely to be a good memory of the experience. However, if it occurred impulsively, not planned, and there were unmet expectations, blame and some hostility then our attitude towards sex can be rather jaded from the start. This of course doesn't begin to consider the wide range of input we get from our parents or care-takers, friends, teachers, clergy, society and the media.

When we are very young sex abuse is a trauma that derails the young person's perspective on sex, control, safety and self-respect for the rest of their lives. While there is no responsibility on the part of the young victim that they were abused, the shame of the experiences produces very difficult memories to accept and many use coping mechanisms like denial and memory suppression.

When the abuse is later in life, when we are more able to have a choice, we still may not exercise it or we may not have the luxury due to coercion or force. Unfortunately, family gatherings, vacations, camp, boarding schools, camping trips, parties and dates are all the possible scenes where peers or adults introduce uninvited sexual activity. If friendlier than forced, the experience may initially seem fairly pleasant. However, when the age gap is great and/or the nature of the experience is one where we were forced to do things we did not want to do, then the outcomes are much more destructive. If the experience is pleasurable, then there is a likelihood that the victim will seek additional opportunities to repeat the experience. However, if it was unpleasant, then the resistance can possibly keep the uninvited overtures from resulting in more sexual encounters, but it may also create a repulsion to normal consensual sexual relations later in life.

A traumatic memory of sex as an experience of force, pain and unpleasantness can lead to a lifetime of avoiding relationships or avoidance of appropriate similar sexual behavior.

Sometimes the association can be very specific and only cause strong feelings of repulsion, fear or avoidance for certain sexual acts or it can be more generalized to mood, location, pace, noise, etc. The possibilities are endless depending upon the combination of the abuse that occurred and what parts of it we were affected by the most.

Not all sexual abuse occurs in alleys or parking lots or as a part of home invasions by common criminals. The majority of it occurs by someone we know and unfortunately it is often a family member. It often occurs with our romantic partners when **no** is not respected and force is applied. This is sexual abuse as well. At any age we can be abused and significantly impacted. Abusers do not wear signs and they typically don't advertise that they are sexual predators. As a result, it is not uncommon to have encountered some aspect of sexual abuse in our lifetime. It might not involve a completed act of intercourse, but it might be a forced intimate touch, or kiss or restraint that is ever so brief and yet ever so distressful nonetheless.

Most abuse goes unreported by children and adults alike. Few want to battle the shame to report the event since the predator is often so well known by friends and family. The shame feeds our self-doubt and eventually the option to report seems like no option at all. So time passes and we put it out of our mind with other activities or if we are really struggling we may medicate our way to force down the painful memories and emotions. If we have spiritual beliefs, we may turn to them for comfort or we may see the lack of protection from such an awful event as a betrayal and begin to resent God for failing us when we needed protection.

Most cope with denial and repression of the memories with the hope that they will never resurface. Then one day, in a much more appropriate setting, we are about to have consensual sex and we are overwhelmed by fear, confusion, repulsion or maybe even anger. This can even be the case for those who became very promiscuous sexually after the abuse appearing to take to the active sex life without issues. And yet when the act becomes emotionally intimate with someone we really care about these incredibly strong emotions come from out of nowhere.

If we are partnered up with someone who is very patient and understanding, we may have the time to identify the source for such issues and work through them. However, identification usually has many obstacles. All the effort we put into denying and repressing our memories of the original events often continue to do their job very well, even when we have an appropriate relationship and want to have loving sexual relations. The abused continues to feel the repercussions of the past experience and still may not know why unless they get assistance with putting the pieces from their painful past together. Sadly, too few seek help and eventually settle for much less desirable partners, continue a promiscuous sex life, a sexless life or no life partner at all.

All can be addressed where a very natural and healthy sex life can be experienced and continued, but not without putting these past experiences in their proper perspective. While extremely intimate, even sexual baggage can be unpacked and its haunting effects upon our current lives eliminated.

Addictions

There is one insidious event that creeps into our lives and infects it in more ways than most can ever appreciate before it is even detected. Others may be able to see it, but typically nobody close to the situation. A Father, a Mother, a Sister, a Brother, a Son, a Daughter or ourselves, all of us are susceptible, all of us are vulnerable. What appears, as isolated incidents of lapses in judgment slowly become a regular event. By the time it becomes regular we are so invested in the denial that we can't see the intoxication, delinquency, incarceration, threats, beatings, being passed out in the chair, on the floor or in the yard, the loss of food and rent money. Addiction has become a part of the fabric of our family.

Slowly as the addict gets sicker, so do we. Making excuses, avoiding appearances, calling in impromptu sick and vacation days, seeking out and throwing out liquor and drugs, all the while becoming more determined to hide this embarrassment and take whatever means necessary to extract promises that it would stop. Yet for quite a while any suggestions of outside assistance that cannot be our own terms seems too high of a price to pay to right our world. Only one person may be abusing the drugs, alcohol or even food, but all of us have been sucked into the darkness of the family's secrets that bind us.

Sometimes things do not change until the addict is dead. Even incarceration is now merely a pit stop of the constant merry go round. When treatment is proposed or forced usually family treatment is recommended because the addiction affects everyone in the family.

If the addict wants to get help, the family often instinctively fights it. They may proclaim, "No hospital is necessary", "a lifetime of meetings isn't necessary", "they can still work in the family business", "what do these people know", "they act as if we are the problem". And they are partly correct, the family all become a part of the problem. Like a hanging mobile each family member is a part of the delicate balance of the family. If one member tries to do something radically different, like getting help, it is like cutting the string that ties the family together and all of the other members are thrown in disarray. If one tries to get help, the others may instinctively try to fight it. Other family reactions may include, "How dare that person decide that there might be something wrong with the rest of us? We all know the alcoholic/addict just needs to stop". It doesn't matter if the one seeking the help is the addict or just a family member or close friends who cannot take it anymore. Everyone can be motivated to fight it to keep the balance and not make waves, usually to protect secrets.

And thus, the addiction has its own self-perpetuating protection mechanism. It is as if the family and close friends at times form a symbiotic ecosystem that is both unhappy with the addict and interwoven with things not changing too much. This effect can be weak for some members and extremely strong for others, but denial is an intricate part of the system that is connected to the addict. If you had an addicted parent, even if they have been dead many years, there are effects from the addiction. You may very well have no addiction to drugs, alcohol, food, gambling, or sex yourself, but you will have many driving factors in your life still that stem from the addiction.

If one of your siblings is an addict who lives across the world and you only deal with the rest of the family, there are still many driving effects that shape your life. Living together creates more intimacy certainly, but the reach of the addiction's impact is limitless when it happens to ones we love or have loved.

When it is us who is addicted, comprehensive change is required to regain our life. What may seem distasteful is the relinquishing of a life that has become a mere shell of itself. Typically, others are aware of this when we are not. There are those few whose outward appearance yield few indications even to the trained eye, but the shattered life inside is the key symptom.

You alone can decide you have had enough. If you are unconvinced, consider having an open mind. Often, it is when we are certain that we have no problem that one actually exists. No matter how minor things appear or how devastated and lost we may think of ourselves, there is hope that this can get better.

Criticism

Receiving criticism is something we all encounter, but when it far outweighs the compliments or it is interwoven with what we hear from others, we can build this into our view of the world and ourselves. If the content and the delivery of the criticism are not put into their proper perspective, then we can internalize some devastatingly warped perspectives on what is appropriate, normal, acceptable and good. Before we have a choice, we are at times subjected to age inappropriate criticism and for those not so fortunate it may have been encountered on a daily basis if not nearly every interaction with a parent or guardian.

Living in an environment where the barrage of criticism is constant the world is a very dark place. For many, the constant posture of attempting to please becomes a way of life only to be repeatedly shot down. While the venues away from home, like school, and the homes of relatives and friends can be a great relief, often we take our criticizer-in-chief with us in our head constantly replaying what we have heard. To the extent we let ourselves relax while away we are jolted back to the onslaught of rejection and insult awaiting us at home. Beyond the shell-shocked posture we take on when constantly put down by our parent/guardian we also have the content to contend with in our heads. Am I really that clumsy, silly, fat, stupid, ridiculous, noisy, irritating, messy, worthless, ugly, weak, or unwanted?

Well, to hear some of the things that come out of adult's mouths to children can seem that way to those in their care. People who are constantly frustrated, angry, depressed, in pain, overworked, stressed out, have their own critical voices in their heads and are simply not thinking about the impact their words will have. As a result, our frame of reference is way out of proportion. We can never measure up, be good enough, never succeed enough, and no matter how much success we achieve it is never enough, never fully appreciated or enjoyed because the voices in our head are still calling us _____.

Those voices may never be forgotten, but we can stop playing the tape over and over. We can identify the triggers that start the tapes day after day and learn how to dismantle them. This type of baggage is one of the most common and undermines so much of our sense of accomplishment, what is acceptable, what is desirable and simply what we want from ourselves. Our brain is like the digital player that needs no batteries. It can run forever if we do not take the steps to turn it off. Some may think the only way to quiet the tapes from playing is to drown them out with fun, drugs, alcohol, sex, dangerous activities, or constant emergencies. The messages can be taken off repeat when they are put in their proper perspective. Just because they have been playing in your head for years doesn't mean they can't be taken off a constant repeat setting.

Just like we can learn new information, we can also learn to stop doing things that hurt us, no matter how much we are used to it. A life without constant self-criticism is one where we can relax and enjoy how much life has to offer us in this given moment. It can be done and there is no reason it can't happen for you.

Some of the more destructive and significant events in our lives can be forgotten or we may think of them on a very regular basis. Conscious or not, they likely are motivating us in very undesirable ways. Just because they happened and are a part of our past does not mean they have to control or haunt our future. Events, no matter how traumatic and painful, can often be put into a more appropriate perspective that frees us from the baggage it created.

9. FLAWED CONCEPTS

Beyond people and events that can divert us to a path of a baggage-burdened life, there is the most effective destroyer of lives, the believed lie. They are everywhere. They are in dialog of movies and literature, they come out of our parent and friend's mouths, but the clincher is that we choose to believe them.

When we believe a lie, we set ourselves significantly off course all the while believing we are not only doing the right thing in the right way, but also for the right reasons. We can be amazingly steadfast in our poor sense of direction in life. Whether it is saving up for a lifetime for a few moments of exhilaration, never planning for our future, discarding the most important relationships in our lives for an ideal, we can be stubborn. It doesn't matter what the specifics are, or how well intentioned we were, if we are on the wrong course and we mean well, the results of being on the wrong course are still ours to experience.

In this section we are going to review those flawed concepts we often cling to and as a result we allow ourselves to be thrown off course. Sometimes these are called old wives' tales, conventional wisdom, common sense, yet most of the time they are convenient maxims that delude us into making very poor choices again and again. While our limited time is passing we are investing in directions that are flawed, in maps that are inaccurate and in philosophies that lead us to ruin. They shouldn't be unfamiliar to you, most are very well known, but not as flawed concepts and yet they are probably undermining your life already and you are blissfully unaware of it.

Comfort

No matter how good things are we instinctively seek out what is most comfortable. While it sounds innocent enough this tendency has an inherent flaw for those of us free to make our own choices, just as we instinctively ask the parent who is most likely to say yes. Unless we have some sort of odd reason to motivate us to seek rejection, we will gravitate towards whatever we perceive will bring us the most comfort.

The downside of this tendency is usually experienced in our early days doing chores. As soon as we are out of eyesight the tendency to slow down or stop kicks in. Unless this tendency is overcome by the payoff of completing the task assigned, we will find whatever way possible to reduce our discomfort. Then when we are in school the opportunities for this conflict increase. Show up, put our stuff away, sit in our seat, be quiet, pay attention, follow instructions, and do our assignments. This transition is a big leap in responsibility for most of us compared to home and it can take a while to adjust. If we never quite adjust, then as the responsibilities grow, we can chronically leave tasks incomplete and suffer the consequences. Most of us however, do adjust and learn to see our responsibilities through to completion most of the time.

These areas where we tend to accept the risks tend to be repeated and usually get noticed by those around us. We may not pick up after ourselves, we may focus on appearance rather than content of the completed task, or we leave certain areas as ones of little to no concern. This may translate into a tendency to risk speeding tickets, performance reviews, our health, our safety, the security of our family, the character of children and potentially the love of those most important to us.

We may have overcome the tendency to slide on our responsibilities as a general practice in all areas of our lives, but when faced with a great challenge we revert back to options that appear to bring the most comfort. Conflicts in relationships can be where this shows up when our sense of responsibility is increasingly painful to execute. The challenging romantic relationship, a stressful job, or the parenting of a strong-willed child can all tempt us to take the easy way out. If we do, and the repercussions are not associated with our choices, it is easy to start a practice of once again seeking to be comfortable over carrying out our responsibilities.

This is especially understandable when otherwise responsible people are confronted with others who are mentally ill or consumed by addiction. No matter how skilled or resolute we have become, these situations can reduce the best of us to doing anything to stop the discomfort. This usually translates into giving into the demands and manipulations of these more challenging individuals. The same can be said for work scenarios where we are requested to perform tasks counter to our beliefs or sense of ethics, or perception of the law. While many tend to compartmentalize this behavior, we may allow it to become a practice in more parts of our lives once again focusing on just wanting to be comfortable in order to be happy.

For some, seeking comfort has become a constant and high priority criterion. As a result, a long series of unintended consequences has occurred. We may not see or acknowledge the connection, but they are there:

- The many things not said in order to not make waves, thus our perspectives and desires are not clearly communicated.
- The invitations refused because it involved meeting new people, thus we severely limit our opportunity to make new acquaintances that could result in new friends.
- Doing for others what they can do for themselves, we rob them of the dignity of the accomplishment of self-reliance.
- We stay with abusive people because we are more afraid of the unknown than the brutally painful known world we live in.
- We spend holidays with families that are hate-

ful and demoralizing because we are supposed to spend them with family.

As counterintuitive as it is, our attempts at comfort often lead to extremely unpleasant results. Here the baggage can be twofold; 1) we cannot bring ourselves to be uncomfortable to stand up for others and ourselves and 2) we are blind to the consequences of our actions.

While we are actively living a baggage collecting lifestyle we often are not able to see the connection, but in time the connections can become clear. These patterns of behavior can be changed and the results significantly improved. However, it will require steps that are not comfortable.

Busy Life, Happy Life

Having a busy life can be the envy for many people. We make it a point to look busy, schedule too much, work too much, play too much, worry too much and as a result rob ourselves of a much more pleasant life. Yet the default message for most of us is that if we have things to do, people to see, places to go, then we have a desirable life. And maybe we do, but if it is done for the sake of it and it can easily get there, then it can be its own special version of torture. Nothing is worse than being in a desirable situation and being miserable. Like being lonely among others, bored at a party, distracted at a movie or play, all these things can look desirable from a distance, yet our life is not for others hopefully, but for us.

What good is it to be envied when we are miserable? None. So how do we get here?

Sometimes we start off doing things for a good reason, but as we have described already we can have some pretty faulty ideas based upon our baggage. If we made a habit of trying to look good for the sake of it, then we may still do this from time to time or regularly out of habit. If you have ever seen someone from many years ago that you didn't really care for, but envied you may be tempted to look like you are having more fun than you are. We can be silly and petty sometimes because we still can feel like we did when we were in college, high school, junior high or even grade school if the trigger reminds us of that time in our lives.

The first time we hear of, see or remember someone from many years ago it will often catapult us back to that time and often the emotions and a few characteristics of our lives associated with this person back at that time. The memories may be pleasant ones, but when they are unpleasant it can motivate us to do some pretty odd things. Like buy things we don't need or can afford, instantly act differently or just hide and attempt to be unnoticed. Sometimes we can come up with the lesson that being busy is what makes us happy when that is rarely the case. Being busy just makes us appear like we are important and maybe have a full life. A full life can be just as miserable as an empty life.

We may like the constant activity to a certain extent, but we also need down time to process what we experience, to rest our bodies and our minds, to interact with those around us and to make time for those things that we can't plan for such as being there for friends and family when they need support. Being there for others is something we can rarely be available for when we are constantly busy. This is a common regretful result from working too much, or doing anything too much that takes us away from our family and friends. Sometimes we avoid others because we are uncomfortable or it is too hard to deal with the natural conflicts that arise in every relationship. Everything we choose to do we are not choosing to do everything else. So it is important to choose wisely and make sure we are choosing to spend our time in a way that is in line with our priorities.

Even technology improvements that initially appear to save us time can be a greater potential demand upon our time if we become to enamored with it. While new devices are not inherently bad for us they can distract us from our responsibilities to ourselves, our loved ones, our friends and family and even our employers. Same can be said for most anything that we get a payoff from that is less difficult than relationships. If our relationships are viewed as being too difficult, then we might gravitate towards things that keep us from pursuing or investing our relationships with others. If we are too busy working, reading, crafting, exercising, traveling, or anything that severely limits our interaction with others, then our business may be a way we undermine investing in the things we would really prefer.

So as we identify what is really important in our lives, it often helps to write them down and occasionally take the list out and review it to see if our recent choices are in line with what people, places or things are truly important to us. Our baggage gives us a tendency to get off course, so beginning a practice to be more conscious of our priorities and how we are doing to align our daily choices to those priorities can help have better results.

Isolation

If you avoid commitments to spend time with others in any fashion except when absolutely necessary, isolation may be a concept you have bought into. It may be a concept you in part learned from your family or friends. It not only involved social engagements, but any opportunity to become closer, involved or acquainted enough for more to be revealed about ourselves than we desire. The greater likelihood is that a combination of modeled behavior by others and by personal experiences have shaped our posture towards engagement with others.

The people we observe are executing all kinds of behaviors as are we and we make note of what happens as a result. We may not be all that observant and we may not appreciate the variables involved in their motivations, their approach and why they received the results they did, but occasionally we will make observations and take away a lesson.

Let's say that you as a younger person early in your social

development were a bit insecure and you end up meeting a few other children your age at home, school or daycare etc. The interaction doesn't go quite the way you hoped, you end up getting your feelings hurt when the others exclude you from their chosen activities. Many would probably withdraw for at least a little while upset that we have been rejected and excluded. This can happen at home with siblings or visiting friends or even parents, but it is more likely that it happened with people outside the home.

A significant part of the development of friendships depends upon the action of both parties. Sometimes friendships are hostage situations where one person makes all the moves, but typically it involves effort from both players. The more interest or effort we put into a new relationship the greater potential there is for hurt feelings and disappointment if it fails to continue.

When the early relationships end it may be experienced with unexplained absence of one of the parties. They are no longer around, no more visits to the house, no longer in our classroom, or no longer on the playground in our neighborhood. However, most endings are more direct. We are told we are no longer welcome, sometimes with an explanation and sometimes without. We may be told we are mean, stupid, ugly, weak, scared, a baby, the wrong color, too young, the wrong gender, too poor, too rich, too neat, too dirty and the list can go on and on. It really doesn't matter why. We were rejected and it hurt.

It would be pretty rare, but not unheard of, that we only have to have an experience like this once to decide that people are just not worth the trouble. However, it is much more likely that we have experienced a series of rejections over time and at some point, and have come to the same conclusion. We may realize that we have to live with our families for now, or work with other people or ride the bus or share the street with other people, but we can choose to keep it all to a bare minimum. This way can minimize, if not totally eliminate, the opportunities that other people can hurt us.

We may choose to forgo friendships and any kind of romantic relationships, simply because they are just too high risk. We may learn to fake interest, social graces, fashion, poise and even sincerity and empathy, but ultimately, we keep people unimportant and at least at arms distance all the time. No secrets, no emotions, no tears, no hopes or dreams or desires are shared in order to eliminate any chance of being hurt again. Even if we manage to collect friends to hang out with or romantic relationships that end in lifelong commitments, we still protect ourselves in order to not get hurt. Occasionally we may get weak and almost share something or begin to care about someone again, but we know better and seek to re-correct our perspective as soon as possible before we allow ourselves to be hurt again.

This makes for a very lonely life. This isolation can become our home. It is comfortable and it is our prison. We may seek comfort in literature, hobbies, pets or vocations, but not people. They are not an option, not really. The very steps we have taken to protect ourselves when we isolate are the same ones that keep us from realizing that there are other options. We may employ psychiatrists or therapists, but we may tell ourselves they are only there because we are paying them to be there. They don't really qualify as a person, not really. And this is how we stay alone.

The pain of rejection and disappointment are ever present and possible in all relationships. The happy couples and families that really do exist have the same pain of rejection and disappointments. They just respond to it differently. They choose different responses and so can everyone else. Isolation is a flawed life strategy because it cuts us off from the most basic human desire to connect and share experiences. Besides, no one ever died of rejection or disappointment. If you are a practitioner of the isolation strategy in life it can be changed and the rewards are endless.

Emotions

If you are a person who has become someone who no longer feels or can express emotion, then you have probably bought into the flawed concept that we can keep ourselves from having emotions. We all have had those encounters where we were overflowing with emotion and we either didn't want to be or we were being told we shouldn't be so emotional. When we are born, with few exceptions, we show our emotions freely. Babies from the start hold nothing back, but we soon learn and continue to learn as toddlers, children and adolescents that showing your emotions is not always the best strategy. The downsides cause loss of privileges, affection, opportunities, friendship and even love.

So we adapt if our parents or caretakers don't like our displays of emotions and if they make it unpleasant enough we learn to adapt, determined to stem the tide of consequences of being soft or weak. You may be told, "you will not cry", or be scared or hurt or angry or you may just tell yourself over and over until somehow some way the emotions begin to diminish. First, they diminish enough to mask them from others. They may still surface when alone where it is safe to let it out, but eventually we all learn that you can never be entirely safe from being found out, especially as a child. Usually, as a child we do not control our own world enough to make sure we are never observed expressing our emotions.

If our environment and experiences are not too severe, our reprogramming of our emotional selves may stop there where we can feel our emotions, but they are so tightly controlled they never show or so we think. However, as we age there are more hard lessons out there for us with acquaintances, friends, enemies, authoritarians and romantic relationships. People get close, conflicts get more complicated and relationships become more multifaceted. If our perceived need to conceal increases, it drives us farther inward. More and more we tell ourselves we will not feel, we will not cry, we will not be hurt, we will not be afraid and we may decide to even give up being angry, but more of us hang on to that one since oddly it is so much more socially acceptable. However, every person's situation is unique. So after pushing our emotions farther and farther down we begin to notice we no longer are aware that we feel at all. We are numb. Now while many accomplish this feat by the shear will of survival there is a much larger group who turn to alcohol and drugs to numb the pain of our emotions.

So, what appears as a problem solved comes back to bite us. We are navigating emotionless like a machine. Depending upon how good we are at learning the social, educational and business ropes, we may very well become very successful in the eyes of the world with a family, money and power or we may be barely able to support ourselves alone much less attracted to a mate or support a family. If we managed a more successful life where we can make money, fix problems, be super parents, be super community servants, and even have plenty of friends, we still can't do one thing, feel. And the funny thing, eventually, we all have that need.

Having the emotional faucet tightly closed off robs us of the very thing that we sought to eliminate, the ability to rise and fall with the world around us. Dissatisfaction with a life without emotions is what you can call a 100% club. Eventually, everyone wants them back. The only problem is that they haven't been as tightly sealed off from the world as we thought. It turns out that people who have reported not being able to feel their emotions for decades actually were feeling them. They had just turned their brain off so they were never acknowledged. What appeared to us as a mature powerful strategy in our youth and young adult life actually turns out to be a con on the one person you thought you could trust, you. Our denial of our own emotional existence was not the elimination of anything more than the experience and the opportunity to maturely process our reactions.

The realization that we have been fooling ourselves can come to us in the strangest of places, empty nest homes, jail cells, courtrooms, custody hearings, funerals, hospital beds and anytime when we are all alone. Being estranged from all of our family and friends doesn't happen overnight, it happens because we did not choose to give of our emotional selves to our loved ones and they are tired of being shut out. At these moments, we sometimes start letting ourselves feel again, we may even shed some tears in private. However, for many the tears won't come for fear that we will never stop. And we have no idea how we feel about anything since everything is blank.

This is an indication that you will need assistance to reconnect with your emotional self. The blocks some people construct are so crafty it takes a great deal of time to pry the stopper loose. Then once they are free to be expressed then there is the backlog of emotions to process. While this is quite a job for most, you will find no shortage of people who will describe how meaningful it is to be able to enjoy the highs and lows of life freely as they occur.

Once we return to a life of allowing ourselves emotions, we will find that many more things become possible, most importantly the ability to connect intimately with others. Sometimes this can even occur with family members and friends who were cut out for much of our lives. Just because we got so comfortable at denying our emotion doesn't mean we can't learn to be just as good at letting them exist and enjoy them as the asset they are.

I Can't Change

We have all heard the expression, "This is just the way I am", when someone is confronted with a less than desirable quality. We have likely heard this from our parents, caretakers, teachers, TV, friends, practically everyone.

Depending upon what is being referenced this can be an accurate statement, but too often we end up using this statement in response to criticism when we have no desire to change things that are possible to be changed.

We may be embarrassed that the characteristic has been pointed out or we may not like the characteristic either, but believe it can't be changed. Even though innovations are developed every day to enable changes to our bodies and our lives, many things about us are really not possible to be changed such as our height, our age, our family of origin, our history, and how the people around us act. We can mask or lie to others about ourselves, but in a practical sense going beyond hair dye, cosmetics, exercise, eating habits, education, getting inspiration or coaching is not very realistic. But when it comes to the way we live out our future this is totally open to change even when it comes to the way we act.

Think back to the times you have heard this same statement and it was about the way the speaker behaves. "I can't help that I am so nervous, this is just the way I am". Or...

- I can't help it that I am worried...
- I can't help it that I am jealous...
- I can't help it that I am secretive...
- I can't help it that I am suspicious...
- I can't help it that I am gullible...
- I can't help it that I am stupid...
- I can't help it that I am uncertain... It is just the way I am.

We say it so matter of factly and we believe it, and worst of all.... it is NOT TRUE.

When you break down the word can't, it should mean cannot. However, in these instances we are saying to ourselves, I will not.

We can change these things. We see people around us change like this all the time. If we do not know someone personally for inspiration, we can read about it in literature, or see it in the real life of famous figures who reinvent themselves in the face of adversity. I can't is what we often say when we mean we will not try.

We may not know what to do, we may be afraid to do anything, we may even fail the first attempt or two. The one thing that will keep us from making any changes is to not try. If we say we can't over and over to ourselves, then we believe it and there is no more needing to discuss it or think about it. It is simply out of reach and therefore we might as well move on. Nice and convenient since changing would very likely make us uncomfortable, very uncomfortable.

Being human seems to naturally motivate us to strive to be comfortable. We fight discomfort all of our lives. We buy clothes that feel good on our skin, we establish routines to make our lives predictable, avoid certain people and situations just in order to preserve our comfort, so why would we all of the sudden want to become uncomfortable? For a more important goal of having a baggage free life. One where few things keep you from the things you want to be in life.

Change is nearly always uncomfortable. And yet change is another one of those things that won't kill you. And yet we will avoid change as if it might.

The truth is that we can make all kinds of changes, but in order to do so we have to leave certain things behind. Just because we have decided in the past that something is permanent in our lives doesn't mean it has to stay that way.. Nervousness, worry, jealousy, things we are ashamed of, the inability to trust, or trusting too much, buying into lies about our capabilities or allowing the unknown to keep us from moving forward are all things, like many others, that can be changed in any of us, even you.

The people who make changes are simply willing to do what it takes to do things differently. So all it takes is being willing, no skills requirement. You will likely need some direction like a guide, but change is possible even for those who have never believed change was possible before.

Unrealistic Expectations

We all have expectation of things many times a day if not

hundreds of times a day. We can develop expectations about the people and events in our life and the world based upon our previous experience or just because we prefer things to be a certain way.

Most expectations we choose to have can be either realistic expectations or unrealistic expectations. Right away you might think that all of your expectations are realistic, but that is often not the case. We all have some unrealistic expectations often for a variety of reasons. We may adopt unrealistic expectations due to unreliable or incorrect information. We may choose to count on somebody to show up at 6pm for dinner, but we know they don't wear a watch and they are rarely on time. Or we may choose to rely upon a person we like for advice about buying a car when there is nothing to suggest they have any special knowledge or expertise about cars.

Instead of letting facts direct our decisions about what to expect, we often will allow other factors to influence what we choose to expect of the world around us. Someone who is likeable, well spoken, holds or appears to hold similar values as we do, or we perceive as having our best interest can win our ear when it comes to making decisions and forming expectations. Then, even when we do have a great deal of data about the people, places and things around us, if it doesn't agree with what we want from them we may elect to simply expect things to magically be different and as a result be disappointed when our expectations are not realized.

Whereas, when we elect to ignore facts or allow ourselves to be swayed by other factors we simply are increasing our risk of being disappointed. If this risk was one that is well thought out that would be one thing, but often we take big risks with the expectation we select to have without giving it much thought at all. And yet what we choose to expect in life and make a priority can have a significant impact on our sense of wellbeing. If for instance, we decide that someone in our family suddenly ought to begin acting in a different way and we make it important to us that they meet that expectation, we are likely to become very unhappy when they continue to act as they please. And yet we do this all the time. We will say to ourselves my mother/brother/son/daughter/sister/father know that when they act like that it drives me crazy. Why do they continue to do it? Maybe they are just being themselves or they may be out to irritate you, but why they are doing it doesn't matter. What matters is that we allow it to make us crazy.

If we walk up to a wall and bang our head on it, it hurts. Why would we want to do it again? Do we think if we do it again tomorrow it will be softer and not hurt so much? Do we think we can change the hardness of the wall? Apparently, because we do this all the time.

Now when we are parents of younger children, having expectations of them behaving and conforming to a parent's guidance and rules is very appropriate. However, once they become adults or have become accustomed to making their own decisions, then it is time to stop expecting behavior that is no longer likely to bend to our will. Parenting, much like mentoring or coaching, is our role for a season that has a natural beginning and end. When we try to play that role with our children, or some similar role with others who do not agree with our lead, it is time to update our expectations.

Spouses develop unrealistic expectations of each other constantly, bosses do with employees and vice versa, siblings, friends, and family members all do it. And some of us also do this with institutions, government, corporations, the justice system, our local civic and religious leaders, our neighbors and the list goes on and on. If they exist in our world, we probably have some unrealistic expectations about them. So, our expectations probably seem justified to us regardless if they are realistic or not, but on top of that is the amount of importance we place upon those expectations being met. Here are some examples that you may have allowed your expectations to become too important in your life.

- If you get really upset or angry when the traffic lights do not go your way.

- If you get really upset or angry when people drive differently than you think they should.
- If you get really upset or angry that there is injustice in the world.
- If you get really upset or angry that there is corruption in the world.
- If you get really upset or angry listening to the same news program you watch every day.
- If you get really upset or angry that your government is not in line with your priorities.
- If you get really upset or angry that your job has aspects to it that you dislike.
- If you get really upset when people are not as neat as you are.
- If you get really upset that people are always cleaning up around you.
- If you get really upset or angry when your adult children don't do what you tell them to do.
- If you get really upset or angry when your adult children don't call as often as you would like.
- If you get really upset or angry when your spouse does not take out the trash, make the bed, pick up their clothes, put caps back on containers, or whatever else you would like them to do.

There is the old saying if it hurts when you do that, stop doing it.

Much like the evidence presented in a court of law we are presented with a version of the facts and we are to decide if they are true. If we carelessly decide these presented facts are true or not true, then we are likely to base many decisions upon this judgment until you have some compelling reason to rethink your judgment. The criteria for the evidence in a courtroom are based on three characteristics: authenticity, relevancy and credibility. Yet, we rarely give this kind of scrutiny to the information that comes our way. Additionally, a judge, an arbitrator or lawyers representing either side are supposed to remove themselves if they have any personal connection with the matter under review to eliminate bias. This is something we cannot do. As a result, we will always have a degree of bias through which we see our version of the facts.

Expectations created based upon first expectations are likely to not serve us as well as ones we choose to create after we have had more time to refine our observations. When we observe something personally it seems so real to us that we often will take it as fact when it could very well be that we have misinterpreted the events entirely. Our versions of the facts are often different from the actual facts.

A lifetime of unverified facts and unrealistic expectation can make for a pretty unhappy life. So much so we can vacillate between being angry and believing the world is about to end at any moment. This is baggage no one needs and it can only be unpacked by methodically reviewing how realistic are our expectations.

Reciprocity

The sayings, "if you scratch my back I will scratch yours" or "an eye for an eye" are often the basis for some fairly destructive viewpoints on how we think the world works. While in the case of kindness and consideration this can be a healthy inspiration, but it also leads to our healthy behavior being dependent upon the behavior of others towards us. Whether we like it or realize it, many of the actions we are exposed to have nothing to do with us. Someone who approaches us angry and mean has often been wronged in some way before we came upon them. They may take it out on us, but we are not their problem. When we take this into consideration we can easily see how we can get ourselves into a fairly nasty cycle of treating others badly.

Let's say you are heading to work and a patrolman pulls you over for a reason unknown to you. Before you can respond respectfully, they are chewing you out and acting as if they are going to throw the book at you for something that you really believe you did not do. This would be upsetting and probably cause you to be irritable towards the next few people you encounter on the roadway and at work. You cut off a few people and yell at someone who gets too close to your rear bumper and slam on the brakes. At the next stop light the guy gets out of his car and angrily comes toward you when the light turns green and keeps you from having to deal with him. As you enter the office someone asks you for something you are late on and you snap back at them that you will get to it when you get it. Your boss hears your exchange and asks you to come into their office to talk about your attitude. Reminding you that your performance has been suffering lately and is there anything they should know about that might be causing your outbursts and tardiness?

What you may not have considered is that you had just passed the police station right before you got stopped and that officer might have just been chewed out by his boss for not filling out some paperwork and was docking his pay. As he was leaving to begin his patrols, your car was the first one he saw on the road. You just happened to be the one he took his frustrations out on. This was only a description of a single hour, but in real life the chain of frustration and poor behavior, cycles through millions of us every day and among family members, co-workers, friends, acquaintances and strangers all day long. In a sad perverse sort of way we treat others poorly when we are treated poorly and in turn we become the person people want to avoid because we are irritable, angry, explosive, sarcastic, negative, depressing, etc. all because we have chosen to do unto others what they have done unto us. Now, we aren't always willing to just pay each individual back or we may not want the consequences of treating our boss poorly, so we may wait to take it out on the next person. The people we take things out on the most are the ones who can't get away from us. Our family, our employees, people who are stuck with us for one reason or another and we let them have it.

Sometimes we are conscious that we do this, but often we do this without realizing it. Our feelings will get hurt and we attempt to cause the same kind of pain in return. It is almost instinctive and we may even find ourselves apologizing with the statement, "I couldn't help myself, you hurt my feelings and I wanted you to feel bad too". The key thing wrong with that statement is that you could help yourself, but you chose to take your problems out on the next person that came along.

When we do this, we teach all those around us to keep their distance and protect themselves from us, since who knows what has happened today that we may have to suffer for since we are their personal punching bag. When we are feeling hurt or threatened it is very easy for it to translate into anger. If we allow it through at a minimum to sour our attitude or on the other extreme by taking revenge on someone else entirely, we simply perpetuate the cycle of bad behavior. Those we mistreat will either be motivated to dish it right back at us or worse yet go away vowing to never voluntarily interact with us again. This is how we can end up without many friends and acquaintances.

However, we can start choosing differently by refusing to take our irritations out on others. Once we can conquer that hurdle, then we can set the bar to not allowing irritations to cause our attitude to be wrecked for weeks, days, hours, etc. It takes practice and often the assistance of a coach or therapist, but it is possible for those of us who have been irritated and angry most of our lives to stop the cycle of mistreatment towards others and ourselves.

For instance, let's say you are once again heading to work and a patrolman pulls you over for a reason unknown to you. Before you can respond respectfully they are chewing you out and acting as if they are going to throw the book at you for something that you really believe you did not do. This understandably would be upsetting and probably tempt you to be irritable towards the next few people you encounter on the roadway and at work. However, you think to yourself, "Well whatever that was about, it wasn't about me. He probably had something really upsetting just happen to him. I am not going to let it ruin my day." Then, as resume your drive to work you let people in when lanes are merging and they wave in gratitude. Someone who gets too close to your rear bumper and you gently reduce your speed until they go around you. They appear not too happy and you choose to listen to the song on the radio instead of returning any words of correction. At the next stop light the guy looks back at you and shakes his head and you smile at him and he shakes his head again. As you enter the office someone asks you for something you are late on and you apologize, commit to do it first thing and make a written note about the item. Your boss hears your exchange and tells you good morning. You head to your desk and begin to work on the late item, finish it and deliver it right afterwards to the person who requires it and you go on with your day feeling like you have accomplished something already.

It doesn't take much to create a radically different day for ourselves and the ones around us.

God is Punishing You

One of the most unfortunate faulty concepts is the idea that God is punishing us and or has rejected us in some way. Many adults have managed to miscommunicate faith-based concepts to very young, impressionable children leaving them with some extremely damaging concepts to be recalled again. The most vulnerable of us all are our children. And when we were children we were the vulnerable ones. Whether it was malicious or not when our parents, grandparents, aunts, uncles or any other adult relative, friend of the family or worse yet a member of the clergy carelessly used the name of God to instill fear, guilt and shame, we were handed the most insidious gift of all; the idea that God cannot love us or forgive us and we are cut off.

In the study of communications, we are taught that the

responsibility of ensuring the recipient gets the correct message relies with the one delivering the message. And the one concept of effective communication is to know your audience. And yet year after year, adults will bend down to very small young children within inches of them with angry faces, yell, scream, hit and use the name of God as the one who is disappointed, ashamed, unhappy, and is probably not going to let you go to Heaven with Mommy or Daddy.

Our young psyches cannot handle this kind of messaging and come away with anything but a positive lesson learned. Rather some learn from these careless instances that God is an angry, hateful, inconsistent, irrational, erratic, judgmental, unforgiving, sadistic monster that no longer provides a safe refuge from the rest of the world that we still do not understand. We also often have the same sad impression of the people who passed on the message.

If that was not our experience then we may have got the idea that we are unlovable from a more innocent source, age inappropriate sermons. Children can easily misunderstand messages that are appropriate for adults. If we were within earshot of a message that described topics involving fear, guilt and shame, then the idea may have come from here. Then of course there are the instances where someone maliciously tortured us mentally and emotionally with stories of damnation, unworthiness, and being beyond forgiveness. Nothing is worse than a destructive concept cemented in the young mind of a child. The event may be forgotten, but the concept and the self-condemnation usually haunt us for a lifetime. Lifetimes of believing we are not worthy, not lovable, not capable of being forgiven and so we have no hope of the life others appear to have.

When we are very young our parents seem like gods. They seem to know everything, hear everything and are all-powerful over us. As we grow we come to learn that these characteristics are not true of our parents, but we may still attribute these characteristics to God. If we somehow acquired a perspective that God is an angry, hateful, all knowing and unforgiving, then it is like still being very young with our parents that have those same characteristics. We can never get away from him. He is always there haunting us, so we may try to be good and do all the right things and try to make no one ever unhappy with us. Or we may try to outrun the fear and pain with music, delinquency, promiscuity, alcohol and drugs.

Numbing the pain with adrenalin or altered states is a dangerous direction, but one that has its short-term payoffs. For a little while the fear and the pain are dulled or neutralized. Often the path we take is somewhere in between and eventually we start to find our own way in life though still haunted. The more impacted we are by the concept of a vengeful God the more baggage we will continue to collect. Usually this amount of weight causes us to have a fairly tortured life, but we may have found ways to mask it.

Often a painful version of God keeps us from attending any kind of faith community or it may drive us to explore others. Unfortunately, our pained perspective will often make anyone who has a favorable perspective of God very unattractive to us. If that is not the case, then we may simply be the one who does not partake if we managed to become friends or a spouse who isn't haunted by an angry and judgmental God. When you grow up with a nasty version of God in your experience then anyone who has a more positive concept appears like saps who just have yet to experience the slaughter. Instead we seek to fill our lives with things that we think will work. We pour ourselves into pleasing others, working hard, our children, sports, our children's sports, TV, work, or things that don't seem so productive. When we believe God is punishing us we tend to over compensate either to numb ourselves to the pain or to attempt to displace it with an over the top pursuit of things we at least partially enjoy. The extreme effort can cause us to have some pretty disastrous results like alienated family and friends, poor job performance, divorce, addictions or emotional problems.

Doing life with the tortured psyche of a young child trapped in the body of an adult who seemingly should have it more together makes for a pretty miserable life. It doesn't have to stay that way, but we often require a significant event before we will reach out for help and start doing enough things differently. The good news is that misconceptions like this can be made better at any age.

Trust

Trust is something everybody seems to approach uniquely. Some people who have had bad experiences with certain types of people, places or things will tend to not trust them while people who have had good experiences with people, places or things will tend to trust them.

The key question we often don't answer is "Trust them to do what?" What we are willing to trust will happen is often very general while our experiences are very specific, but instead of adjusting our trust according to the specific area of our experiences we tend to trust all the way or not at all. We may do this no matter how many times we experience that certain people, place or things are unreliable and unworthy of our trust.

Both extremes are very damaging to us. If we tend to trust despite our experiences, we tend to pile more and more heartache over all the disappointment we experience from having our family and friends let us down by stealing from us, lying to us, or maybe being disloyal. The possibilities are endless, but if we trust those around us and they do not honor that trust, then we would create less baggage for ourselves by learning to be more selective. And despite the idea that you are supposed to trust your spouse, family, children, friends, authority figures, etc. if they are not trustworthy, then continuing to trust them is not healthy for us.

More than likely if we are not willing to withhold our trust, then there is probably something else going on that is holding us back from making a stand that might make waves. Maybe we are afraid of being rejected or not being perceived as a friend. This can be an especially dangerous trap for parents who may enjoy being popular with their children and their friends, but when it comes to actual parenting they are reluctant to say no and administer discipline.

On the other end of the spectrum we may be a person who cannot bring themselves to trust anyone. We share nothing; expect everyone to betray us if they get the chance and we cannot even allow people to know the slightest detail about our lives without the suspicion that they are in some way going to take advantage of us. If we were surrounded by very inconsistent behavior throughout our very young lives, we may have never developed a healthy practice of establishing attachments to others. This inability to make the most basic steps of trusting another human being can lead to a lifelong pattern of secrets, mistrust and isolation from much of the world. We may have this perspective, but have learned to put on a socially better-adjusted face, but still refuse to share anything truly important to us. Sometimes we may even fabricate substitute details about our past and ourselves in order to not have to divulge anything about us. As a result, we often will negate anything positive anyone will say to us because we believe that if they really knew us they would not think so much of us. This is especially destructive when we have difficulty believing anything anyone says about us. If we hear a compliment, we may wonder what they want in return. If we hear the words "I like you" or "I love you" we may tell ourselves that if they really knew me they wouldn't love or like me.

We may also compartmentalize the areas of our lives where we are willing to trust and areas where we are not. For instance, at work we might trust in a very fact based and discerning manner whereas when it comes to our personal life we may be all over the place, trusting when we shouldn't or not at all. Trust is a decision that we can exercise at any time anyway we want, but we rarely think of it this way. Typically, when we are more erratic or stuck in one extreme or another we are allowing our trust decisions to be based upon emotion which is rarely a good idea.

One of the related, flawed concepts we can buy into is that we can't trust, or that it has been too long, or that we have been too hurt that we are incapable of trusting anyone ever again. Whatever the line is these statements are not true.

Being able to exercise trust in an appropriate way is something we can be taught at a fairly young age or a very mature age. Trust is often a very central issue for those of us who are significantly burdened by our baggage. It may not make any sense how overwhelming it can feel to ever consider trusting someone in the ways we have avoided for so long. The extreme stakes are in part overblown by the well-practiced avoidance of letting others in.

The secret is tackling this issue with someone who is easily verified as trustworthy. It may be a friend or family member, but often if we have been in the practice of not trusting these people, then you may want to consider a professional to help you begin the journey of learning how to trust appropriately. No matter what the circumstances are there is hope that it can be improved. You do not have to continue to live a life without meaningful people you can trust. They are out there, but they are human and can make mistakes. Part of relationships with others is being willing to forgive others when they prove they are human.

Rules

Rules are everywhere. We learn early on there are rules for how to crawl, walk, talk, ask for things, eat your food, act in public versus at home, play games, and how to act when we are in trouble. Many of these are unspoken rules.

Before we enter a classroom, we are bombarded with rules. Regardless of our environment it is a lot to take in and master and some of us do not do so well. We have all seen the variety of rules parents can have and how they all seem to break down at one point or another. Some children are very good at following all of their parents' rules for unknown reasons, but the majority of us can only sit still for so many seconds, stay quiet for so many seconds, keep from touching something for so many seconds and you get the idea.

Young children need a lot of grace, but some of us did not get much grace when it came to our inability to strictly follow the rules. Some of us were gently assisted back within the lines while the rest of us were hit, slapped, yelled at, screamed at, grabbed hard and whisked away to another room and spanked or just spanked right there on the spot. Then, there was the correction that would go on and on. In most homes this was only moderately successful at best. Impatient or inexperienced parents often struggle to get us to follow the rules while we are often clueless to all the ambushes of punishment that seem to come out of nowhere. Just when most of us were getting a pretty good handle on these ever-evolving rules, we begin school.

What was either an exciting or traumatic separation soon becomes a whole new host of rules that seem to be just for school. While this may have come gradually for some of us, for others it was quite abrupt and harsh. For those of us where it was extremely harsh at home, school became the relief. For those of us where home was very easy going, then school may have become the new challenge. While we may have had siblings at home to learn from, at school this was greatly magnified by the large number in our classroom.

It is in these observations we are introduced to the input of other people's experience as opposed to simply our own experience. Things we wanted to do but were never brave enough to try, we now could see what happened when someone else did it. Likewise, when others did exactly things we had done before, we soon found out that the results were not always the same. This may have been observed at home between Mom and Dad and thus began our preference for adult attention and favor. If such a difference existed, then we quickly learned who was the nice parent and who was the mean parent. Who was the kind parent and who was the angry parent, which parent talked to us and explained why we couldn't do something and which parent yelled and or abruptly would lunge at us and give a spanking. Sometimes there were even more rules if we had siblings that chose to impose themselves upon us when no one else was looking.

Then in the really unfortunate circumstances there were those households where the consequences were very extreme, such as beatings, naming calling, constant berating unless there was another adult present, the withholding of food, affection, privacy and even control over our own bodies. If the people raising us were treated brutally when they were young or if they were mentally ill or in the grip of addiction, then treatment they dished out to us when we were very young could have been very severe.

In no way does any young child deserve anything less than a loving, secure environment where lessons are taught with consistent gentleness and kindness. However, all of us were occasionally the recipient of a tired, frustrated, over worked, hurt, angry, worried, scared or worse yet mentally or emotionally disturbed parent, authority figure, sibling or friend who would take their pain out on us. These are experiences that teach a very distorted set of rules. Rules that breed fear and insecurity and in more extreme cases excessive shame that we allowed people to hurt us, take advantage of us and rob us of our innocence. A young psyche cannot process any of these extremes well, but they will adapt in the ways that make the most sense to survive. How can we get through this day without getting ambushed, abused, yelled at, hit, spanked or have something of mine taken away?

When we have been raised in environments or join them later in life where the rules are constantly changing and we cannot get a handle on what works and what doesn't, we cope in ways that monopolize our lives. We may learn to totally focus on everybody else and not take care of ourselves. With having to expend so much energy studying others and being on guard, we lose our natural sense of self-care. As a result, we lose ourselves often in anyone who is around us. Usually, this is a spouse later in life, but can be a sibling, parent, child or even a friend.

These people we attach ourselves to in later life are typically always in some sort of drama, either being very over the top in their everyday actions or they are in constant crisis. When these people who we have made the focus of our lives somehow get abruptly separated from us, we often will have the sensation of a loss of purpose. Although the break can be initially invigorating a sense of aimlessness often arrives soon thereafter. This is in part why adult children of alcoholics are often attracted to, and often marry, alcoholics since they are what they are used to. Despite any conscious effort to avoid anything like their parents, we often go with what we know. Not always consciously, but it happens more time than not.

People who discover this mode of operation, where rules are either an object of hyper focus or we don't follow any of them, tend to go with what we know. Despite the negative things we might tell ourselves, like I must be defective/crazy, why do I keep getting involved with bad/messed up people? This can be changed. This strange tendency is reversible.

No matter how messed up your life is now or was in the past with help, healthy social choices and relationships can be made again and again. No person is doomed to repeat the past unless they take no effort to make significant changes in the way they do life. Even if you have considered yourself too messed up, damaged or defectively wired, we are all just a comprehensive rewiring job away.

Faith

Flawed thinking related to faith is probably one of the more common stumbling blocks for people. Most of us should be familiar with the concept of having faith in something or someone. Usually this faith is a belief based upon evidence you have observed and believe will continue to exist. Spiritual faith however, is for the most part, based upon things that often cannot be proven, but can be personally experienced. Most of us probably do not give this distinction much notice, but the difference can make or break one's ability to have a successful spiritual faith, while having faith in someone or something is usually quite a bit easier. Explaining something to someone who has yet to experience it can be challenging. And the explanation received may not be the most accurate or meaningful to the person receiving the message. Add to this that not every person of a faith are knowledgeable about the religion they are associated. As a result, it is easy to see how varied the impressions people can get of even a single religion through a single person's faith.

Given that there are so many types of faith that have common elements, it is easy to get confused when trying to understand how they relate to each other. This is not only a significant problem for individuals outside of all religion, but even for those within a particular religion. Additionally, some religions maintain that all other religions are false religions, while others embrace parallel beliefs.

The two most prominently practiced or claimed faiths in the world are Christianity and Islam, which both along with Judaism are what are referred to as the Abrahamic religions which all claim their origins with the God of Abraham. While many members will often passionately point to the differences between their respective faiths and religions, there are many common characteristics such as their ancestry, major figures and the concept that their god is the only true God. Other prominently practiced or claimed religions fall into groups such as Indian religions like Hinduism, Jainism, Buddhism and Sikhism and East Asian religions like Confucianism and Taoism. The rest are religions that are also closely tied to their regions of the world.

It is understandable how a member of a major religious group might have misconceptions of another major religion, but it actually is more complicated than that since there are many diverse sub-groups within each religion and most of them have enough of a difference about what they believe that they have split off and created a new sub-group/denomination or sect. Sometimes these differences were specific or may have been rooted in a portion of the group being more conservative or liberal that the rest. However, even after a group breaks off and creates a new sub-group they still will have some variation of some being more liberal (who see their religious beliefs in many shades of gray) to some who are more conservative (who see their religious beliefs as either black or white with no middle ground). This applies to all the major religions of the world.

There are a range of ultra-liberal to ultra-conservative Christians, Muslims, Buddhists, Sikhs, Jews, etc. This natural variation applies to all groups. So depending upon the perspective of your parents, the other significant role models in your life, you may have been exposed to a fairly wide variety of representatives based upon your location in the world. Some are warm, kind and loving, and some yell, are mean and hateful. No matter what religion or sub-group/denomination/sect a person represents they can be any of the above based upon their personality, their personal preferences and, of course, their baggage.

So if we didn't grow up in a faith centered family, then we were likely exposed to a very small, insignificant, disjointed sampling of the various religions or sub-groups within a religion and some portion or all of it likely had little to do with spiritual faith. If our family was very faith centered, we would have gotten a good deal of input about the one sub-group/denomination/sect they belonged to, unless they changed them from time to time. Yet this home-based input will often be all we have to base our concepts of spiritual faith until we begin to encounter people in the world apart from our parents or caregivers.

If your parents were faith centered and they were kind, loving and they chose to provide you with age-appropriate instruction about their faith, then you probably adopted that same faith and it, at least at one time, was meaningful to you. However, if they were centered on their faith, but they were not very kind, loving or the method of teaching was not age-appropriate, then you likely got a much less helpful impression of their faith and probably didn't adopt it as your own. The crueler they were towards you and others, the greater the likelihood that you came away with strong negative emotions and opinions of their God. If you were punished, in ways that were frightening such as locked in a closet, not being allowed to eat or drink or go to the restroom, berated, or physically abused in the name of God, their faith or with any reference to God, then you probably came away with a very negative view of God, religion as well as your parents. The younger we were and the more severe the negative experiences we had associated with faith, religion, religious ideas, leaders or figures.

If on the other hand, if it was our parents or caregivers that had those bad experiences and vowed they would never put their children through such an ordeal, they likely spared you the direct abuse, but they may have passed on the negative impressions about faith, religion, certain religions, certain subgroups/denominations/sects etc. When our role models don't like something, we tend to not like it. After years and years of influence that a parent typically has, once we are on our own as adults we may avoid those same things, convinced we don't like them either. However, under these circumstances we may actually have a different opinion, but we may never give those things a chance unless we hook up with a new influence from friends, a mentor or our spouse.

So our family of origin experiences can have a significant impact upon our attitudes and our openness towards new things. When it comes to faith, it is like preparing to receive a signal over the airwaves for a radio, phone or computer in that you have to in technical terms, have the right equipment and in human terms be open minded and willing to receive something new.

Even those who have chosen and developed a spiritual faith can sometimes run up against old ways of thinking about what God is supposed to be or what we are supposed be like in regards to faith. Many people with faith centered lives still struggle with the old impressions they got from places they can't recall. Someone can be active in a faith and become once again convinced they are undeserving of good things because the hateful things said to or done to them when they were younger. It can be an insecurity triggered by a slight rejection that brings back a deep pain from a very significant rejection early in life and can convince them that their faith can't help them. And this is how the unfortunate impressions tied with faith and religion early on can create a minefield for the adult believer.

The reactions later in life are very real and impactful and often the early life experiences are not even remembered or have not been thought of for decades, but they are still there like a landmine waiting to be stepped on to go off in us with an extreme wave of emotions. The wilder the early life experiences associated with faith and religions were for us the more there is to investigate and sort things out with the assistance from someone who been there as well. There is always a way to free ourselves, but it starts with realizing that what we have been thinking all these years has been based upon a faulty concept or misleading experience that we just absorbed because we either trusted them or what we came away with was the best we could understand at the time. These perspectives can be changed.

Shades of Gray

There are stark differences between the way some people look at things in the world as opposed to others. It is known by many names, but probably the most common are Black and White versus Shades of Gray thinking. "You are either with us or you are against us" is an example of black and white or false choice thinking. If you tend to be a black and white type of thinker, then you tend to see things as either right or wrong, for us or against us, hot or cold, wise or naive, etc. The Shades of Gray thinker sees many steps or options in between the two extremes with allowances for variation, exceptions, extenuating circumstances. Of course, these aren't only two ways of thinking, but they do appear to represent a continuum of a characteristic I'll call the Perception of Options. On one end of the continuum there is the perception of only one correct choice and all else is choosing otherwise and on the other end of the spectrum there is perception of many, if not an infinite number of choices.

Where we fit on this continuum depends upon our experiences, our preferences and the topic. It is possible for us to be black and white on one subject and believe there are an infinite number of shades of gray on another subject. However, there is a fairly common tendency for us to link subjects together or to treat them in a similar way. So, if we are more of a Black and White thinker on a few key topics then we may take that approach with all other topics without much thought. The same goes for where ever we are on the continuum. However, most of us vary from topic to topic. For instance, if we were treated cruelly by a parent as a child, we may have the opinion that there was nothing good about them when they may in fact have facilitated a significant skill in you as a child. And yet we may have a much greater appreciation of the contributions from another parent who was more kind and loving.

The upside of the Black and White approach is that decision making is easier with fewer choices to evaluate. However, there are often pesky details that are not easily explained away and they often have to be ignored, underappreciated or undervalued. While a Shade of Grey approach is open to all details, nuance and variations, there is the sometimes-overwhelming breath of choices and variables to consider. While ultimately a more refined or holistic choice may be identified it might take a considerable amount of time to select. Ultimately, these two extremes have downsides that most are unwilling to live with and as a result they become less committed to one approach or the other and begin a more moderate approach in an attempt to get the best of both approaches. Unconsciously, we may shift our way of thinking once we discover that our natural way of approaching our outlook may not produce the results we prefer.

Downside examples of Black and White thinking vary, but examples include things such as, I can't be friends with people that are not like me enough. I love them and I miss them, but I just can't hang around someone who isn't in law enforcement, believes in God like I do, likes animals, or won't support my charity. I can't accept my child is gay, too smart, won't come visit me for family holidays. If they can't respect my wishes and be the way I think they should, then I just can't be round them. When we are Black and White thinkers, things are all or nothing, there is little to no room for exceptions. While we are certain we are being smart by standing firm on the way we see the world, we also create a great deal of heartache for ourselves because we keep drawing these harsh lines in the sand that we will not cross.

Some downside examples of being too committed to consider all the Shades of Grey is that we can easily lose our sense of perspective with distractions of the next wave of data about some significant issue that needs consideration. Often this approach has no boundaries and literally anything can derail our path, line of thinking or pursuits. Children of ours may have a rough path and need a little support after being on their own, but we can't seem to motivate them to work, contribute or clean their room and they are twenty-eight and have been home again for four years. Or maybe we are the ones who can never say no to our boss or the volunteer coordinator at the soup kitchen and so we neglect our family.

The benefits of Black and White thinking works well when playing sports or following corporate policies or laws and regulations, but it can be very detrimental to personal relationships. While the benefits of Shades of Grey like thinking work well when problem solving, being creative and working with others. However, when we try to use one approach for all things, we can easily leave a wake of unintended results behind us. It is possible to be more conscious and discerning about which approach we employ from one situation to another. We can be very all or nothing about our spiritual faith for ourselves, while we may choose to be very accepting of others who believe and live much differently than we do. It is possible to apply the types of thinking options as the situation best calls for instead of only one approach for all topics, situations and context.

Responsibility

The typical experience most of us have is that while we are very young we are regularly learning more and more about the personal responsibilities we are expected to take on as a part of growing up. While I doubt many remember being potty trained, some of us will recall being taught the responsibilities in personal hygiene such as brushing our teeth, washing our hands and taking baths. We also were introduced to chores like picking up after ourselves and maybe helping around the house. In some families we may have actually been included in the family business and even contributing to earning money for the family to live on. However, some parents do not require any contribution from their children, as if they were doing them a favor by not requiring them to take on much responsibility and being allowed to enjoy being a child. For some who were shielded from age appropriate responsibilities, we can become very spoiled and consequently struggled later as more responsibilities were required of us.

While we are very young we mainly get our input on this topic from our own family or caregivers. Yet as we venture out to school and eventually into the workplace we get input from others as well. Sometimes if we got very little constructive input we may have had encounters with law enforcement as a result of disregarding the laws of the land. Some parents not only model the behavior that these laws are not to be respected, but may also come to the young person's defense, getting us off and still telling us afterwards that it was their fault and we were not to blame. This can create some very unfortunate circumstances, since the child or young person is taught that when they are arrested mom or dad will get them out. While society will hold the young person in jail responsible for their actions obviously the parent played a significant role in not preparing this young person for life in society.

Most of us will never encounter such a shock from a jail cell, but we all will find out there are some things we learned or thought we discovered correctly about responsibilities and find out we are wrong. It is easy to be wrong. With all the sources of data and all the bias that each person holds in addition to the way they delivered the information to us can influence what we learn. We may also have just not been paying attention or maybe we were paying attention to the best of our ability and the person trying to instruct us did not appreciate that. While legal issues are not a problem for most, our responsibilities in dealing with others affects us all. Here is an area where the teaching and mentoring we got from parents, relatives, coaches, teachers, other adults and peers may not have given us all that clear of a picture about where are responsibilities lie.

Typically, we learn that we are responsible for part of ourselves, but in some cryptic way so are other people. For instance, if we are someone's child and we are in trouble, our parents are in trouble. If a family or friend gets in trouble, then we are supposed to help them get out of trouble. If we have a spouse and they spend more money than we have, then I have to help pay for it. And it can go on and on. Basically, we learn with fairly great consistency from all our role models that we are in part, if not in some cases completely responsible, for others close to us. And they are in turn, are in part, or at times, completely responsible for us. Yet, this is not really true in all cases! It is true that if someone is injured and we are the only one there, it is the responsible thing to do to get them to a hospital where they can get care. But if our friend robs a bank and comes tells us about it, we really are not supposed to help them. It gets stickier when it comes to family members who break the law or suffer from some sort of addiction.

If our parent or spouse gets drunk and makes it to the front yard and passes out on the lawn, we generally feel inclined to go get them, bring them inside, clean them up to the best of our ability and put them to bed. Of course, if we do this the person who was sleeping it off on the lawn loses a great set of consequences, which might have been the amount of pain and humiliation required to decide they need to get help. However, if they wake up in bed clean and rested, then they decide they weren't as intoxicated as they thought. Or worse, they may realize that they couldn't have done this and that they can re-peat this over and over and if they pass out in the car or in the yard we will make all OK.

This may sound extreme to some, but some form of this behav-ior happens in most of our families. We do for others because we have somehow gotten it in our head that we are responsible for them and if they won't do it then we will have to do it. Add this to the person who realizes that they don't have to take care of themselves because you are making it your life's mission to do it for them and we have a match that destroys both lives. The destruction comes for both but for different reasons. The irresponsible recipient continues to not take responsibility for themselves and the other person taking all the responsibility ends up not having a life. This is a sad story for families and friends of immature people and others with addictions be-cause the whole family often is sucked in. In the case of milder symptoms, it typically goes unaddressed for a lifetime, but they often manage to pass it on to their children and people they mentor.

Another symptom of not being clear what is our responsibility and what is someone else's, is constant blame. Everything is someone else's fault. This is another very unfortunate way of looking at the world that we can learn from our role models. If we think about how others deserve the blame or talk about how others are to blame constantly and about how our lives would be so much better if it were not for these other people, we have a thinking problem. When we are never wrong. When we never make mistakes. Everyone else is to blame. If you talk like this, then you are confused about responsibility. If you know better than to talk this way, but still think this way, you are still confused about responsibility. This way of thinking is not rooted in reality and to continue it pulls us farther and farther from reality.

Likewise, if we rely upon others for the things we can do for ourselves, then we are not taking care of our responsibilities for ourselves. If we are doing for others, things that they can do for themselves, then we are robbing them of the opportunity to be more accomplished and we are cluttering our lives with focusing upon others when we should be taking care of ourselves. This is a common posture for people who have no hobbies, don't take days off or vacations to actually relax and recharge. Instead, we take care of others, bailing them out of jams, making things right, making sure they are happy, and all the while we are not taking care of ourselves. And no matter how we justify it and convince ourselves that these people can't live without us, they can and they likely will if you let them. And in turn we can actually take better care of ourselves and have more of a fulfilling life since we are appropriately taking care of ourselves.

Disclosure

So many of the tenants we live by are learned when we are very young. Of course, most get refined over time, but the extent to which this occurs often depends upon the amount of relationships and interactions we have with others. However, there is one additional element that is critical to this refinement and that is disclosure. When it has gone poorly at home with our parents, guardians, or siblings, we can quickly adopt the lesson learned of there is safety in secrets. However, this fails to consider that the secrets we have and collect may be not true. So the idea that disclosure can be helpful can be fairly counter intuitive given all the benefits we often perceive from having secrets to avoid ridicule, punishment or abuse.

Based on the impressions we have gathered in life about letting people in on our opinions, actions, thoughts, and emotions, we usually tend to either keep things to ourselves. If we tend to share them, then we often get some sort of feedback that we can use to refine and sometimes correct our perspectives on the world around us.

If we tend to not share these things, then we continue through life without feedback and we have whatever perspective we have about these things based mainly upon limited information and our own judgments. If we are fairly evenhanded and generous with ourselves this may work out OK. On the other hand if we tend to be more critical of ourselves, then the opposite will likely be true where we may be overly critical of ourselves sometimes about the most simple and mundane of everyday things.

Disclosure when used wisely can help keep us balanced. If we tend to be easy on ourselves even to the point of not confronting uncomfortable topics, feedback from others can help bring this to light. Likewise, if we tend to be too critical of ourselves then feedback can help us see our own self-critical views in a more even-handed way. Feedback from others can be very valuable, but if received from a poor source it can also be very destructive. This is why it is very important to be very discerning about who we open up ourselves to for feedback. If the people we are around early in life are insensitive and mean-spirited then we may experience quite a bit of betrayal and ridicule as a result of disclosures. Even if our early disclosure experiences are pleasant, but the feedback was unhelpful or destructive then we can easily conclude that no good comes from opening up.

If our friends and family members are not any better at handling their lives, then they are not very likely to be able to provide us with helpful feedback. Even if we like the feedback they give us, but when we make use of it things consistently turn out poorly this is likely indicating they are not our best resource for feedback.

What we share can also impact even the best source of feedback and can easily undo what benefits it can bring. If we go to the doctor and leave out a few symptoms they are very likely to give us an inaccurate diagnosis. The same goes for feedback about everyday problems. Partial disclosure will mostly yield incomplete or inaccurate results.

If we are reluctant to share our intimate thoughts, opinions and emotions with others, then we have likely had bad experiences with this activity in the past. The problem is not the act of disclosure. The problem is more than likely with the person or persons we chose to let into our world. When we have a few bad experiences, we can firmly establish a practice of not sharing with others because they will: laugh at us, hurt us, tell others, take advantage of us, humiliate us, criticize us, think less of us, think we are weak, think we need professional help, etc.

While some of these reactions may be true of some of the people we share ourselves with, the more mature ones will spare us those painful reactions and treat our disclosure with the utmost care. This is what professional counselor, therapists and coaches are trained to do, but they are not the only ones who are capable of this response. Friends and family may be able to respond appropriately to sensitive disclosures maturely due to having been through a similar experience, having been through other difficult experiences, or they had others model to them how to respond appropriately.

A person who is a good resource for one person may not be

good at all for another. So ultimately you have to vet these resources for yourself. Recommendations from others may yield good candidates, but the test is actually trusting them to keep your confidence and testing the value of their feedback. The value you probably will not be able to ascertain without trying out their feedback. Having the freedom to let others in on either what happened in the past or just recently can be extremely liberating and valuable handling situations in our lives successfully.

If we find it difficult to disclose to others it is likely due to baggage we have accumulated from unpleasant, hurtful, or unhelpful feedback. The causes while not clear at the time can be better managed in future disclosures for healthier outcomes.

Acceptance is Agreement

Somehow the word acceptance has gotten equated with giving up and agreeing with whatever we have been opposing. I can't say for sure how this happened, but it might be rooted in the execution of contracts and agreements and, or the well-intentioned encouragement of others. When we sign a contract, or written agreement, we do document a position of acceptance of the terms and conditions of the contract. And when we receive something from someone we often say the item or gift was accepted. However, when friends see each other struggling they may try to urge a solution to the problem. "You are just going to have to accept it and move on". We have all heard it and we may think it is insulting that such a thing should be proposed because somewhere deep down most of us already know that we really don't have to accept anything. As a matter of fact, getting to the point of standing our ground and not rolling over when things are unacceptable around us is a big step towards taking control of our lives and maintaining healthy boundaries. The only problem is that agreeing to a contract and choosing to accept something in our life and identifying that something in our life is unacceptable are very different things. It may seem odd at first, because it sounds so similar and this may also contribute to how we get ourselves in the position to be so confused about the practice of acceptance, but they are very different actions.

Let's say your spouse starts robbing banks. Now most of us would see this as a very unacceptable behavior. If we are clear on this point we might let our spouse know that we can't be a party to such behavior and that we can no longer live together since being in such close proximity puts your family and possibly your own freedom at risk. However, if we were to choose to not believe that our spouse is robbing banks even though they have admitted to as much, we are choosing to not accept the reality of the situation because it is too uncomfortable to acknowledge that our spouse would put us in harm's way. Both the ability to acknowledge the facts about our lives and identify what is and is not acceptable behavior are two very important actions to maintain our mental health. Yet many of us do the exact opposite.

Due to the pain associated with the reality of bad things happening around us, we tend to put up with unacceptable behavior from ourselves and others and we tend to deny the existence of selected facts just to avoid the heartache of knowing such things. In both instances we are doing the same thing, choosing to disagree with the facts. When we deny something that is troubling we can avoid the trouble and having to deal with it because our denial treats the situation like it doesn't exist (disagreeing with the facts). We all do it at least a little bit. We hear something painful and our kneejerk reaction is, "It can't be true", " I don't believe you", "You are wrong, not my child", "My mother doesn't have dementia", "My sibling can't have cancer", "My Dad wouldn't leave me", "I can't believe they are dead", "There can't be a God if my child is dead", etc. Even if we are pretty level headed about the subject matter, we will likely resist the facts for some initial period of time hoping they will turn out to be different than they appear. Yet until we agree that the facts exist, we can't deal with the challenges they create while we are denying that they exist.

Acceptance is probably best defined as choosing to agree with the facts when it comes to use in everyday life. Most days we are not signing contracts in our personal interactions with others. Yet if we step out of sync with the facts we can become quite disoriented about how best to proceed. If we are driving a car and a large truck splatters a large amount of mud on our windshield we are instantly in a dangerous situation because we cannot verify it is safe to proceed. Likewise, when we step out of agreement with the facts surrounding our life we are also in a dangerous situation.

- If we choose to not believe that our sore tooth is infected, we may lose it.
- If we choose to believe that our teacher will give us another chance, we may fail the course.
- If we choose to believe that only other people get caught, we may be fined or incarcerated.
- If we choose to believe that our friends and family are out to get us, then we will end up alone.
- If we choose to believe that being responsible for our own actions is not deserved, we may become bitter.
- If we choose to believe that our ailing family member is just fine they may die from neglect.
- If we choose to believe that we can stop drinking anytime, but never do, we may be addicted.
- If we choose to believe we can bully others without consequences, we will end up being very alone.
- If we choose to believe that God is responsible for a death, then we will no longer be able to trust God.
- If we choose to believe that our outlaw spouse is not doing anything wrong, we may end up in jail.
- If we choose to believe that our loved one is not dead, then we are unable to grieve their loss.
- If we choose to believe our violent family member won't do it again, we will probably be injured.

- If we choose to believe that our pedophile family member won't do it again, someone we care about will be violated again.

Nothing good comes from being in a state of prolonged disagreement with the facts. Most of us do it for a short period of time as a coping mechanism to deal with the shock of a traumatic event. However, we must accept the facts of the situation as the facts if we are to move forward and deal with them effectively. Dealing with them may involve healthy choices, allowing yourself to grieve, leaving a bad situation, calling the police, or making a mental note that the line between what is acceptable and unacceptable is now clear. Once the windshield is now clear we can better judge how to proceed.

Love of Self and Others

For a modern civilization with all the advances we have made in technology and understanding the human condition we still are mixed up about loving ourselves and others. First off, we are more likely to believe love to be an emotion that comes and goes mysteriously with the wind or at least in ways we cannot control over long periods of time. As a result, statements like, "I fell in love" and "I just fell out of love", or "I just don't love them anymore and I can't do anything about it", are common. Embracing love like this makes a long-term relationship or marriage virtually impossible. Much less subjecting ourselves to an unreliable regard for ourselves.

Despite what you have read in novels, great literature, seen in movies and heard from family and friends, we don't fall into love like a hole in the ground. We choose to love. We choose to care about people, places and things. Even ourselves, but I will get to this a little later. Despite all the passionate tales of miraculous whirlwind romance, love is a decision. We may choose to care fairly quickly and carelessly, but it is still a decision that we can control. For instance, let's say your fantasy mate is attractive, talented, and rich. Well from a distance many celebrities will fit those requirements and you may have a strong regard (love) for a few. If your criterion is more selective then you will find that you have to actually get to know them to find out if they are trustworthy, emotionally stable and mature, have similar spiritual beliefs and are kind to animals and others.

If we leave our definition of love to a mix of emotions that stirs in us when we think of or are near someone that attracts us, once these loved ones become familiar those feelings will become much less intense, frequent and without significant effort can vanish completely. Emotions are complicated and they shift and change all the time. This is probably why they are so intoxicating and why metaphors like falling and being swept off out feet are so often used.

For most the idea that love is a decision really takes the excitement out of it all and most resist this simple concept in deference to the fantasy we have built up over years. Yet real relationships built upon concepts supported by fantasy are doomed to serious challenges if not failure. Despite what we prefer to believe, love takes effort and often it is very hard work. For instance, parenthood is very long-term commitment to love and train children to navigate the world on their own. Now some people are not good parents. They may prefer to be with their friends, or have fun or they may not stay around at all and leave the child with their spouse or to fend for themselves. While most of us would find it hard to relate to being like this, these people have simply decided to care about other things more than their child or to not care/love their child at all. That is a choice a parent can make. It is rare and it has some disastrous consequences, but it is an available option. Sometimes we see this when a child is very troubled, difficult to raise or has some significant disability that one of their parents just can't seem to handle. Love is a decision.

Also, the opposite is true. Many of us know people or know of people who have faced extreme hardship in relationships with parents, siblings, children, spouses or friends and still they choose to love them. Love is a decision. It is not always an easy decision, but it is a decision. Without this knowledge we may be waiting for love to come along. We may be waiting for the emotions we think of as love to come back to save our marriage or to make our children easier to tolerate, etc. Waiting for love to just happen or for us to fall into it is a flawed concept that will bring us nothing but heartache. Love is a decision.

When we decide to love someone (either quickly or after careful consideration) we act differently towards them. We think about them in different ways, we will often choose to be with them and support them over others we don't love or don't love as much. As a result of this behavior we tend to feel many of those feelings we often associate with love. The spouse that now appears less wonderful now that we know what they look like without their clothes on and what their little habits are may be less attractive. If we choose to stop loving them our attitude and actions towards them can change drastically. So it is often the case that over time, the commitment to long-term relationships towards a spouse, a child, a parent or even a friend will require a continuing choice to love them. If the child becomes very unpleasant or different than we hoped for we may have to deal with our disappointment and choose to love them anyway. If a parent becomes in need and is very demanding or challenging, we may have to deal with these new challenges and choose to love them anyway. If a spouse struggles with addiction or fidelity, we may have to deal with our disappointment and pain and choose to love them anyway. Likewise, if a friend makes some choices you dislike we may have to deal with our disappointment and choose to love them anyway. Unfortunately, because we often have a much more mysterious view of love, we may consciously choose to not love them anymore when their behavior is less than desirable and we may just let them become less important in our lives and let the relationships deteriorate. Loving others takes effort, but the rewards are more than worth it.

When it comes to ourselves we may have been taught that it

is vain to love yourself. Yet there is a natural instinct in us to care about ourselves. Loving ourselves is natural and healthy. When we are convinced that we should not love ourselves we tend to neglect ourselves and redouble our efforts upon others. This is a no-win strategy since most people are going to gravitate towards taking care of themselves and let you fend for yourself.

Most of us get it that we need to care of the basics like personal hygiene, so we brush our teeth on a regular basis every day and have regular checkups. However, when it comes to more delicate matters like developing our own image of ourselves and taking care of other responsibilities like paying our bills and keeping other commitments we may tend to neglect these things if we chose to not care or love ourselves. A common refrain we will hear from someone who struggles with self-love is they will be overly critical of themselves when it is not warranted or accurate. Such as statements like, "I am so stupid", "I can't believe I even thought someone could like me", "I am ugly", "I am an idiot", "I am never going to meet someone", etc. This type of self-talk, or self-abuse, is a very common symptom of denying ourselves our own love.

Choosing to love ourselves works just like with others, it is a decision. If you are a person who has consistently denied yourself any self-care or consideration, then a way to start showing yourself love is to do things for yourself that are good for you and that you enjoy. Refraining from negative or inaccurate self-talk is a good start, but it can also involve eating well, grooming ourselves better, getting out with others, going to social events or other events of interest. Ultimately, it should occasionally include you being able to see yourself in the mirror and you choosing to say I care about you (me), I love you(me).

While this may seem a bit unusual, it is actually very healthy to care about yourself like you might like others to care about you and that you want to care about others. We all deserve love and we are with ourselves twenty-four hours a day, seven days a week. If we don't love ourselves, then we are choosing to be with someone twenty hours a day, seven days a week that doesn't love us. This is never a good idea, yet many of us live like this because we somehow bought into the idea that caring about ourselves was egotistical, self-centered, selfish and just wrong. It is true if taken too far it can become all those things, but it can be just as bad, if not worse, to not love ourselves at all.

There is an appropriate degree of self-love and it is not vain to care enough about ourselves to treat us like we would treat someone else we really cared about.

Sex is love

There is often a much-maligned view of sex, but one of the most central issues is how we confuse it with love. Just to make sure we are on the same page I will use a fairly conservative definition of sex as being the intimate touching between individuals for the sake of obtaining or giving physical pleasure. One of the likely reasons for such confusion between sex and love is that love is not the same for everyone. Love is often referred to in a general way with little clarification if mentioned at all, thus leaving much room for interpretation.

One significant disconnect comes in the language we use to express our love. While other languages have multiple words for the different kinds of love, English has one. Ancient Greek had eight to nine different words for love and in the Greek language today the more common words for love are: agape, philia, storge, and eros. While these words translate to English as love, friendship, affection and intimate love, if you grew up with English as your first language you probably have noticed that the word love can mean many things to us and to those around us. Yet if we use it outside the context of romantic love we can get some surprised reaction.

In more recent times love styles have been defined by social scientists as a means to categorize our love behavior. In 1973,

John Lee, a sociologist, identified six basic love styles in his color wheel of love in interpersonal relationships. These styles are very closely linked to the Greek words for love with **eros** based upon romance, **ludos** based upon conquest, **storge** based upon friendship, **pragma** based upon practicality, **mania** based upon obsession, and **agape** based upon selflessness. But none of these help us with what love means to us.

We as individuals can have a wide variety of experiences that we associate with love. If we are raised where the subject matter taught and the interactions modeled for us are age appropriate and nurturing, we will likely come away with a view of love that shows itself in various ways, such as described by Dr. Gary Chapman in his book The Five Love Languages. Dr. Chapman suggests that we tend to perceive love when others provide the following:

1. Words of Affirmation
2. Acts of Service
3. Gifts
4. Quality Time
5. Physical Touch

If you grew up watching your parents or caregivers expressing what you associated as love with affirming words, then you will likely interpret that same behavior later in life with someone showing you love.

If you grew up watching your parents or caregivers expressing what you associated as love with acts of service, then you will likely interpret that same behavior later in life with someone showing you love.

If you grew up watching your parents or caregivers expressing what you associated as love with gifts, then you will likely interpret that same behavior later in life with someone showing you love.

If you grew up watching your parents or caregivers expressing what you associated as love with quality time, then you will likely interpret that same behavior later in life with someone showing you love.

If you grew up watching your parents or caregivers expressing what you associated as love with physical touch, then you will likely interpret that same behavior later in life with someone showing you love.

Now if you grew up in a setting where you were not raised by well-adjusted parents or caregivers or if they were significantly distracted, then you may have had a much different experience. If this was the case you may have been neglected or exposed to information, images or experiences that were not age appropriate. You may have gotten a much different impression about love.

If you observed or were provided intimate details of a broken parental relationship, which may have included descriptions of infidelity, addiction, emotional, physical or sexual abuse then you may have a developed a very dark picture of love. We tend to absorb the behavior modeled for us about how adults behave and treat each other and they tend to be instinctively imprinted upon us for a lifetime. With determination we can ensure we act nothing like these adult role models who were caught up in such destructive behavior. However, if we are not careful these types of experiences can impact our outlook on love. Worst case we may refrain from love or commitment or repeat the behavior we witnessed even if we didn't approve of it then and don't like it to this day. Less destructive results might be a lingering insecurity of a spouse's fidelity or social interaction. Most will end up somewhere in between with often destructive results in our personal lives and relationships.

If we were sexually abused with or without either critical or instructive comments, we may have emerged knowing how to use our bodies to get what we want and typically a deep seated shame of being responsible. Worse yet if the only relationship we had with a parent or caregiver was one of emotional, physical or sexual abuse, we may adopt a highly distorted view of the world that intermixes emotional pain, physical pain and inappropriate sexual behavior with love. This can, and does, occur in homes of all sizes, in institutions, in slavery and on the street. While it might sound farfetched to some, the product of such a set of experiences can create a very unfortunate view of the world. The resulting confusion does not have to be permanent, but it does often take professional help to reprogram those very destructive past experiences and the impressions they left upon us to replace them with a healthier perspective and behavior.

So, the confusion of sex being love is possible from many sources. What we experienced, what we were taught and what we had modeled for us about the expression of love has everything to do with what it appears to be to us today. We also can reinforce whatever concept we have by looking for confirmation in our everyday world. Whether it is in magazines, movies or online, we can always find what we think are examples that the way we think of things is normal or correct. However, destructive behavior, while it may be familiar and thus comfortable to us, is not the best we can expect of ourselves or deserve.

Everyone deserves to be loved in a kind, patient, nurturing, and encouraging ways that provides a safe environment that protects us from harm. If this sounds foreign to you, please know it is possible for you too, especially as we start to shed some of our baggage.

Forgiveness

Most of us have been on both sides of a situation where forgiveness was the solution, but it never occurred. When we were the one to be forgiven we may have wanted it a great deal or we may have been perplexed that someone could stay upset at us for so long. However, when the roles are reversed and we are the one that is upset the idea of forgiveness is one that often seems inappropriate. It is a common perception that withholding forgiveness punishes the other person. Yet in many instances the other person is unaware of our perspective and emotions related to their actions. Even when they do know, if we withhold forgiveness for a long period of time the other person will often move on with their life without us while we stay irritated, angry or even resentful most of the time or at least when we are reminded of this person, place or thing that upsets us.

Some spend their entire life choosing to not forgive someone and are miserable as a result. When it comes to matters of behavior forgiving real or perceive slights or wrongs is always an option even when the circumstances are very serious and the amount of pain is very great.

There are probably few people who had more reason to not forgive a person than Aba Gayle. Her 19-year-old daughter was brutally murdered and the anger and desire for revenge was in part fueled by the promise that her daughter's killer would be found, tried and convicted, probably receiving the death penalty. After eight long years of hate and anger Aba began exploring options to regain her life. That exploration soon introduced her to a new perspective on forgiveness that eventually led her to correspond with and visit the man who murdered her daughter. The instant she dropped that letter in the mailbox she knew her daughter's murderer did not have to be executed for her to be healed and she once again began getting on with her life. The man she met in prison was not someone she excused for his actions, but she did realize on her first visit that the day her daughter lost her life he lost his future.

What Aba learned is that forgiveness is a choice and for her it was a choice to regain her peace of mind and release herself from a life consumed with anger and hatred.

Few of us have as much to forgive, but many of us carry a continuous grudge against other people, places or things. Yes, it may sound odd at first but we can get pretty upset with even inanimate objects such as broken washing machines or cars and with places where we are reminded of unpleasant memories. We can even hold grudges against people we don't even know personally. All we have to do is listen to a news story or better yet a broadcaster, who repeats story after story about the ills of a certain; person, movement or institution and pretty soon we will be angry and upset as well. So much so that we start getting upset when we repeat the story to others. While it all may seem perfectly justified and correct to do so, one thing is happening all the while. We have lost our peace. As long as we open ourselves up to the idea that we should be angry and we should hold a grudge and we should stay that way until things change to our liking, we will have little joy or peace.

When we first hear of something outrageous we usually have an emotional reaction. During this reaction we may embark on a line of thinking that may choose to stay worked up, because it seems like a good idea. It is at this point we are choosing to trade our peace of mind for whatever the issue is that originally got us worked up. Sometimes they are real things that happen to us like Aba and sometimes they are things that happen to others that we hear about from others. Most often they are things that happen to us or to those around us, our family and friends.

Most of us know of someone who will not speak to another member of their own family because of something they said or did many years before. Sometimes all parties know the original offense and sometimes it is unknown even to the person who holds the grudge. So when asked about it, the reasons vary. Choosing to not forgive always destroys our peace because we are allowing a known solvable issue to continue and cause us pain. Choosing to not forgive can destroy families as well. Spouses, children, parents, siblings, etc. all can be banished from our hearts with the simple choice to not forgive.

Some of the myths about forgiveness include things such as forgiveness equals agreement and it definitely does not. Or that forgiveness is letting them win. Win what? When we are all upset and we hold someone else responsible we have given them the power to keep us tied in knots. That isn't a winning strategy. It is a losing one. What's even worse is often the other person is blissfully going about their lives rarely thinking about you or what you are upset about if they are even aware of it at all.

Another belief is that forgiveness is for the weak. This is not about forgiveness, this is about power and poor boundaries in relationships. Sometimes these myths come from people just being confused about their choices. If a spouse is being battered and throws out her abuser, she may choose to forgive her spouse. But they are making entirely different choices if they reconcile without setting some clear limits and changes to address the abuse.

Forgiveness is not forgetting. A parent may forgive their teenager for wrecking the family car, but they are not getting to take it out again until it is repaired and probably on a much more limited basis.

Forgiveness is not giving up or giving in, it is about letting go.

There are a lot of directions we can focus our unforgiveness, but the most destructive and most common direction is ourselves. We judge ourselves as wrong about something and we are upset with ourselves. As crazy as it sounds we do this all the time. Think not?

Let's say that you are interested in someone and you want to get to know them. So you walk up and start talking to them and out of nervousness you say something insulting or unkind as a careless attempt at humor. When the encounter falls flat and no connection is made, then we get on to ourselves for the poor choice of words. If we think about this over and over for a few days, weeks, months or even years, we have not forgiven ourselves for that silly mistake.

We do it all the time. And if we don't consciously choose to forgive ourselves on a regular basis, then the weight of unforgiveness can really weigh us down. Just think of all the wasted time thinking about how we screwed up when we could be out living our life. We are all human and we all make mistakes nearly every day, if not many times a day.

Once we get tired of letting these things steal our joy and peace of mind we will become more resolved to adopt the position of forgiveness and its forgiving line of thinking.

Guilt

Guilt is one thing that most of us are very conscious of experiencing. We do something that is wrong, not OK or that brings pain or discomfort to another and we feel guilty. There are natural and healthy instances of guilt. Guilt can be a great feedback mechanism for us when we make mistakes and need to correct them. However, many of us also experience guilt when we have done nothing wrong and thus creating a no win scenario for us that rarely, if ever ends. One of the more common sources of guilt is the fabrication of an offense, which another tells us about and we never can seem to correct it. These instances are almost always a manipulation to keep us in the other person's debt, such as, "we need to make them happy".

As a result, we may spend a lifetime driven to make up for past actions we never committed. For instance, the mother who struggled with a terrible childbirth may use this hardship as a manipulative tool to drive their child into doing their bidding. Every time the child or young adult starts to exert their independence the mom reminds them that because of the great pain caused just bringing them into the world they owe her to behave as she pleases. While as powerful as this claim is, this is a lie. It was not the responsibility of the offspring that the childbirth was difficult, as they had no say in the matter. Two people made the decision to have a child and along with their medical histories, conditions and assistance they had available to them determined the severity of the childbirth. Is the child never guilty of causing great pain to their parents? Absolutely not. Once they are making their own decisions they can do many things that are a source of great pain, but not before. Often these guilt-creating behaviors are unconscious or at least not completely understood, but they were likely learned in their family of origin.

We often first learn about guilt in the home and these lessons include both the realistic guilt that pertains to real events and the unrealistic guilt that does not. Sometimes unrealistic guilt centers on events that have not even occurred yet. A father may say to a child that if they do a forbidden act that it will kill their mother. If this was in regard to throwing her off a bridge this might be true, but usually this is said to manipulate a child to do the preferred bidding of the parent such as attend a family dinner, use their manners, or continue their education. While these are all reasonable things to ask of a child, the motivation being applied is inappropriate. When we use manipulation on a child to create unrealistic guilt, we are teaching our child that manipulation is a normal technique for getting what you want from others. Even if this type of manipulation is used only between the spouses, the children will observe this and pick it up very quickly.

The flaw in most of our perceptions about guilt has to do with the idea that there is only one type of guilt and that the only way to resolve and extinguish guilt is to get the agreement from the person, place or thing that our offense has been erased. Impressions like this are impossible to carry out when we no longer have contact with these people or if they are dead. As a result, we can carry a load of guilt for something we never did and we were not responsible for its occurrence. The good news is that all guilt is resolvable, but depending upon the type of guilt it is and the situation, it may require different responses.

The other side of the coin is that some experience little, if any guilt. And while this may seem like a great way to be, they can at times not experience guilt even when they are responsible and consciously committed the offense. Some of these folks are mentally ill and some were never taught a more standard set of what is right and wrong in the world. This is in part what many of the world's philosophies and religions attempt to address in that they describe what is considered right or wrong and the consequences that can occur if offenses are committed.

The same thing happens in most homes of young children. The rules of right and wrong are communicated and re-communicated, as well as enforced, until they are learned. This is why we often hear that being consistent as a parent is important. If the rules keep changing, then a sense of there being no rules is learned.

If we experience no guilt what so ever, then we probably have trouble with relationships since we are likely to act without regard for others. If we experience very little guilt we may have a good sense of right and wrong from our childhood, have continued to refine it through relationships with others and mentors, and focus on behaving appropriately. However, both of these circumstances are less common. More common is that we experience realistic guilt on an occasional basis for mistakes we have made and we have some unrealistic guilt that we have gained as a result of our own misjudgment or from the help of others. Less common, is the experience of intense guilt both realistic and unrealistic. So much in fact that we rarely go very long without experiencing guilt. If this is occurring, then most moments of each day are filled with trying to please or pay back others and even ourselves for past offenses. As a result, there is little or no time for a life of our own. If this is the case it can easily lead to extreme or reckless lifestyles which can include abuse of alcohol or drugs to escape the torment and possibly a life of crime since doing wrong is already a significant part of our self-perception.

Usually it takes the assistance of another person or persons to help us see our guilt for what it really is. Which of our guilty offenses are realistic and may justify an appropriate response and which are unrealistic and simply need to be dismantled and banished from our minds. If we continue to live in the proximity of people, places or thing that tempt us to experience unrealistic guilt we may have to develop certain boundaries or distance to keep us from picking back up that unrealistic guilt.

There is no simple answer and it may take a great deal of energy to find the correct perspective, response and course of action, but the life free of unrealistic guilt is worth it since it affords us the time and freedom to choose our own lives.

Shame

Shame is one of the more debilitating experiences we can have. Shame leaves us with the impression that we are unworthy of a normal life. Shame targets not our actions like with guilt, but rather that we as individuals are fundamentally wrong, broken, ugly, tainted, dirty, not OK, not normal, or a mistake. Sometimes the shame is attributed to our actions, or the actions of someone in our family or even the actions of someone in our community. If someone close to us does something really awful we may experience shame in being associated with them and as a result, choose to avoid them. Unlike guilt, shame is rarely appropriate and it can have devastating results upon our lives. When it goes untreated it can significantly cripple our ability to function in the family, with friends, at work and in the community. Worse yet, shame rarely has anything to do with actions we have taken.

One of the more common ways we experience shame is with our emotions. We share or express our emotions in an open way and someone important to us criticizes us. It could be a parent, and older sibling, a teacher, a relative, or any authority figure. If we are carelessly told, "we shouldn't feel that way", or that, "big boys and girls don't cry", we can walk away thinking that something is wrong with us even though we are having perfectly normal human emotions.

Another common way we can experience shame has to do with our bodies. Are we strong enough? Tall enough? Is our hair a popular color and type? Do we have freckles or not? Are we good at sports? Are we handsome or pretty? and Are we the right shape? The shape of our head, torso and the length of our legs is not something we can do too much about. Even our feet can be a source of embarrassment and shame. People and especially kids can say very mean and critical things. When we take those comments seriously we can fall into the habit of repeating these statements over and over to ourselves. The more we say it the more we can experience the shame again and again.

Sometimes a family or a set of friends or business associates can be bound together because of a past event. This is not uncommon in families where there is an untreated addiction. One member is addicted and the rest of the family or group becomes consumed with either helping, hiding or blaming their misfortunes on their common problem.

While shame can emerge at any age probably the most common shame is rooted in experiences we had as a child. We are very young, let's say from the age of three to ten years old, and we fundamentally lack the ability to understand much less deal with complex problems that arise in the family, with friends and in the community. Regardless, whether if we are a willing participant, a coerced participant or a forced participant while we are very young, we can still emerge with a tremendous amount of shame.

Leaving it bottled up can cause us to have significant impacts on our personality, our social choices, sexual comfort levels and preferences, family life, professional life and our ability to be successful part of our community. What happened could have been fairly limited such as being mean to a friend or sibling, expressing an emotion, crying, the minor damage of property, lying about an event we witnessed, rejection of a friend or family member to much more serious events such as the significant destruction of property, theft from person's outside of the family and causing significant harm to another human being or animal. However, the worst-case scenario that creates shame, which happens much too often, is the sexual abuse towards us by another person especially when it is an adult and threats of physical harm.

When we participate or have these things happen to us at this very young age we are not able to deal with the complexity and confusion nor are we even capable of credibly calling for help. The resulting dilemma is often a no-win situation that can cause severe mental and emotional trauma. Because of our inexperienced position in the world we can easily misunderstand some of the facts surrounding what happened to us. If we were told that we were hurt or abused because it is our fault we may very well believe it. We may grow up keeping a very deeply protected secret that we are dirty, filthy, dumb, defective, and will never have anything good happen to us. We can also end up believing that we will destroy everything we touch. Whether we do or not we will as a result look for signs that we have once again created a mess of things only to reinforce what we mistakenly believe.

As odd as this might sound this can be the secret life of successful business persons, professionals, scientists, and entertainers. No one is immune from the misunderstood events that occurred to us when we were very young. Even the most mundane things such as knocking something over which nearly everyone child does can turn into a torture that can go on for a lifetime convinced we are clumsy and uncoordinated. Shame is not like the size of your foot, it can be resolved even vanquished, but it will have to be shared preferably with someone who is experienced in helping people with such experiences. There is no shame that cannot be lessened and most can be eliminated altogether.

Being with Others

The way we interact with others can also be a very common source of baggage for us. From a very young age we begin making observations about how people are supposed to interact with one another. For most of us this is a very instructive trial and error-based set of experiences upon which we assemble our ideas about how we are supposed to interact with others.

A significant input into our concept of being with others comes from observing the people around us when we are growing up. Depending upon the number of siblings you have greatly affects this learning environment as well. If you have brothers or sisters, then these interactions are plentiful and may or may not be under the watchful eye of a parent or guardian. If the interactions are mostly pleasant, then we can have one set of impressions, as opposed if one or more of your siblings are especially mean-spirited and take advantage of you on a regular basis. If you are an only child your interactions are mainly with your parents or guardians and later, you are exposed to others closer to your age. The circumstances of our company as young children can create impressions we develop about how we are supposed to react towards one another. We find out early that some people are like us and some are not. Some we enjoy being around and some we don't. Some are entertaining and some are mean. Some include us and some don't.

Then there are the people we observe who are much older than us like our parents or guardians. We see how these people interact with one another and we form impressions about how people are supposed to treat one another, react to stress, disappointment, kindness, correction, surprise, friends, employers, neighbors, strangers, people with less resources and people with more resources.

Whether we realize it or not, we base our impressions of new people, places and things upon how we think things should be in light of what we have experienced and observed. The less we experience and observe the narrower our ideas about how things can occur. The baggage created by this experience is the limited experience perspective we have about the ways of relationships.

If we grow up with nurturing parents and have few if any tragedies in life, then you may think that bad things happen to other people. You may likely be quite challenged to deal with and relate to others who have had a much different set of experiences. If we have not grown up in a family but were raised without our blood relatives and we also experienced many tragedies then the perspective we may have may be much more resilient, but unfamiliar with the certainty that comes from long term relationships.

Probably a more common scenario is that we grew up with a family, experienced to some degree tragedy, heartache and rejection and expect that others have as well. Our experiences with others build a lens through which we see the world. When our experience base has been painful, scary and maybe degrading we are not likely to be that interested in venturing out for more of the same. When our experiences have been more moderate in its ups and downs we tend to be more open to see what else is out there in additional relationships.

Here are some examples of the various lessons taught about being with others:

- We may have been taught that there is no time for play, because there are too many chores that need to be done, while others are encouraged to divide our time between play and work.
- We may have been taught that our family are the only ones we are supposed to trust and yet our experience may be that family members are not always trustworthy.
- We may have been taught to welcome our neighbors into our lives or that we should be very private because others may try to take advantage of you.
- We may have been taught that there is little in this world to be learned past what our parents, guardians, siblings or some other isolated source can provide or we may be encouraged to be open-minded and learning throughout our lifetime.
- We may have been taught that emotions and crying are not to be displayed or we may have been taught that these are natural parts of life.
- We may have been taught that it is us against the world and we are to grab, hoard and protect everything we can accumulate or we may have been

taught to share what we have with others less fortunate in this world.

- We may have been taught that laughter is disrespectful and immature or we may have been taught that laughter is welcomed and that it is one of the most healing behaviors between people.
- We may have been taught that living with other people just happens and is easy, hard, fun, miserable, lonely, heartwarming, demented, safe, abusive, or hopeless.

Those who are better prepared to navigate playing, working and living with others are the ones who are taught that it takes appropriate and intentional effort (also known as work).

Whatever we have acquired as ideas as to how being with others should be, we probably have a lot more to learn. Some of us grow up with great role models when it comes to interacting with others from the sandbox to marriage and our professional lives, but many don't. It is far more common to be limited in our impressions about the way people are and how we should interact with them and this causes us many problems. The negative results can range from a life of isolation, failed marriages, estranged family members, the inability to keep a job or make new friends. However, no matter what poor results we have had up until now, it can change for the better.

10. NEGATIVE SELF TALK

The person who speaks to us the most has the most influence and that person is ourselves. Our self-talk occurs whether we are conscious of it or not, but most of us are at least somewhat conscious of what we are saying to ourselves. We may have become calloused to the voice. We may deny the voice, but it remains. The prominence of positive and uplifting thoughts in our past will likely bring about the presence of positive and uplifting self-talk. Likewise, the prominence of negative and defeating thoughts in our past, will likely bring out the presence of negative and self-defeating self-talk.

What we choose to repeat to ourselves is based upon those things that made a significant impression upon us in our past. And we repeat those most central thoughts to ourselves over and over with the tireless precision of an endlessly powered computer. For many of us, these topics are repeated from our first waking moment to the last conscious moment each day. Of course the events of the day interrupt this self-conversation often and trigger other subjects of self-talk when reminded, but we return to the most prominent thoughts that we for some reason or another choose to focus on. And therein lies the key. What we say to ourselves is a choice, but many of us have lost consciousness of this choice and sometimes of the self-talk itself.

If the thought is that we are stupid, we will tell ourselves we are stupid again and again. It makes no difference if we are highly intelligent or well educated if it is a prominent thought in our past we may still repeat this to ourselves constantly. If it is not one of your prominent thoughts, then it might be an often-triggered thought. You may use this particular one yourself. However, if you don't you likely know someone who does. Occasionally it slips out verbally when some of us make a mistake with the utterance, "I am so stupid". Despite the facts a prominent or easily triggered thought can be habitually repeated again as if it makes perfect sense.

Negative self-talk can cover a very diverse set of topics, but the more common fall into a few categories: self-judgment, self-consumption, focus outside of ourselves and hopelessness. All of the baggage we are carrying is likely feeding our negative self-talk. The first category self-judgment, is where we say that something is wrong with us such as, I am so stupid", "I am so ugly", "I am so fat", "I am so clumsy", and really devastating one, " I am crazy". Mean children, acquaintances, adolescences, adults, society, and even sometimes parents will tell us this and out of shame we will let it stick. It is often very far from the truth yet even staring into the mirror, winning the adoration of others, or being intellectually conscious of our own contrary qualities we may still have the habit of repeating to ourselves that we are so stupid/ugly/fat/clumsy/crazy. We occasionally will hear it slip out from the lips of very well educated, attractive, fit, coordinated or sane people when their self-talk actually becomes verbalized.

Also, very devastating are the self-consumption statements that are repeated far too often to ourselves, "nobody likes me", "nobody loves me", "nobody will ever like me", and "nobody will ever love me". Whether we are told this explicitly or infer it from abuse or the lack of kindness, attention or affection, we are reinforcing the belief that we are undesirable. This one can be pushed down deep, so many are not that aware they are saying it to themselves, but all too often it is there. Even when we encounter friendship or love, the statement can often become, "they wouldn't like me if they really knew me", or "they wouldn't love me if they really knew me". So when we have the company of others who love and care for us, if we have latched on to this line of self-talk we can undermine most of the friendship, love and affection that comes our way by discounting it as based upon a lie.

Other self-talk can include repeating to ourselves the things we are afraid of like the world coming to an end, losing our job, our loved one has been in an accident, etc. Repeating the thoughts just heighten our fear sometimes to a hysterical level. Repeating the things, we see ourselves as guilty of such as hurting someone, saying a careless comment, worse yet we can torture ourselves that we are guilty of things we did not do or were not our responsibility. Some of us like to be historical and review our disappointments over and over as if they just happened.

We can occupy ourselves with our thoughts about other people, places or things that we are suspicious of, fear or hate. This type of self-talk is often triggered by simply hearing the news. Much of the published news is dramatized to get our attention and nothing gets our attention more than things we need to be suspicious of, fear or get angry about. Often this centers on the typical sensitive topics of sex, politics and religion, but it can be about anything. These objects of our suspicion, fear or anger can be so effectively stoked that we stay in a near state of irritation or rage constantly. When this happens we naturally drive away people who may not agree with us or we avoid people who have different options.

As you can tell so far with the key phrases I have highlighted so far, by repeating these negative thoughts to ourselves relentlessly we can set the stage for the very thing we fear to come true because we allow it to become our perspective. Privately we hold ourselves in unyielding judgment that no one can break and often we keep this whole line of thinking a secret because we developed a fundamental distrust of others. And while any of these thoughts can be a harmless passing thought as a result of reading literature, the news or seeing a movie. Negative self-talk, when it describes a perspective of hopelessness, can become the basis for some of the most unfortunate of destructive life choices.

The most destructive line of self-talk is one that involves hopelessness and considering taking our own lives. While it is not unusual to having isolated and fleeting thoughts about sui-cide, it is another thing entirely to consider it seriously. This line of thinking that there is no hope and we might as well end our own lives, is not only untrue it is the quickest way to end-ing all possible options of getting sustained relief. Just because you believe you have tried everything does not mean you have. Your hopelessness is a by-product of your negative self-talk. If you are seriously considering suicide right now, please call the National Suicide Prevention Hotline at 1-800-273-TALK (8255). This is not something to postpone. At the same time if you have toyed with the idea, but have not developed a well thought out plan you are still in serious danger and should seek counseling as soon as possible.

When we experience a great deal of pain, grief or anguish we eventually will consider most anything to relieve the pain. Yet taking our own life is a permanent and failed attempt at a solution to a temporary problem. While it might not seem so simple, the basic underlying condition that lays the path for this type of extremely destructive self-talk is depression. De-pression early on may be recognizable as depression, but when it has been experienced for extended periods of time it can at times become forgotten or unrecognizable. This disoriented state is what makes us so vulnerable to making the ultimate unwise choice of taking our own lives. As simple as it may seem this all starts with the destructive line of self-talk, "there is no hope", and this is never the case. There is always hope, but what is the case is that we are at times unable to see it.

Our baggage keeps us from seeing the world and ourselves as we really are. We are that person that got lied to, hurt, abused, ridiculed, threatened, criticized, disappointed, aban-doned, manipulated, and had love withheld from us. Yet there are ways to still break through this onslaught of deceptions and not buy into it. You are worth saving. You are worthy of love and you are better than the things you tell yourself. You may have had careless people tell you things and have done things to you that no one should ever have to endure, but you have. Instead of continuing to just endure you can flourish by choosing to stop repeating their lies and the ones you say to yourself. There is hope and you are worthy of a better life.

The sources of our baggage are different for each one of us and yet many of the basic building blocks we all experience are the same. Identifying yours and dismantling them is a journey, but a worthwhile journey of ever-increasing freedom and joy.

PART 4 – CONVERTING OUR BAGGAGE INTO LUGGAGE

Agents of Change

To reverse the baggage collecting lifestyle that we have become accustomed to will be hard. However, it will come with a new-found sense of peace and freedom you will value. If you have not made many significant self-directed changes in your life these suggestions may be the hardest thing you will ever do because it will be at times very uncomfortable.

Reversing this lifestyle will set off nearly every alarm in your head, telling you that you need to stop because this is wrong. However, just keep one thing in mind. Nobody dies from being uncomfortable, however they do die prematurely from undue stress of carrying a load of baggage that no person was ever meant to carry.

It is hard to make changes when the prospect of doing so sets off alarm bells in our heads that something bad is going to happen. Worse yet, we may not even consider sound advice simply because we have dismissed it long ago and reinforced our baggage influenced alternative with years of negative self-talk. Repeated self-talk statements such as: Things never change, I will never change, I can't change, I am not supposed to be happy, etc. lock us into a frame of mind that blocks any sound advice that might help us make new productive choices.

This is what the Agents of Change are: a roadmap of principles and actions to put into practice to reverse our baggage collecting lifestyle.

11. KEY CHANGE PRINCIPLES

Change is a Choice

Despite what you have heard or believe, anyone can change. Many may choose to not change, but that is the essence of this change principle: Change is a choice. However, our baggage of convoluted lessons learned can easily lead us to believe we are trapped and unable to change. Trapped by the belief that we can't change,

Trapped because change is too hard,

Trapped out of fear of the unknown and

Trapped because we are comfortable with the familiar.

As a result, we may say to ourselves or even out loud, "I can't stop", "I have tried everything and nothing ever changes", "I have no choice, this is just the way I am", "I can't help acting this way, this how I am". "What would I do different? This is all I know", "When they hit me it really isn't all that bad, I know they love me. And none of it is true.

We covered earlier that comfort is a common flawed concept we think is required to be happy when actually the converse is often true. What makes things comfortable is familiarity. We may be treated badly by friends or family, but since they are familiar we may continue to tolerate it despite its wear and tear upon us. Breaking away from the people, places and things that are no longer good for us is hard, because it means change. We know what it is like to do what we have always done. What we can't know is what it will be like if we make a change. The fear of the unknown can be a very powerful motivator to keep us from even considering making a change to improve our lives.

Yet, when we continue to include people, places and things in our lives even though they are very destructive for us, more than likely we are resisting because we have yet to become willing to be uncomfortable to grow out of our unhealthy habits. Whatever needs changing in our lives for things to improve is going to be uncomfortable, sometimes very uncomfortable.

For some of us being in certain entertainment venues or workplaces is really unhealthy for us. And for others, drinking alcohol, eating chocolate, reading romance novels, watching porn, or shopping for entertainment is no longer working for us. Whatever your next best candidate to change is, to make the change successfully you must be willing to be uncomfortable enough to see it through. We don't have to know everything about what the new way will be like, we just need to be willing to be uncomfortable in order to grow out of our old ways of thinking and behaving.

For many of us changing our baggage directed lifestyle means heading into unfamiliar territory and it is hard for this very reason. It is best to be realistic and realize that we will not change significantly over night, but we can improve little by little over time and eventually you will stop taking on more baggage and eventually you can also clean out most of the unnecessary baggage you have been carrying with you for so long.

A way to start off slowly is to begin by doing little things differently. Start off small and work your way up to doing bigger things differently. If you watch TV as a major entertainment activity then start taking days off. If you have always played video games each evening, then take days off. It will be hard, but instead of seeing it as something you have to do view it as training. You are developing your tolerance to discomfort. If you are like most of us, you are so used to indulging yourself whenever you can, that choosing to not do so can be very unnerving. Yet, this is just the beginning because you are in training to become a baggage shedder as opposed to a baggage collector.

Other things can be done differently to develop your discomfort tolerance, for example, avoid your favorite food, If you never exercise, then exercise. If you always exercise, then take a day off. If you always watch the news or listen to the radio take days off from it and do something else. If you never visit your family, then go visit them. If you see them all the time, then skip a visit from time-to-time. More than likely while you are learning to better tolerate being uncomfortable, you will also learn some other things about yourself and the world around you. As well as catering to ourselves in the constant pursuit of making ourselves comfortable or happy, we create a very small world for ourselves. As we open up the possibility of doing things that are not in pursuit of our own comfort we tend to notice a lot more of what is going on in the world. This increased awareness of things outside of ourselves will become very helpful to changing our tendency to take on unnecessary baggage.

So, make yourself a list of the things you can disrupt or do differently to start you on your journey. Take small steps at first and while you begin the alternative path of activity say to yourself, " I am going to do this instead to see what it is like. It will probably be uncomfortable, but it won't kill me and it will help me get used to being uncomfortable. Who knows, I may learn something new along the way". If you can do this you will begin to develop a greater and greater tolerance for doing things you don't necessarily want to do and that will be uncomfortable. This will be essential since you have many other tasks that will require this degree of tolerance.

If you find yourself too stressed by this idea, then take it slower, but still stick with it nonetheless. This is a basic skill for being able to make significant changes in your life.

If you are basically a sedentary person then a significant lifestyle change would be to become a marathon runner. If you are someone who stays at home most nights and watches TV or plays video games, then a significant lifestyle change would be to go out or have people over on a very regular basis. If you are always on the go and vigorously pursuing fun activities then staying in more and reading for entertainment would be a significant lifestyle change.

All of these changes are behaviors of choice. There is a whole other part of us that we have put into a category of, "this is who I am or it is no longer a choice". We may have a wide variety of reasons we tell ourselves why, but most likely things in this no choice category are things contributing to our baggage-burdened life. These can include not celebrating holidays, not eating in public, not discussing painful topics, not saying we are sorry, not admitting wrong doing, not using public restrooms, not accepting complements, not traveling, not taking vacations, not letting anyone get close to us, etc. We have to prepare ourselves for some big changes ahead. But fear not, crime detectives never come upon a crime scene and determine that making personal changes killed someone. We may tell ourselves it might, but nothing could be farther from the truth. In fact, things are about to get very interesting as you adopt this perspective. Let's take a look at another principle that is critical to enable changes in our lives.

Taking Responsibility

Having baggage can make us fairly confused about our responsibilities. Often, this can lead us to taking responsibility for things that are none of our business and denying responsibility for things that are clearly ours. When we are younger we get plenty of instruction about our physical responsibilities, such as what to touch, when to be gentle, washing our hands, what to keep out of our mouths, what is hot and sharp etc... Yet, as adults we may discover we are still learning about how to take care of our bodies. People die every day from preventable illnesses that had advanced too far along to treat simply because a doctor was not consulted on a regular basis or was never consulted at all.

Sometimes we have had these basic physical responsibilities perfectly modeled for us from a very early age, however we somehow got it into our head that it is still someone else's responsibility to manage them. This can happen with parents that continue to help out with reminders well into their children's adult years or when spouses take over with the reminders. This can easily happen with children who never leave home. It can also happen with families that are not all that close or those that are very close well into adulthood, but somehow the transfer of responsibility did not get consciously accepted. Regardless of how it occurred, if you are an adult of sound mind and capabilities, you are responsible for your own physical well-being. This doesn't mean your parents or guardians necessarily taught you everything, but it does mean that we, as adults, need to proactively manage our physical health and continue to learn about the new information that becomes available about how to improve on what we know already.

In addition to our physical health, we have to keep ourselves safe. We also have to proactively take measures to preserve our fragile life. Where we live, how we travel, what we put in our bodies, all have the potential to add risk to our lives. What we expose ourselves to factors into how secure we are from the things in this world that could prematurely end our lives. Not that we need to be paranoid, but being ambivalent or ignoring these risks is being equally irresponsible with our lives. If we proceed through life with the perspective that it is someone else's responsibility to manage our physical actions, health and safety we will likely have some very undesirable results.

The next area we typically get a great deal of instruction is our social interactions starting with family, friends and acquaintances. We start off with who takes care of us since we can't take care of ourselves for quite a while. Along the way we discover there are others who are not present to take care of us, but rather potential companions like siblings, and others we are exposed to. The more we are exposed to others, the more we learn that each encounter can be different, but the interactions are more enjoyable when sharing, courtesy and kindness are practiced. If we were never instructed to try these behaviors or were never exposed to others that reciprocated well, then we

may have had few if any social interactions turn out well.
Whether our friends or our family are closer to us or more like acquaintances, these relationships come with responsibilities that we may or may not choose to carry out. When we stay engaged and meet those responsibilities those relationships have the potential to thrive. Of course, relationships are a two-way street. The basic practice of staying in touch, being considerate, expressing our regard and communicating about significant events that happen in our lives all factor into successful relationships with others. Baggage can derail our relationships with others by never letting them get established or by disrupting them when mysterious danger signs occur. One of the more self-destructive ways to interact with others is to take responsibility for them where we do for others what they are perfectly capable of doing for themselves. We can develop this way of behaving by being around others who are initially younger, less capable, chronically ill, mentally ill or addicted to the point they appear to not being able to function. What starts off as a helping hand can develop into a mindset that we are supposed to take care of others. If this approach towards others take hold in us, we often can neglect ourselves in our attempt to take care of others. This can also complicate parenting by promoting continued dependency instead of a path towards autonomy. Baggage can cause some of us to see everyone as needing our help when we are the ones that need help the most from ourselves.

Spirituality can be another area that we may have received considerable instruction if we are raised in a religious home or setting. It is natural to instruct children to know what the parents or caretakers believe and how they apply it in their lives. Where baggage can confuse responsibility in this area is by practicing a, "Do as I say, not as I do", approach to guidance. Spiritual and religious topics are best received when the words and behavior are congruent. If the faith related instruction is accompanied with shame, guilt, unkind or cruel behavior then the faith image will likely include those ways of behaving.

Not all parents are aware of, have access to, or are prepared to provide age appropriate teaching when it comes to spiritual topics. Taking responsibility here may include getting feedback about personal preparedness, resources and surrogates to assist with the guidance.

The other two areas tend get the least amount of instruction and we are left to figure it out on our own with how we think and how we experience our emotions. Sadly, these areas are much too important to develop well without guidance. Mental baggage can cause us to be indecisive and to repeat confusing and conflicting trains of thought over and over as opposed to selecting the way we aspire to think and to make decisions based upon the best information available. Our brains are miraculous, but if they are not trained and exposed to well laid out information, it can become confused, disorganized and difficult to use for effective decision making. So, if some of our baggage motivates unorganized thinking, adoption of unreliable data, poor learning skills and poor decision making, it is our responsibility to learn and adopt improved practices for ourselves. How and what we think about is our responsibility. Most people have a near average intellect or better, but the lack of education or a lack of applying our education can result in the mistaken belief that we are not mentally capable. This is rarely the case. Intentionally honing our thinking skills through continued learning helps us to direct our thinking to what we decide as being the most beneficial to think about.

Emotionally we can be pulled on a roller coaster ride of ups and downs or we may rarely recognize how we feel only to blow up with little warning or to be down for significant periods of time. Baggage can treat us to a regular assault of mixed emotions that make little to no sense. Yet many of us still think of emotions as the best guide for our decisions. This is rarely the case. Emotions are the result of what we experience and how we perceive it. This applies to what we have just experienced in real time in addition to everything we have ever experienced all mixed in together. Thus, this is why we can have such a mixture of what appears to be unrelated emotions. Emotions are chemical reactions within our bodies, they are our emotions not anyone else's and therefore they are our responsibility. Poor education about emotions often allow many to consider emotions as our lead and everything else follows. When actually, emotions are the result of what we experience. So, the experience or memory of an experience happens first, we think about it (perceive it) and then we feel it. If we are not all that conscious of our thinking then it is easy to think that we feel the emotions first. As a result, feeling better comes from improving our thinking by clearing our baggage of bad lessons learned based on incorrect or incomplete data or both. So, if you are tempted to say, "You made me feel", Stop and take responsibility and say instead, "When this happened, I felt (emotion: sad, glad, etc..) and I began to think X." Now your taking responsibility for your emotions!

Words Matter

We all can get in the habit of using certain words or phrases often by imitating others. The problem is that if we talk a certain way long enough it influences the way we think and perceive the world. If that line of thinking and perceiving is untrue then we begin to miss out on what the facts really are since we have already convinced ourselves otherwise.

Two of the more common terms we can use inaccurately, we have described earlier are **can't** and **feel**. Often use of the word can't is not a declaration of inability, but is masking a lack of desire to make an effort. Using the term can't can create a self-defeating perception that there is little to no reason to try since things never work out the way we want. What is typically more accurate is that we, will not or choose not, to do something. However, saying we can't sounds less arbitrary because we would if we could, but we can't and as a result we create more baggage for ourselves. It is better for us to get in the habit of saying either I will not or I choose not to as these are typically more accurate.

Using the word **feel** carelessly can also skew our thinking. Saying, "I feel like driving to the store", rarely is challenged, but it is not a feeling. Now we can feel angry, joyful, afraid, anxious, hurt etc. However, we often use the term feel in place of the word think or decided. While on the surface this might not sound like a big deal, it creates a smoke screen for our thoughts and choices. If we consider our feelings are uncontrollable then anytime we conveniently don't want to have to explain our thought process or choices, we can say we felt like doing it. Who can challenge that I didn't feel a certain way? Nobody, but this also adds to our baggage. It is more accurate for us to get in the habit of saying I thought or I chose to.

Another set of terms we can over use and misuse are **always, never** and **should**.

Statements using always and never are rarely accurate especially when we are referring to ourselves. These statements can include: I always say the stupidest things. I can never get things right, things always go their way, people never notice me, etc. Being human, we all make mistakes and have results we may not like, but it is extremely rare that we do anything with such accuracy that we always do it or never do it. When we tell ourselves things about ourselves or in relationship to ourselves using these absolute terms we create a false perception. Using these absolute terms rule out the possibility of variation. The terms rarely and usually are probably more accurate, but may still be off. However, we may have had little success with something or I often get this result. While still an impression it allows for our perception without taking it to an unrealistic extreme that cuts off the possibility of alternate outcomes.

Should is another term used frequently in place of others that lead to very inaccurate communication with ourselves and others. When we think we are supposed to do something we often elect to use the word should. Should carries the weight of judgment that is often not described or entirely understood. If we grew up hearing we should know better, we can associate the opinions of all the parents, caretakers, authority figures, etc. together. As we begin to adopt this term we often will use it to coerce others to our desires or way of thinking. The word should is a perfectly good word if it is qualified when we are supposed to do something. For instance, if you are tired and want to feel better you should get some rest. However, you should do what I tell you doesn't tell you why or the benefit, leaving you to imagine for yourself why you are supposed to do whatever is being requested.

As a younger person, we may have asked for clarification and gotten an outright intimidating answer of, "Because I said so!" While in conversation we can ask and we will hopefully get a better answer that actually clears things up, however with ourselves we can easily allow should statements to just repeat in our heads. As a result, we will often hear ourselves and others say, "I know I should do this or that", without any clear reason of why.

A better choice instead of the word should is to say "have you considered X /to ensure or in order to, etc." When we suggestion someone consider an action followed by the benefit of doing this action we are making a clear recommendation without commanding or judgement.

What may make the use of these terms less noticeable is that we may only say these things to ourselves in our head. We may appear to avoid these unhealthy terms if we have made a habit of minimizing how much we speak with others. Yet, speaking these terms is more of a symptom, the real danger to us is when we use them in our thinking or self-talk.

Once you start taking notice how often you say or think in these terms you can start to remind yourself of more accurate ways to say and perceive the circumstance you are describing. Some good alternatives to these common absolutes are:

- I am not willing in place of I can't.
- I think in place of I feel when we are expressing judgments, opinions, choices or thoughts

- Often or frequently in place of always.
- Rarely or infrequently in place of never
- Consider plus the outcome in place of should.

There are other words and phrases we may use on a regular basis, but these five tend to be the most common. Why do we care?

Well, if we are regularly telling others and ourselves things that are not true or accurate, then eventually we begin to believe it ourselves. The more we are not sticking to the facts the more we are causing ourselves to be out of sync with the world. If we tell ourselves we can't speak before a group then we will avoid any opportunity to do so. If we tell ourselves that we always make a mess of things, then we will look for any reason to support our viewpoint. If we tell ourselves that we never get to have any fun then we probably will tend to pass up opportunities to have fun. If we tell ourselves that we feel like everyone is out to get us and a friend tries to point out that is not the case, we will likely tend to defend our perspective with the position that this is the way I feel and I can't help how I feel. Of course, this is not the case. We cannot feel everyone is out to get us, but we can have that perception.

We tell ourselves these lies all the time. And the more we lie to ourselves the more we cause ourselves to become out of sync with reality. The farther from reality we allow ourselves to drift, then the harder it is for us to navigate the world successfully. It is like trying to play a game of baseball with an alternate set of rules. Instead of running the bases when we make a hit, we may consider it our right to run the bases on a strike or before the ball has been pitched at all. While we may be allowed to proceed like this for a time eventually we will be asked to leave. Nobody benefits from such a disconnect from the facts, but if we allow ourselves to become convinced we are right, then we may reach for any explanation we can to justify and support our position and to explain why everyone else at the ball field is wrong. I think we have all been there, being certain we are right and everybody else was wrong. Time usually makes it clear, but in the meantime those who are out of sync with the world are missing out.

Pay attention to the words and phrase you regularly say to yourself and others. Inspect them in a way that you have not considered them before. Do they really hold up? Are they really true? Are they factual? If they are not, you need to begin dismantling them from your speech and your self-talk.

It is hard enough to navigate life with a life's worth of baggage. However, many of us choose to compound that with lies and an alternate version of the facts of the world, creating a box that is nearly impossible to break out of, but it is possible. First, we have to become aware of the hold paints the world and others with a broad brush that is not based in reality. The sooner we break the habit of using these incorrect uses of these words and phrases the sooner we will unshackle ourselves from such limiting thinking.

Shedding ourselves of our baggage and the propensity to collect more starts with these three keys principles: we have choices, we are responsible for ourselves and our words matter. While our baggage may fight the adoption of these principles, your load will begin to lighten the more you embrace them and let them guide your outlook on yourself and the people, places and things around you.

12. BAGGAGE SHEDDING ACTIONS

As we review the many ways we have taken on our baggage and begin to see how we have allowed it to weigh us down, we typically become motivated to make things better. While that simple decision may be all that is necessary for some, most of us need more direction. The unraveling of the aches and pains and poor lessons learned of a lifetime is not going to happen overnight. Most of us are creatures of habit and the habit of acquiring more and more baggage is a lifestyle that keeps us from being free to live our own lives. The good news is that this can be corrected. It is not like flipping a switch or taking an antibiotic. It has to do with charting a course that focuses on being open-minded and exploring ourselves.

Change is often uncomfortable since it takes us away from what we know and those things that are familiar to us. Yet our bad habits are comfortable for those of us with baggage. This baggage weighs us down, stands in our way and tempts us to do nothing different that might break us out of the chains that have been binding us to a series of unfortunate perspectives, voices and memories. So much of what it takes to get different results is that we have to begin living our life differently. Not all at once, but bit-by-bit, little-by-little incrementally changing the way we do life. After a while, results will begin to make themselves obvious, not only to ourselves, but to those around us as well. Sadly, some close to us may not like our changes, but this is not about them or what they are comfortable with either. Some find that as they start making healthier choices that some family and friends will discourage us to stay the way we are. These people are likely valuing their own comfort over what is best for us. As difficult as it maybe, we may find that we need to distance ourselves from these people in order to grow. While some changes will come slowly and we may even back track from time to time, change will occur if we start living our lives differently in a few key ways.

We need to develop a practice of clearly seeing ourselves as we really are and to be able to express that factually to others. Most of us can likely remember countless times we have been upset with ourselves because we had done something, which we promised ourselves we will never do again. And yet, if we are unable to articulate this perspective to others and ourselves honestly and factually, then we will likely minimize the experience until it is long forgotten. Once forgotten we are poised to make the same comfortable decision again.

We need to have a guide who can show us the ropes in this new path of acting differently. If we want to learn a new sport, game, or job we look to someone who knows the ropes who can show us the way and what to watch out for to minimize our mistakes. Not that we won't make them, but it significantly improves our success to learn the new activity as soon as possible.

We will also need a community of support that can provide a variety of perspectives on the new ways we are choosing to live our life. It is not easy to shed baggage that has been our constant companion for most of our lives. Yet having others accessible to us can be a real deal breaker as to whether we will stick with a new baggage averse and shedding lifestyle. We have been a captured student of our own experiences, perceptions and memories and we need to change the curriculum to a new set of ways to view the world.

Finally, we need to develop a practice of activity that has an effective way to bring us hope and peace. Most of our baggage has done a very good job of breeding a sense of hopelessness in us. Maybe not entirely, but it is not unusual for baggage to have such a hold on us that we may tend to see our dilemma as one we are destined to be shackled to for the rest of our lives.

Change is hard and often requires the assistance of others. In the midst of making changes we need hope and we need a break. Nobody can go for long without rest and the same goes for when we are changing our way of doing life.

There are many new lessons you will learn in your journey. While the key concepts are internal actions, the following change agents are external actions that will set up the mechanisms in our life that will not only help shed baggage, but also make us more baggage resistant.

Are these the only agents of change we can use? No, but these are the essential ones that will ensure your progress. If you leave one out, you will significantly risk your chances for significant results. So, keep an open mind about these topics and remember, it is supposed to sound foreign and uncomfortable. Expect it to. Just remember, no one has ever died from being uncomfortable.

In addition to embracing the Key Change Principles, there are a number of essential actions to breaking the cycle of a baggage collecting lifestyle. They are:

1. Being of Service
2. Practicing Gratitude
3. Practicing Honesty/Disclosure
4. Accepting the Facts
5. Engaging a Support System
6. Engaging a Mentor
7. Practicing Forgiveness
8. Allowing Ourselves to Grieve
9. Research and Study
10. Prayer and Meditation.

While they may not sound like much, these ten practices are extremely powerful in allowing us to process the painful experiences of our past, present and future life. The first two, being of service and practicing gratitude, are baggage disrupters that pull our attention from our negative self-talk and towards something good that often lifts our spirits and builds our self-esteem. Getting into the habit of these two actions will make the discomfort of the other actions much more tolerable. The remainder of the actions are the intentional behaviors that confront our baggage and begins the process of putting it into its proper perspective.

We not only need to release ourselves from our past baggage, but we also need to resist the temptation to collect new baggage for any longer than necessary. It is not that it is reasonable to make ourselves impervious to the pains and heartaches of life, however as we experience them we can process them in a timely fashion and put them in their proper perspective. All the difficult things that have happened to us and that we have been carrying around with us can begin to be dismantled in an appropriate way that does not seek to deny they ever happened, but does diffuse its power to control our lives today.

Being of Service

The idea of service as a baggage-shedding action may seem counterintuitive while its effects are quite significant. Providing someone or organization a helping hand when they are in a situation of need can bring a small, yet meaningful opportunity to see the world through a new perspective while executing an act of generosity. It can also open the door to having new relationships with others as a result of our kindness. If we are a person who likes to get credit for everything we do, then the act of service can be more beneficial to us when kept a secret to take the requirement for something in return off the table. Unselfish acts towards other people, places, and things gives us a sense of accomplishment and builds our self-esteem. All of these benefits better prepare us for a lifestyle that is less focused upon seeking comfort.

How we are of service can vary from helping someone with their coat, to picking up a dropped pen, to repairing someone's faucet, lubricating a squeaky door, listening to someone who is lonely, or providing a meal to someone who could use one. As a part of a service organization, we can join others to help build houses, provide clean water, support critically ill children, seniors or the disabled, mentor students, collect eyewear for new owners, fight disease, poverty or hunger among the many services needed by our communities.

Generally, our service falls into one of three categories, time, talent or treasure.

When we spend time with someone we are giving a great gift, our time and attention. We can talk, walk, shop, go to a movie, share a ride, have a meal, visit someone in the hospital, take someone to the doctor or to an event or we can honor them by listening. It really doesn't matter what the activity as long as we are present and spending time with others for their benefit. We may possess a talent or skill that we can share such as eyeglass repair, cooking, how to interview for a job, how to tie a tie, or even reading to someone who is blind or too ill to sit up. Anything we know how to do can be a talent-based act of service that is for their benefit.

We may also have resources we can make available to others as an act of service. While this can mean money, often we have a roof over our head we can share for a meal or an event or we may have possessions we can share with others. We often hang on to items that are no longer needed, like clothing, old tools, kitchen items, sporting equipment, furniture, musical instruments, even old cars. Whatever treasure we have at our disposal we could share it with others, either temporarily or permanently, for their benefit.

As we make our time, talent or treasure available to others a few things happen to us. We are instantly thinking about others and seeing the needs of others and what we might be able to do for them. While we consider this, we are giving our busy minds a break from thinking about ourselves and concentrating on others. This in itself is an act of charity that lightens our heart with the compassion we are choosing. When we identify something that we can actually execute, we get to deliver the news about our offer and if accepted then we have the pleasure to deliver it. Now a word of caution about expectations. When we offer something to someone we have no idea how they will react. They may be elated, but some may not care for our offer. In isolated instances they may be insulted or embarrassed. Prepare yourself for the possibility that you may not have or choose to offer something that your intended recipient will desire. That said, most will be grateful and you get the joy of their appreciation and their enjoyment to make use of your gift.

Not only the act itself, but the memory and the knowledge that you made someone's day, enabled a child to play an instrument, made repairs for someone who could not afford them, etc. is another source of joy for us. Just like a memory of cherished accomplishment, the memory of an act of charity can be a great addition to the stockpile of healthy and uplifting memories we can choose to start building for ourselves. To consider all of the memories we have, if we were able to create a surplus of cherished memories, then we would be less likely to remember unpleasant events. This can be a result we all can create by regularly making it our practice to be of service to others. As time goes on, we not only remember these events ourselves, but others remind us occasionally about them as well.

We probably all have witnessed the appreciation of someone to someone else who has been charitable towards them. The more we are of service to others, the more we are appreciated and thanked on a repeated basis. Again, another benefit.

Practicing Gratitude

In addition to being of service, another action that builds and helps maintain a sense of well-being is practicing gratitude. Gratitude is simply choosing to be glad about the people, places and things around you. However, practicing an attitude of gratitude requires mental muscles most of us have not developed. Like many of the characteristics of the baggage shedding lifestyle, you have to develop the habit of gratitude.

If you notice your discomfort kicking in already, relax this is normal. In our fast-paced world of wanting more and never getting enough, it can seem very counterproductive to arbitrarily choose to be glad about the people, places and things around us. You might be right, especially if you don't want to be happy more of the time.

The secret is simple. Just look around you, think about the people, places and things around you and acknowledge the ones you are glad about. Can't do it since you are not glad about anything? Not a problem. It can still be done. Just say the words, "I am grateful for the air I breathe". You don't have to do a happy dance or be reeling with joy, just say the words, "I am grateful for the air I breathe". Congratulations, you have just selected something you can be grateful for anytime. Gratitude is a choice, not a feeling. It can start with feeling upbeat, fun and happy, but it can also begin with a simple choice when you can benefit from it the most when we need a lift.

The next step is to make a list of things for which you are grateful. Can't think of anything? Stretch yourself and try some things on for size. I am grateful for the trees, the grass, the breeze, my favorite ice cream, something you enjoy eating, a place to sleep, shelter, my health, etc. you get the idea. Work on the list for a while and then keep it out where you can see it. Try adding a few new items to the list every day. If you have no good place to keep it out, then carry it with you in your wallet or purse. Many find this works well on whatever electronic device you access most often. Just don't file it away so well you won't run across it. The point is that you should easily run across it and read it every day if not multiple times a day.

I know it will be easy to resist, forget, think it is stupid, etc. Trust me this makes a difference even if you can't tell it right away. We have been in the habit of being dissatisfied, disappointed, disgusted, and probably depressed at times for so long that we naturally want to fight doing things that just make you feel better.

You may want to take an alternate approach of making sure you read the list every morning and every evening just before you go to bed. What will start to happen is that you will begin to be more and more sincere about these very natural things to be glad about in your life. Starting and ending each day with this practice can go a long way to redirecting how you approach your day and end it. After a while you are going to want to add to the list. So do it! Or maybe you might want to make a new list. Maybe someone smiled at you today, you heard a song that you had not heard in years, read something that inspired you, or maybe you have figured out that you are grateful for some of the tough things that have happened to you because you have learned something positive from it.

Whatever comes to mind add to the list, remake the list, make multiple lists, keep making lists and leaving them where you can see them and find them. In your place, on your bike, in your car, on your mirror, in your locker, on your desk or on a board at work, on your calendar, on your refrigerator, or on the wall by the door so you see it as you walk out the door. Whatever works for you, do it.

It took me years to get it so ingrained in me that I naturally think and speak aloud things I am grateful for many times a day throughout my day. In the early days of the Internet I started a web site called The Gratitude Page. Setting it up and adding things to it became another motivation to identify new things for which I was grateful. Others started commenting and adding thing they were grateful for which was very motivating for me as well. I heard from students, men, women, nurses, clergy from around the world. This was back in the mid to late 90s and I got busy with other things and lost track of it when I changed Internet service providers. But every once in a while, I will think back on it or run across a blog or an article that mentions the website and the inspiration it brought to them. Who knows, the list you post on the wall might inspire others as well.

Practicing Honesty/Disclosure

The first step in making any change is realizing that there is a problem. Fundamental change is usually not made unless we have a good reason. Especially when the thing we may be changing is something we are comfortable with and we can't imagine doing anything differently. The Baggage Sources section of this book provided you with many common potential sources of baggage for your life. You probably recognized some, skimmed over others and avoided others. Early on picking anything is fine; eventually we become willing to change the things that are more challenging. We all have to start somewhere and there was probably at least one source that reminded you of something that has stuck with you for quite a while. Make yourself a note that will make sure you remember this observation.

There are different audiences and levels of honesty that you may or may not be familiar with that will be important in your pursuit of a baggage shedding lifestyle. The audience is simply who we are, or are not, honest with about a topic. The audience, while it can be endless, given the number of people in the world, but to keep it simple let's group the audiences into ourselves, confidants, friends, family, acquaintances and everybody else. Some people probably came to mind when you read this list. Some who you might like to trust and probably more that you trust very little, if at all. The truth is that all of us have been burned by the betrayal of others at one time or another. And while many of us eventually get over it and begin to trust again, some of us decide trust is a luxury we cannot afford. Here in lies the first big stumbling block.

We cannot heal ourselves and we don't trust anyone else enough to let them help us. I address this issue up front since it is so key to the burden we acquire with our lifetime of baggage. Trust is not something we can either can or cannot do. It is simply a choice. We make choices every day. To get up or not, to go to work/school/tend to our families or responsibilities or not, etc. Then there are many little decisions we make every day such as how to travel, to and from places, what routes to take, who to smile at or not, what to drink, etc. Each of these decisions has implications. If we pick wisely things go well or at least as desired. If we choose poorly then there are consequences: we are late, laundry piles up, our stomach is upset, relationships fade, we are alone or worse yet we feel alone among others.

When we have been betrayed by others by either making fun of us, judging us or telling others when we have shared intimate secrets with them, that experience is good information that we often use poorly as a generalized lesson that people in general cannot be trusted. When actually all we learned in reality is that person cannot be trusted in the way we were trusting them at the time.

If you think back to the times you trusted others and your privacy was not honored, think about what these people were like. Did they appear trustworthy using the description above? If not, then your experience is in part based upon your choice of who to trust. We who continue to trust occasionally still may run across a betrayal, but the vast majority of the time the secret to not getting burned is choosing whom to trust wisely.

If when considering the criteria above you still cannot identify a candidate that you know, then there is always the professional route. When our current circumstances have not yielded great trustworthy relationships then professional mentors, coaches, counselors and therapists make a great substitute. The vast majority honor their ethical code of their professional role of confidentiality.

Ultimately, when we have been betrayed and we have arrived at the conclusion we cannot trust anyone again, we are working with flawed data. What we need to do is pay attention to the facts and choose to trust wisely among our friends or professionals to begin being honest with ourselves. We do not have to feel like trusting someone to choose to trust them, we can do it because it makes sense based upon the facts and because it is important to our well-being. This way we can break the practice of our own perspective being the only reviewer of our thoughts and actions.

The problem with never letting anyone in is that we are our only judge. And because of the often poor or limited perspective we have on the events of our lives and of ourselves we can be a very harsh and inappropriate judge. So, if we are to correct any of the poor perceptions and self-judgment of ourselves we need to begin to let another person in on our thinking, so they can give us some feedback. Just having a different opinion based upon the same information can be enlightening.

While it is not necessary to be completely honest with everybody, many of us develop a habit of guarding our secrets so well that we have nearly become experts at hiding things about ourselves from others. Part of changing our baggage clutching and gathering lifestyle will involve letting a select few in on our secrets. This is probably a very uncomfortable topic, but remember the reason this is uncomfortable is that you have become an expert at guarding your baggage. Who can be trusted is discovered by choosing wisely. What is important is that we begin to let a select few in on what we are dealing with.

Why?

So, we can be introduced to reality. Most of our baggage is a very distorted view of the facts that has not been put in its proper perspective. To do this, it takes selected individuals you choose to trust to give us an alternate perspective on the facts we have burned into our psyche. Unfortunately, the first person we often need to start being honest with is ourselves.

At this point we should consider the different levels of honesty and it is probably best to consider the range of honesty and whom we are honest with. The parties we can communicate with varies from everyone to just ourselves with friends, family and other confidants in between. Likewise, if we are completely dishonest at one end of the spectrum and completely honest at the other then we can map out our options.

	Mostly Dishonest	More Often Dishonest	Half And Half	More Often Honest	Mostly Honest
Ourselves					
Confidants					
Friends					
Family					
Acquaintances					
Everyone else					

Figure 12-1 Honesty map

Each category can fall anywhere on this spectrum for a variety of reasons. Maybe we have become convinced that being honest only gets us into trouble and we keep things so secret that we have managed to even hide most things from ourselves. How is this possible?

There are a number of ways we can be dishonest with ourselves. We can ignore the facts, choose to believe a most desirable version of the facts, or disregard the facts and create our own version of the facts. We often unconsciously filter out the information we don't prefer, dislike, hate or that causes us pain. If we filter out the vast majority of what we have available to us, then we are on the far left of the spectrum when it comes to being honest with ourselves. How honest we are with ourselves sets the baseline for our interactions with everyone else. Typically, we are somewhat less than completely honest with ourselves due to our current biases. If our preferences, opinions, baggage (issues) or biases are profound, then we may be much more dishonest with ourselves than honest with ourselves.

If you have locked everything away for a very long time it may be the case you have never dared to speak of things for fear of telling someone. If this is the case you may have managed to forget or suppress many of the things that trouble you. This doesn't mean they no longer affect you, but that you have managed to think about other things instead. Yet we are still impacted by these experiences.

The first thing you attempt to share with someone else should be a small or relatively minor thing for you, but still something you have not shared with someone else. This way you can start off slowly and you are also not over burdening your relationship with the person you are choosing to trust. While the person you choose to trust may be entirely trustworthy, they may simply not want to or have the time to have this type of relationship with you. Pick something minor and ask if you can share something with them and would they be willing to keep it to themselves. If they agree, go for it and see how it goes. If it goes well then you can then consider what else might be shared. If it appears to go poorly, take some time before rendering final judgment. It may be that the person was having a bad day, was really too busy to talk at that time or simply was not feeling well.

If you get feedback, don't expect to like it. However, think of it as a gift, a different perspective. Try to consider that someone else's perspective might be more correct than your own. Thank them for their feedback and let them know you want to think about what they have shared with you. If you feel relieved because you have gotten this off your chest feel free to tell them this. Getting into the practice of trusting others with your sensitive experiences is a big step. Take it slowly and don't give up if things don't appear to go well. If friends do not work out, seek out professionals. This is what they are there for, to be a sounding board. They are not there just for people that are mentally ill. They are there for all of us.

Interacting with others about the experiences and perspectives we have about our own lives has a similar benefit as engaging a guide or mentor on a new activity such as skiing, photography or quilting. While it might be easy to say some people are just better at those things, but it is just not for me. When we have not done something before or have not done it for a very long time we can easily not know how to get started and any attempts can be uncomfortable, frustrating and maybe even painful. Yet as we do life many of us pretty much try to do it alone and as a result we can often get started on the wrong foot or in the wrong direction and without a guide or mentor we can become lost, discouraged, resentful, unfulfilled, alone, and dissatisfied.

However, just like with activities such as skiing, photography or quilting we can learn how to do these activities successfully. We may not become Olympians, professional photographers or quilters, but we can be successful enough to enjoy the journey and our accomplishments. This is what interacting with others does for us. We share about how we see the world, what is challenging us, what we struggle with and we get feedback from others who have a different perspective. A perspective that we don't have to adopt but one that can present an alternative from which we could benefit. It is often the case that our pain, fears and heartaches are in part, if not entirely, from a perception that can be improved upon. Your baggage may have convinced you that your problems are too great to be resolved, but this is not true. There is no problem or unhappiness too great that it can't be improved upon if we keep an open mind.

The idea of being honest with others and ourselves often conjures up painful memories of betrayed trusts, embarrassing moments socially or in our families and yet as an adult we can choose who and where we are sharing ourselves. Whether we are opening up to ourselves in thought or talking to a friend, a support group or a professional, we can take some comfort in that our choices today are not the same as those past events. We are not considering blurting out some guarded secret upon a whim. We are talking about carefully selecting what to share and with only the best of candidates who can probably help us. Now you might be thinking to yourself, "if I can't trust my friends or family members that I like who can I trust?" The answer is simple. If we do not have good people to confide in, then we need to expand our circle of acquaintances, make better friends, visit a support group or hire a reputable professional counselor, therapist or coach. Not every group or professional are a good source of feedback either, but if you can find good reviews from multiple independent sources then they are likely to be a good candidate. Beyond that, you have to take a risk with any new resource just like you do with anybody else.

Will it be uncomfortable?

Absolutely, but the benefits far outweigh the risks. If you don't have any friends or family you dare trust then seek out a professional that has made it their life's vocation to help others process their experiences. Are they all great? Sadly no. However, most are very competent and have ethical practices that keep them from betraying your confidences. So, what is shared in a counselor or therapist's office will not get back to your family or friends unless you tell them yourself.

But there is an intermediate step to talking with others that might make it a bit easier. This may sound a little strange, but you can test making your first disclosure by practicing what you will say to yourself first. You may find yourself hesitating with the thoughts that you don't know where to begin, or that you simply do not know what to say. We often have so many preconceived ideas about how these mysterious conversations may go that we can barely get anything out of our mouths. So, practice. Just like you would a presentation, practice how you would open up about one or a few things that bother you. Often, if we can come up with a basic outline of what we want to share, then that can get us past the anxiety when we are actually beginning to disclose something to another person for the first time.

Also, keep in mind those being honest and practicing mindful and meaningful disclosure is a process that occurs a little at a time. One of the likely experiences from opening up to another person is a sense of regret or maybe even panic of "What have I done?" Many of the thoughts and emotions surrounding this reaction are based upon our past experiences when our selection of when and where to share things about ourselves were not safe choices. We are not the young child anymore or the awkward teenager. We may still be awkward and insecure, but we are capable of making better decisions.

When our emotions flare up reminding us of situations years ago that went horribly wrong, we know we want no repeat of that to occur. Often, we are already making sure that the situation will not repeat by making better choices. The first time we burnt ourselves on a stove we probably stayed away from the stove for a while. However, unless we choose to avoid cooked food for the rest of our lives we learn to return to the stove. We learn that we need to pay attention to which elements are hot and what has been heated by them. Not only are the elements hot, but other items like pots, pans, their handles and any utensils near them can be as well. We can use the same learned and adapted behavior with ourselves in the way we look at our interactions with others, our perspective on our past experiences and how we choose to act from this moment going forward.

Just because we have been on one course for a very long time doesn't mean we can't change courses. We can change how we choose to think and act regardless of how we feel. Anytime we do something different than we have done for a long time it is uncomfortable. At a minimum, it is the lack of familiarity that is behind the uncomfortable feeling. So, we have to remind ourselves that any change will be a bit uncomfortable and the more radical of a change it is for us this sensation of discomfort will be increased. However, this has nothing to do with the outcome or the potential benefit it can provide us. Our mind may leap to bad imagined outcomes because we are uncomfortable, however we have to remind ourselves of the facts.

We are doing something new or something we have not done in a long time. As a result, I will be uncomfortable. However, I am interested in getting some new and different results and that is why I am trying something new. I may not like how this feels, but I have to do this to see what other outcomes are possible when I try this different approach. If it doesn't work out, I can re-evaluate it later when I have more facts.

While you may not be used to giving yourself a pep talk, most of us have to do this when trying something new. We all have the negative talk in our head, so it only makes sense that it will help us to counter this with positive fact-based pep talk. People who talk to themselves are members of the human race. The only ones that look crazy are the ones moving their lips, talking out loud and moving their arms when no one else is there. As long as we don't do this in public we are safe from appearing crazy.

Accepting the Facts

Another key action that is essential to putting difficult experiences into their proper perspective is acceptance. We may not like the circumstances we are in, but unless we are acknowledging the facts that surround us, we are choosing to live in an unproductive world that is fantasy based. Denial is a very effective coping tactic when we just want to kick our problem down the road and add them to the mountain of baggage we carry around with us.

Denial is simply choosing to ignore the facts. If someone we know gets intoxicated on a regular basis and is often getting in fights, losing jobs, getting arrested for disturbing the peace, driving under the influence and we are uncomfortable with those facts, we might choose to deny that they have a problem. We might say things like, if he just got a break he would stop having trouble, if his girlfriend hadn't left him he would be alright, if he would just get a good job everything will be alright. No, it won't because this person shows many signs of having a serious drug and/or alcohol problem. Until we accept the facts that this person is getting intoxicated, getting in fights, losing jobs, and getting arrested we are not going to be able to join the real world and be a part of the solution. Wishful thinking gets us nowhere.

Acceptance of the facts is not a personal endorsement, condemnation or even any agreement with any particular conclusion. It is simply agreeing that the facts exist. My loved one is having trouble. They are getting intoxicated regularly, getting in fights, losing jobs and getting arrested. We can disagree on what the facts are, but that is another issue. Just like in a court of law both parties bring into the case what they claim are the facts that support their side of the case. We will do the same thing. However, when our version of the facts does not align with reality, but is rather wishful thinking, then we are in trouble.

Acceptance neither changes the facts nor resolves our issue with them, but it does do one important thing, it puts us in alignment with the facts to the best of our understanding. This gives us a great advantage, the ability to become a part of the solution. Before acceptance of the facts of the situation we can only be a part of the problem. If we have a dog who doesn't feel well and we assume they have a cold, we might not take them to the vet. A neighbor might mention that it could be heartworms and it could be very serious. If we continue to assume it is just a cold and the real problem is heartworms, the dog could die. Yet when we accept the facts, our dog is sick and our neighbor suspects it might be serious, then we are empowered with the knowledge to be a part of the solution and get the dog to the vet. If we continue to deny the facts, the results can be disastrous.

Likewise, if we are the one who is sick and we continue to discount the suggestions and diagnosis of our doctors, then we are continuing to be a part of the problem. This happens a great deal with people who see the possibility of being sick as so bad they choose to pretend there is nothing to be investigated or treated. When the illness itself clouds our judgment like some mental illnesses and addiction, it can be quite challenging to accept the possibility we may be sick. Yet when we consider if the same facts were happening to someone we care about we might find that we are much more accepting of the facts.

We can use intentional self-talk to check how we are doing with our acceptance of the facts around us. Some sample questions we can ask ourselves are:

- Am I choosing to have a perspective that is not consistent with the facts?
- Do I have someone in my life that hurts me on a regular basis?
- Do I pretend that my actions have nothing to do with the results I experience in my life?
- Do I spend time with people who create dangerous situations for me?
- Do I acknowledge how others have treated me and how I treat people in my life?

Acceptance of the facts of our past experiences can often be painful, embarrassing and can even be experienced as threatening to our current life and self-perception as we know it. This is another source of discomfort that is all a part of the process of putting the events of our past into their proper perspective. Acceptance of the facts about our circumstances and our past enable us to begin updating the lessons learned formed with incomplete or incorrect data. If we are unwilling to accept there may be additional or updates to the facts as we know them we can lock ourselves into taking responsibility for things we had little or no influence over. So once we are honest with ourselves there may be new data concerning a significant impression, judgement or decision we made in our past, and we accept this new information, then we become enabled to update our mis-guided past choices and let go of some more baggage.

Engaging a Support System

A support system is a collection of people that you can count on and you get to see and interact with regularly. They may be individuals that do not know each other or they may all be members of some sort of group or multiple groups. If they are unrelated individuals, they may be people you have enlisted to provide a listening ear, advice, or just companionship. One or more may be professionals you have engaged for support. The alternative is to engage groups to find support. The group's purpose for being might be surrounding an interest (making art, crafting, woodworking or restoring cars), a pursuit (learning an instrument, birdwatching, mountain climbing), enjoyment (playing music, attending sporting events, dancing, fishing), self-improvement (organization skills, meditation, community classes) or recovery (from a injury, trauma, addiction or a loss). The members may include family or friends, but often they start with new acquaintances, and sometimes include friends or professionals. Whatever the purpose for the group's existence, it's going to be necessary that there are members of that group that are doing better at leading a baggage shedding life than we are. This way we have others to observe and interact with to update our knowledge of how relationships and life works. Once we are open to sharing some of our lessons learned and perspectives on things we can also benefit from feedback that may update us on our impression of the facts in our life.

We may actually find it to our benefit to be a part of more than one group. Some may be a little bit more entertainment oriented and then some may be a bit more seriously pointed towards self-improvement or recovery. As mentioned before, working with others and listening to others actually improves our ability to learn lessons that we could not learn all by ourselves. While we might best learn from personal experience, the stories told by others and the feedback from others helps us to understand how we could do things better. This can be a valuable resource, in the midst of our journey.

The groups geared towards personal improvement tend to have the most potential to become a meaningful support system for us. These groups tend to be issue oriented, so if you have never thought of yourself, as having an issue, then you may have never considered such a group before. However, there are groups that are just for helping everyday people just cope better with everyday things that can easily be called baggage.

These groups, while they number in the thousands, tend to fall into a few easy to consider categories. One aspect is the issue they focus on helping people with and the other is how they are organized and facilitated. The issues fall into the categories of chronic illnesses, significant loss, addiction issues, family and friends of those with chronic illness, addiction issues and those seeking personal growth. The type of organization and facilitation are private/professional led and public/peer led and within each these two types can be either religion affiliated or not affiliated. Given the intersection of these characteristics you can find most support groups that will have a higher potential to help you find an effective support system. Some of the support groups are more temporary in nature, but many find them helpful.

The issues I would suggest you consider in order to guide you are as follows:

- Do you have a chronic issue, challenge or illness?
- Have you ever suffered a significant loss?
- Do you have addiction issues?
- Does someone important in your family/friend's past or present have addiction issues?
- Do you have personal growth issues?

After you have asked yourself those questions, for the ones you have answered yes or maybe, put a star by that issue along the left side of the following table. Now consider what type of organization and facilitation is a better fit for you (private/professional or public/peer led). Next consider your preference for the provider to be affiliated with a religion or not. Once you have made these three selections, you will find in the cell where your selections intersect and some suggested options for groups to investigate.

Issue \ Type	Private / Professional Led	
	Religion Affiliated	Not Affiliated
Do you have personal growth Issues	Issue specific support groups led by affiliated counselors and psychologists	Hospital/ treatment center/ community center sponsored support groups
Do you have a chronic issue, challenge or illness?	Illness specific support groups led by affiliated counselors and psychologists	Hospital / treatment / community center sponsored Illness support groups
Have you suffered a significant loss?	Grief support groups led by affiliated counselors and psychologists	The Grief Recovery Method. Hospital/ hospice/ treatment center sponsored Grief support groups
Do you have addiction issues?	Addiction specific support groups led by affiliated counselors and psychologists	Alternative Peer Groups, Hospital/ treatment center sponsored aftercare support groups
Does someone close to you have addiction issues?	Pastoral counselor or psychologists led groups for family addiction issues.	Alternative Peer Groups, Private counselor or led groups for family addiction issues.

Figure 12-2 Private / Professional Support Groups

Type Issue	Public / Peer Led	
	Religion Affiliated	Not Affiliated
Do you have personal growth Issues	Celebrate Recovery, Issue specific support groups led by affiliated members/staff	Emotions Anonymous, Co-Dependents Anonymous, Obsessive Compulsive Anon.
Do you have a chronic issue, challenge or illness?	Celebrate Recovery, Illness specific support groups led by affiliated members/staff	Illness specific support groups led by fellow sufferers using a set format, NAMI Connection
Have you suffered a significant loss?	GriefShare, Grief support groups led by affiliated members/ staff, DivorceCare, Beginning Experience	Compassionate Friends, SOS – Survivor of Suicide,
Do you have addiction issues?	Celebrate Recovery, Jewish Alcoholics, Chemical Dependents and Significant others (JACS), Millati Islami	Alternative Peer Groups, Alcoholics, Narcotics, Gamblers, Overeaters Anonymous, SMART Recovery, HAMS
Does someone close to you have addiction issues?	Celebrate Recovery, JACS	Alternative Peer Groups, Al-Anon, Gam-Anon, Families Anonymous, SMART Family and Friends

Figure 12-3 Public / Peer Support Groups

The Public / Peer Led Not Affiliated category probably has the greatest number of unique support groups by chronic issue (anxiety, mood, eating, etc.), challenge (sensory, cognitive, physical etc.), illness (cancer, autoimmune, neuromuscular, etc.). To locate one that might relate to you search on the issue/

challenge/illness and the words 'support groups'. To begin identifying your candidates for groups to check out, search on the names or keywords in the chart above. To identify a group that might benefit us, we have to visit them. We have to try them on for size and see which one(s) appear to be a fit for us.

As we try them out we give them an investment to make sure that we are not allowing ourselves to be put off by some selected individuals. Most groups have a lot to offer, so I usually try to stick with a group for at least a few months to give it a good chance of being fully appreciated for what it has to offer. Sometimes with the group that we are checking out we will find that it provides the opportunity to serve others rather than to necessarily learn something from them or to gain acquaintances and friendships. Good friendships usually take time to develop, starting with the acquisition of acquaintances and getting to know them over time creating an opportunity for friendships to develop. Sometimes it takes a little bit more than just a chance meeting to find out enough about somebody to determine we have a good deal in common. Sometimes it takes being out with a group, being a part of a work project, or volunteering to find out that much about somebody.

If I am in the middle of checking out one group (a few months in) and I come across another group that might be a possibility I start involving myself with that one as well and just continue to expand my circle of acquaintances. Being part of a group gives us a sense of belonging and at the simplest level gives us a place to go. It is amazing what it does to us to have people glad to see us, recognize us and welcome us.

If groups have never been your thing or if you have had really bad experiences with them, I won't tell you it will never happen again because it is possible. Some don't work out and some do. Think of it this way: if your best lessons learned taught you to avoid groups, then consider the possibility that they are part of the baggage that is keeping you where you are. The best thing about being around groups is that they offer many perspectives in a brief amount of time and usually we walk away appreciating our own life more. Learning about other people's issues has a powerful ability to make ours not seem so bad. That is worth the trip in itself.

Engaging a Mentor

Most of us need a guide of some sort, even when the new thing we are interested in is fun and exciting. However, many of us resist this approach due a litany of negative self-talk statements like: "I don't need a teacher", "How hard can this be?", "What will people think? I'm through with school", "Most people don't get a guide for this kind of thing". When actually most successful people have had multiple guides, mentors and or coaches along the way, if not continuously throughout their journey. Every few years the airways are profiling Olympic champions who readily give credit to the people who guided them through the years or during critical times in their journey. The same applies for all who achieve great accomplishments, they had a guide, they had a mentor if not more than one. Business leaders, musicians, teachers, writers, spiritual and civic leaders, doctors, lawyers, actors, and comedians, all have had mentors to help them accomplish great success.

It is not enough to have a great desire, equipment or talent, we also need to be shown the way. For the athlete it may be the guidance to a rock-solid training regimen, for the business leader it might be the guidance to focus on intrinsic value and strategy, and for those of us drowning in our own baggage it is the guidance from someone who has been there that lets us know there is a proven path to a much better life.

We need to have a guide who can show us the ropes in this new way of navigating. Having that experienced sounding board doesn't solve all of our problems, but it does give us that advantage to help get back up when we feel defeated or can help us learn from lessons we are struggling to understand. Some guides are so accepted they and their craft create entire industries: realtors, clergy, college preparatory programs, interior and landscape designers, counselors, and any kind of consulting. The list goes on and on, but what is important is that you dispel the notion that most people don't get a guide for this kind of stuff. This is nonsense.

People who get help get better, they make better decisions and they have more success. They feel much less alone and know that someone has their best interest in mind. These are powerful things to have experienced, much more powerful than someone learning about the mentoring relationship and wanting to make fun of it. People who have little in their life often seek to put down others for attempting to better themselves. The fear of what others may think of us is often rooted, if not reinforced, by spending much too time in the presence of these types of people. If you look around, you will always find someone who is willing to put you down or make fun of you. Not because you are defective, but because you are there. If you were not there they would be making fun of someone else. It is usually not personal for them; they are just trying to feel better in a very destructive way.

Getting a mentor is choosing to spend time with someone who will show you how to improve, instead of choosing to listen to someone who will tear you down to make themselves feel better. A mentor feels better by helping others find their own way by sharing their experience, strength and hope. Which makes more sense to spend time with for guidance, the mentor or the tormenter?

A mentor isn't just anybody. They are somebody who knows the ropes. They are somebody who has been where you have been and knows a method for getting from where we are to where they are today. Being old doesn't make you a mentor, being smart doesn't make you a mentor. A good mentor is a person with a history of adversity, struggles and failures. They persevered and acquired a new set of lessons learned that when acted upon provided a different, more successful, and desired set of results. Mentors are not usually waiting around waiting for protégé's. More often they are busy, well thought of and recommended by others when people like us start inquiring about who might be able to help us.

Word of mouth recommendations are often the best source of where to find a mentor. People who have been helped by a mentor are their best advertising. So, you have to ask around, but whom you ask makes a difference as well. But a likely good start is to ask people who obviously are navigating life much better than we are. They will have a much better idea of how to guide us than most. Infrequently, mentors find us or are assigned to us, but this is more likely to occur in our work life. Usually, we have to seek out mentors ourselves. Often the best sources for mentors are often groups of acquaintances and support groups. As we get acquainted with potential mentor candidates, we can verify they have been though similar circumstances and no longer seem to be as burdened as we are. These candidates are the ones to consider asking them if they are willing to mentor us. Not all are willing, so you may have to ask a few candidates before you gain agreement from one. Once you have one we need to engage them regularly to gain as much as we can from them without encroaching upon their time too much.

It can take more than a lifetime to learn all the significant lessons to living a baggage free life, so the insight from others shortens the number of years, months and days it takes to help us get on a path to not only shedding baggage we have been carrying for years, but to begin a way of navigating life where we are acquiring less and less new baggage as well. This collection of baggage didn't show up just overnight. It was acquired over our lifetime, so it will take some time to reverse it, but progress is the key to improving our lives along the way. Just as we have experienced a greater weight of all our baggage over the years, when we begin reversing this trend we start noticing the weight is beginning to decrease. Just like the tendency to become more and more discouraged by things getting worse, it is also very encouraging to have things getting better.

A mentor makes all the difference and there is nothing like

having an experienced guide in your corner, however we have to do the work of shedding our baggage. Some well-intentioned individuals, who are willing to help us, but are not mentors may try to solve your problems for you or fix you by doing some of the work themselves. While this sounds like it might help it actually robs us, the protégé of the experience, of learning how to navigate our lives ourselves. So, a good mentor will share how they accomplished putting their past into its proper perspective, but it will be up to you to actually try their techniques to put your past into its proper perspective. Bit-by-bit you will open up and view with the help of your mentor those flawed concepts, painful experiences, and negative self-talk and begin to unpack that unhealthy baggage and put it in its proper perspective.

Most of us have baggage from all over, our childhood, our adolescence, our young adult and maybe our adult years as well. We also have our family, friends, enemies, authority figures, and events of all kinds and then we have the particular way we have chosen to repeat it all to ourselves over the years. All of this is usually too much for one mentor to guide us through. You will need many mentors over the course of your life and so as attached and as comfortable you might become with a mentor that has walked with you, it is likely they will only be with you for a season. This is no reason to not invest. This is the way most relationships are, they begin, they run their course and they end. Few exist for a lifetime and when they do they are very special, but shorter relationships can be just as meaningful and valuable, since longevity is only a single characteristic of a relationship.

So, our first mentor will help us for a time, then when that relationship ends either by their request or ours, we can go in search of our next mentor. We may be tempted to leave mentors for many reasons, but some reasons are not that wise. If you begin to think your mentor is describing actions and methods that are just too hard, scary or just not you, then I would advise you to refrain from ending the relationship.

Rather, I would suggest talking to your mentor about your thoughts and feelings and they probably will be able to relate to having the same reactions at times themselves. However, if your mentor no longer has time, energy or interest to continue working with you, then it is time to move on.

For some issues, I have used clergy, counselors and therapists, especially when I was in between mentors. While these professionals can often make great mentors, it is also a great baggage shedding practice to cultivate new acquaintances and relationships in ever widening circles. It is from these new relationships we can identify and acquire our future mentors. This may be uncomfortable, but you may be surprised where you will meet people who have learned to put their baggage in its proper perspective.

Accomplished people may already have many people they are already mentoring and they can only devote so much time to others outside of their families, friends and other responsibilities. It is rarely personal, but if a transition is a significant challenge you have difficulty overcoming, then you may want to enlist the services of a life coach, counselor or therapist. You can meet with them and simply tell them you want to enlist the assistance of a mentor or a new one and that you are struggling with identifying and securing one. They should be more than willing to assist you with this goal since this is closely related to what they do for a living.

Practicing Forgiveness

Much of the baggage we hang onto is linked to our judgment of others who have hurt us in some way or another. In most instances, they really have done something to us, but there are instances where we perceive we have been hurt by others and they have not done anything to us at all. However, we had an expectation that they have not lived up to resulting in us feeling hurt or angry at them for not meeting our expectations. While this most often happens with people that are close to us, it can also happen with acquaintances, public figures, companies, governments, and groups of people such as races and nationalities. The end result is the same. We perceive that something happened and we are upset and believe they are to blame.

The thoughts and feelings surrounding this can be very consuming and the common reaction is anger. When we think about how we were unjustly treated we relive the event and re-feel the feelings and tend to stay angry. This is often referred to as a resentment from the Latin words, re (again) and sentire (to feel) or *to feel again*. When we are angry about one thing then we are more likely to become angry about other things. This can create a huge burden in our lives since every irritation can serve as a triggering experience as we are emotionally reminded of our unprocessed anger. Sadly, often the things we are mad about happened years ago and are often long forgotten even by us.

This is where forgiveness becomes so valuable to us as a practice. First off, our resistance to forgive is often rooted in our misconception of what forgiving means. While the forgiveness of a debt means to grant relief from payment, forgiving a person, place or thing about some injustice is a much different act. When we forgive acts of injustice towards us it has more to do with us releasing ourselves of the judgment and negative emotions associated with being the victim.

The more we think about how we have been wronged the angrier we get. No matter how victimized we may be, our hyper focus on the person, place or thing we associate with us being taken advantage of becomes our prison. No matter how much we yell, bully, protest, intimidate, throw things, torture, kill, or hurt ourselves with reckless driving, dangerous stunts, drug or alcohol use or cutting, we are the one in prison. Forgiveness is the way out. No matter how out of control it is it can be defused with one simple act. Forgive whomever we blame and walk away.

I know the first words that come to mind when I say this is, "I can't", and we know this is not true and it is time to open our eyes to the trap we have created for ourselves.

Someone either does not meet our expectations, threatens us or hurts us and we decide to let it control us by fuming for hours, days, weeks, or worse yet years, decades or a lifetime. Nothing is worth this self-created torture. Not even if we are really angry at ourselves. Sometimes we just have to forgive ourselves. We all make mistakes, say careless things, act poorly, and take advantage of situations and maybe others at one time or another. We may also need to forgive ourselves. It is not about deserving it and, IT IS NOT ABOUT THEM.

Questions you can ask yourself to see if you have any people, places or things you need to forgive are: What people, places or things am I angry with every time I think of them?

- What people, places or things do I yell at every time I think of them?
- What people, places or things do I get into arguments about with every time the subject comes up?
- What disturbing people, places or things do I frequently post about online to make sure others know what I know?

We who stay angry or are often angered by the same things over and over have become a prisoner to these people, places and things. It is like a cancer that just continues to spread and devour what is good in us. For those who have to live with us, we typically scare them. They never know what is going to set us off next and if we own firearms, drive angry, or tend to break things, we may very well be terrorizing our own family because they are never sure if a tirade is going to result in a shooting, a bad accident or broken bones. Despite being convinced that we are making the accused suffer, they often can lead perfectly pleasant lives while we continue to judge them especially when we have little or no contact with them.

Forgiveness is for us. It is a choice and we can make it at any time.

So, what if I am not sure how to forgive someone or something, what is involved?

Forgiving is the act of choosing to no longer engage in the line of thinking that takes offense or is angry about an event related to a person, place or thing. Before we are offended or angry we are thinking about the event. We may be saying to our self, "That really makes me crazy", " "I can't believe they don't know how much that bothers me", "I can't take this anymore I am going to make sure I am never nice to them again".

So instead we can adopt new thoughts to think about the object of our forgiveness. Such as, "I am going to let this go and forgive them. I am tired of being all upset over this. It is not worth my peace of mind. From now on they are getting the benefit of the doubt from me. They don't even owe me an apology since it may be that things didn't occur entirely like I thought."

Then as we begin to think of them again, we choose to think along these lines, "I know they are human and make mistakes just like I do", "They may not even realize the things that bother others", "I am wondering what they are thinking, I will go ask to see if I can better understand what is motivating them to do this", "They probably are thinking about something else entirely and don't realize what they are doing, I do this sometimes myself." If you are a praying person, then begin praying for this person, place or thing that you are wanting to forgive. Then begin to say to yourself I forgive _____. Just a simple thought programming change will begin to cease the incitement of offense or anger.

A powerful way to reprogram our thinking is to visualize taking a prison cell key ring off the wall, unlocking and opening your cell door, looking into a mirror right in your own eyes and saying, "I forgive _____". You may have to say over and over for a while until you really let go of the judgment, but believe me YOU ARE WORTH IT!

If we catch ourselves slipping back into the old thinking that is easily insulted and put out, just return to the more forgiving line of thinking. Sometimes we forgive and we take it back, if we do return to the judgement free line of thinking.

Allowing Ourselves to Grieve

We all experience loss, both big and small. Some of the common little losses are the missing shirt button, the missed opportunity to do something fun, or to see someone at an event. None of these are earth shattering, but we do experience loss when they occur and grieve. Grief over little losses may be limited, but we feel them just the same. We may do our best to ignore our grief, but it is there.

We can be irritable, angry, busy, sullen, intoxicated, depressed or maybe we feel nothing at all, but still we are affected no matter what we tell ourselves. Eventually we return back to our old selves. Many losses are accepted, forgotten, but some of us take note of each one. While more of us selectively hold on to a few petty things and continue to stew, lament, regret, or simply miss whatever was lost.

The grief we experience for big losses is much more significant. The same dynamics apply, but the stakes are much higher. Why, because the loss is much more important to us. We may not talk about it and we may not even think about it, but it can still be tremendously important to us. As a result, we are much more affected. We may tell ourselves we don't care, but typically either our behavior or our emotions reveal the loss we are experiencing.

Our initial reactions can vary from silent and catatonic shock to uncontrolled rage, but most of us fall somewhere in between. Shock, disbelief and denial are more common early reactions. This can go on for days, weeks, months or years. Some of us never stop being mortified over our loss. This is common when we lose a spouse, a child, a parent or close sibling to a sudden death or removal from our lives. Having little or no meaningful explanation can help us set a course of going nowhere with grief, but just being stuck in it.

While many have adopted the idea that grief is something experienced in well-defined stages or phases, most have probably never processed much significant grief. Depending upon who we are, what we have been taught about grief and who we let be with us while we are grieving impacts what we experience. We may be non-feeling, hateful, kind, quiet, loud, spacey, isolated, obnoxious, forgetful, angry, withdrawn, suicidal, violent, or just depressed. The most normal thing is to experience any and all of these feelings and behaviors and more.

Outside of depression most spend a good amount of time denying that the loss even occurred, saying to themselves and others, "I can't believe they are...", "This can't be happening" and, "There must be some other explanation". We all have our own path through grief, however it can become destructive when it ceases to be a journey and it becomes our destination. We can stay busy, angry, isolated or depressed for decades, if we get stuck where our grief is a destination, or we can begin the process of putting our loss in its proper perspective. While we may be in agony, even the loss of the dearest child, spouse or parent is not the end of our life. It just seems like it is. If we feed it, we can create a monster of flawed thinking that traps us in our grief.

Grieving well has a lot more to do with living than letting our grief guide our actions. When we let our emotions guide our actions we tend to believe things we know are not true, make poor choices, and place unrealistic expectations on ourselves, others and especially God. This last move is one that often cuts us off from those who can help us stay on the journey through the darkest days of our grief.

Yet for us to grieve in a way that continues the journey of putting our loss in its proper perspective we have to take actions we do not feel like doing. The same things that can help us emerge from a life full of baggage are the same ones that help us to grieve well. We have to be honest with ourselves. We have experienced loss; it really did happen. It is a fact and nothing is going to bring them back. However, it is also a fact that we will always have our memories of them. So, in some ways we will always have them with us, but what we have lost is a future with them. And we still have a future whether we like it or not without them.

We need a mentor to guide us through this haze we call grief. What are the pitfalls? How do I get unstuck? Why am I still so angry? A mentor can guide us through those questions and those times when we just don't know how to put one foot in front of the other. Grief can blind us to the clearest of facts and a mentor can help us open our eyes when we are not capable of doing so on our own.

We also need a support system. While we may be uncomfortable attending church, work, small gatherings, Sunday school, socials, etc. we need to go. Staying home all the time is not embarking upon a journey. It is choosing to make grief a destination. We may not be able to keep the same groups, but we need to be around others to stay grounded in the here and now. While we are hurting, there are others who are hurting too. We now have a greater sensitivity to other people's pain and we have a greater capacity for love. Our best new support system may be a grief-based support group such as Grief-Share or any support group that is focused on supporting each other with the day to day issues we all experience. You may not think of it this way, but grief is a participatory process.

Being of service to others can be one of the most soothing actions you can take to get a break from your heartache. When we do things for others we are taking the focus off of ourselves. When we are hurting we instinctively focus on ourselves and our pain. Yet being of service to someone else pulls us away from the constant urge to focus on ourselves and our pain. Volunteering, walking your dog, doing chores for others less capable, spending time with someone who needs guidance can all be acts which get us away from the constant self-focus that the great pain of loss can bring.

Learning more about your dilemma, by doing research and study can also be an extremely helpful practice when journeying through our grief. Reading about grief and how others have navigated it can be helpful as well as learning about some of the more typical reactions people can have to grief. While we all grieve differently, there are common experiences that may be disorienting to us unless we can read or hear it described. Gaining this knowledge can help us to help ourselves by not fighting the natural grief process, but allowing it to take its course.

Finally, prayer and meditation can also bring us peace. While we may find that our typical results no longer occur while we are grieving, the continued practice can provide a forum for us to converse with ourselves and God about the challenges we are experiencing,

Research and Study

This agent of change is a natural extension of the others. Besides disclosing information, enlisting a mentor and engaging a support system, a baggage shedding lifestyle involves a life of learning more each day. As our awareness of ourselves and the world around us grows, the need for more information is often required to put what we experience into its proper perspective. The more we grow in our skills and experience we may eventually become able to process significant encounters with people, places and things as they occur.

Key topic categories for this change agent are ourselves, others and spiritual topics. These categories of information are the ones that can help us the most to unpack our baggage. Similar to the advantages to working with a mentor and having a support system regularly researching and studying information about ourselves, others and spiritual topics expands our reservoir of knowledge. And knowledge gives us the power to make better choices. Collecting information from others in person is often more impactful due to the personal connection, unfortunately there is a limit to how many people we can meet and spend time with and absorb the benefit of their lessons learned. However, when they publish we can read or view video of their perspectives. So, while engaging a mentor and support system is critical to shedding our baggage, seeking knowledge outside of these resources expands our knowledge base even further. Additionally, a great characteristic of excellent mentors and members of our support system are ones who are also active researchers and students.

One trap we can fall into is becoming convinced we already know all we need to know about a topic. When we take this stance, we cut ourselves off from being enlightened any further. When we cut ourselves off from other people, their knowledge and their experiences, we significantly limit our learning. Beyond the new information we gain, we are also motivated to be better critical thinkers when we discover the wide variation of perspectives about ourselves, others and spiritual topics. So, if you find yourself limiting yourself to one source for your information you are likely cutting yourself off from learning and you have likely drifted to a pursuit of seeking comfort to only read and listen to what you already know and agree with. Even in the pursuit of spiritual beliefs and relationships where there are sacred texts, it is good to expose ourselves to multiple translations and commentaries to expand on what we know.

For those that are already avid researchers and students about topics that interest them or that are related to their passions or their vocations, they already have an advantage to being familiar with this practice. However, you may find that you may have to shift some of your energy to focus on topics related to yourself, others and spiritual topics to improve your ability to put more and more of your baggage into its proper perspective. We may encounter ourselves through our observation of the choices we make and the results we experience, but some tend to run in more of an automatic mode. From listening to others about their self-observations we will likely be motivated to consider what similarities or differences lie between ourselves and others. Eventually we will begin to observe certain patterns of behavior and characteristics that we tend to exhibit. For instance, some might observe that they tend to be passive rather than aggressive, insecure rather than confident, friendly rather than aloof, thoughtful rather than carefree, etc. Noticing things about ourselves gives a window into ourselves and that opens the door to deciding if we like the characteristic and the results it creates.

While this may sound unproductive it is actually quite important. No correction is made to things about ourselves we are unaware of and just becoming aware is half the battle. In the course of our study of ourselves we begin to see more and more of ourselves and over time come to a judgment as to whether we like what we see or not. Being close to others and disclosing what we were thinking when we did something opens up our understanding of how we have many things in common with others while being very unique as well.

Researching ourselves and others often falls within the same pursuit. There are many authors and educational material you can expose yourself to and gain a better appreciation about why we and the people around us do the things they do. While there are the obvious psychology focused materials, there are also many great insightful, inspirational and biographical works of well-known leaders in psychology, religion, philosophers, scientists, inventors, artists, athletes, and average people who are sons and daughters, parents and grandparents, single or married like many of us.

While you will find your own sources, here for example are some of the more significant resources that shaped my understanding of myself, others and spiritual beliefs in my lifetime so far.

Cheaper by the Dozen by Gilbreth and Carey taught me the value of making good use of my time.

Profiles in Courage by John F. Kennedy taught me that courage isn't just about physical matters, it can also be about unpopular choices.

I'm OK, You're OK by Thomas Harris taught me about my perceptions and my communication with others.

The Bible (Psalms, Proverbs, and New Testament) taught me that God loves me, forgives me and I have a purpose although this took years for this to sink in.

I Ain't Much, Baby--But I'm All I've Got by Jess Lair taught me about self-esteem and that I am not alone.

On Death and Dying by Elisabeth Kübler-Ross taught me that grief, while it may have components most of us experience, we all do it uniquely.

The Teachings of Don Juan by Carlos Castaneda taught me that other cultures have wisdom, such as living each day as it were your last.

The Search for Serenity by Lewis F. Presnall taught me about emotions and pain and the lessons they can teach.

The Greatest Miracle in The World by Og Mandino taught me I am a miracle that I can always be grateful for.

The God Memorandum by Og Mandino taught me that poor simple people have great value.

The Big Book of Alcoholics Anonymous taught me to become intentional and methodical about my approach to life and solving problems.

Sobriety and Beyond and Sobriety Without End by Father John Doe taught me the concepts of letting go and letting God.

Bradshaw on the Family by John Bradshaw taught me the dynamics of family interactions.

The Prophet by Kahlil Gibran taught me that wisdom can be in the form of poetry.

A Course in Miracles by the Foundation for Inner Peace taught me to be much more aware of myself and the world around me.

Codependent No More by Melody Beattie taught me the concept of detaching with love.

The Secret of Staying in Love by John Powell taught me that love is a decision.

Getting to Yes by Fisher and Ury taught me to step back and see the rest of the story beyond theirs and mine.

Celebration of Discipline by Richard Foster taught me about prayer and meditation.

The Material World by Peter Menzel taught me the diversity of the world's families.

The Power of Positive Thinking by Norman Vincent Peale taught me that I have to act to make things better every day down to the very the very thoughts I choose to have.

Boundaries by Cloud and Townsend taught me that it is OK to say no and where the line of responsibility exists between all others and myself.

Speaking the Truth in Love by Dr. Kenneth C. Haugk taught me that people need to always engage one another with love in order to shed their baggage collecting lifestyle.

Forgotten God by Francis Chad taught me that the Holy Spirit is the one to look to for guidance and strength.

Touchstones Daily Meditations for Men by Hazelden taught me to take five minutes each day to be inspired.

Network by Bugbee and Cousins taught me about the gifts that God has given me.

The 10 Commandments of Dating by Young & Adams taught me how to take it slowly.

The Five Love Languages by Dr. Gary Chapman taught me the unique ways we all perceive and receive love.

The Purpose Driven Life by Rick Warren taught me the value of knowing your purpose in life.

Journeying Through Grief book series books 1-4 by Dr. Kenneth C. Haugk taught me there are many instructive and comforting messages for the first few years when grieving the loss of a loved one.

Factfulness by Hans Rosling taught me that the news about the world is often very misleading and things are much better than I usually think.

The Body Keeps Score by Bessel van der Kolk M.D. taught me that the impact of baggage wreaks havoc on our brain and bodies and how professionals are now well equipped to help us leave behind the war zones of our past.

Prayer and Meditation

If you managed to get through the previous sections on spiritual topics, but generally are weary about such topics I want to urge you to stick with me just a little way further. Spiritual topics are often polarizing and thus they tend to be some of the most devastating types of baggage we can carry. Additionally, any group whether it be atheist, agnostics, monotheists, or polytheists have a wide range of behavior and perspectives on these two practices. This is in part why there are so many divisions, denominations, sects, and variations of behavior and lifestyles within each of these groups.

The topics of prayer and meditation for some are just nonsense since they are associated with religion, although meditation has become a bit less controversial with the mindfulness focus away from religion. There are some practices common in most religions and spiritual pursuits that have great potential to bring a person great benefits and these are prayer and/or meditation. The problem is that many of us bristle at the context or the specifics employed. However, there are many applications of these common practices.

The rejection of anything we have not heard of before is a form of baggage. Some methods of prayer and meditation may repeatedly use the name of their God over and over while others refrain because it is considered too holy. The greatest divide comes between those of different beliefs and between any belief and the non-believers or irreligious (the ones that are atheist, agnostic or believe nothing in particular). As strange as it may seem, to some there are atheist prayers, agnostic prayers and prayer for people who believe nothing in particular. Likewise, there are atheist meditation practices, agnostic meditation and meditation for people who believe nothing in particular.

While we may have always been presented with prayer and, or meditation as religious they are practices that are used by a much broader population because they bring benefits of focus and calm that many find pleasant and helpful. So, if you have not explored the practices of prayer and/or meditation then I would urge you to consider them for the benefits they can provide as you change your lifestyle to a baggage shedding lifestyle.

This chapter is about to fork into three paths. The first path is one for the readers that are certain there is not a God or that it is something that is not possible for us to know. I want you to read the rest of this chapter and then skip to the chapter called, The Journey Begins. For those readers that believe in God, God(s) or something more specific, but you don't make it a very active or central part of your life, I want you to skip the rest of this chapter and read the next chapter called, For the Inactive Believer, then afterwards skip to the chapter called, Addressing Root Causes versus Symptom. For those that have an active faith In God, multiple Gods or something more specific and it is a very central part of your life, I want you to skip to the chapter called, For the Active Believer.

For the Atheist or Agnostic

Most of us were exposed to one or a limited number of spiritual perspectives or practices either in the home, school or socially. Many of us often form an impression of religions and their practices as being without proof, merit or common sense.

When we reject religion or other spiritual perspectives, we tend to reject the belief and anything we associate with it. This is another form of baggage. Instead of learning something specific from an experience we tend to generalize the lesson and create a larger set of associated things to avoid. A cruel man of God is not necessarily representative of all men of God. Likewise, a cruel atheist is not representative of all atheists. Rather, all we can reliably take away from those experiences is that those individuals were cruel.

The same can apply to activities such as prayer and meditation. While members of one religion will reject people praying to a

God since they have no God in their religion. Others will reject meditation as being a secular practice offensive to God. Yet prayer and meditation have great benefits for people of all spiritual persuasions, including atheists and agnostics. How can that be? Well not all prayers are to a God and not all meditations are exclusive to any spiritual practice or perspective. We may have only been exposed to these practices in association with a religion, but these practices are far more universally practiced. Prayers can be affirming, encouraging, inspirational, requesting, thankful, as well as unspoken, written, printed on flags and wheels, disk drives, fans, leaves, steps in a dance, lyrics in a song, chants, movements, silence and stillness. Prayers can be to God, a spirit, a group, nature, you name it.

Likewise, with meditations, some religions and spiritual practices have meditation as a central practice. However, there are many people in the world that have been introduced to meditation simply as a relaxation technique without any connection or reference to a particular religion or spiritual belief. If the idea of praying or meditating offends you, then it is likely you have spiritual baggage telling you that these practices are not OK.

Not all prayer starts with God. Not all mediations start with or include religious passages. Some just have words of guidance and motivation to carry on with the new path we are undertaking. The people that you have begun spending time with for support, the mentor(s) you have engaged, will likely have shared with you what they have found serves as a regular guide and motivation for them. It may be literature, poetry, inspiring passages in daily readers, songs, music, or phrases. So, while people who have represented all that is repulsive about religion, faith or God to you may have also been encouraging, readers of literature, poetry, inspiriting passages in daily readers, songs, music or phrases, that is no reason to discount or reject all of these practices. And yet we often do it because it is our natural reaction to avoid anything associated with people, places or things that have caused us pain.

Meditation also has a diverse array of techniques, approaches and reputation. While it is mainly a practice to learn how to better focus one's mind on something or nothing for a purpose such as being present in the moment, gaining insight or a new or preferred perception or state of mind. Meditation can take many forms based upon the desired result. Non-religious people can see it as a religious or non-religious practice while some groups within religions may practice and approve of certain types of meditation while rejecting others seen as conflicting with their beliefs. Meditation is a practice viewed by many as simply a relaxation technique without any religious or spiritual connection while others associate it significantly with religious or spiritual practices. Those that see meditation as only being a tool or practice of a specific religion, faith or non-faith persuasion are simply unaware of the many ways and variations of practicing meditation. In its simplest form meditation can be the choice to focus on a thing of nature and simply appreciate its beauty in the present moment.

Keep an open mind that maybe not quite everything we have come to reject is necessary to exclude from our lives. Consider that maybe our inability to put our previous experiences in their proper perspective may be cutting us off from things that could bring us great encouragement and hope. Keep open the possibility that there may be a form of prayer and or mediation you can try and maybe embrace today to assist you on a journey to a baggage shedding lifestyle. Occasionally, people may refer to God or Higher Power or greater source of wisdom, but instead of rejecting everything else they have to say consider that the strength, wisdom and encouragement you get from your support system and mentor may collectively be that source for you.

Here are some example sources of support systems and mentors:

- Belonging to a club focused on a hobby or interest area so I can hear about, learn more, improve my practice and interact with others who can help me grow and provide insight when I encounter difficulties with my hobby or interest.

- The same can be said for a professional group or society, a support group for a specific condition, illness, dilemma, etc.
- Participating in a yoga or meditation class for the peace and calm it brings to your life.
- Attending a support group for recovery from a loss, intense emotion, an addiction, alcoholism or trying to cope with loved ones who are in recovery.
- Attending a retreat or support group because of a great loss or life change.

As we are around other people we are exposed to others, who can and often will share with us their experiences. When this happens, we benefit a great deal. Yet as soon as we spend time with others we will encounter people who think differently from us and we may be tempted to think they are wrong, naïve, or misled if they believe differently that we do.

Resist the temptation to reject the experience of others specially when they appear to have good results. I am not talking about wealth, fame, or popularity. I am talking about the results of a peaceful, purposeful and rewarding life. When you see those results in someone, they likely have something valuable to share. They may describe a path that seems repulsive to you, but it may also bring you similar results if you have an open mind and try some of the same practices yourself.

Next, skip ahead to the chapter called, The Journey Begins.

For the Inactive Believer

For those who believe in God, but for whatever reason do not actively practice that faith, we have a source of hope and direction, but are isolated from it. More than likely we were raised in a situation where faith was taught to us or we were exposed to it in school or socially through friends and we accepted it. And while we chose to believe in God we may have never taken it beyond that or if we did things didn't work out quite the way we thought it should. When we experience disappointment and heartache in the proximity of faith or religion, we tend to question why our faith or our religion didn't keep it from happening.

It is a pretty natural reaction to look for what is to blame when we are disappointed or hurt. When we are younger, newer to something, inexperienced or even a much older veteran with experience, we can easily look for some person, place or thing to blame other than ourselves. Yet, the vast majority of the time our pain or disappointment occurred because we chose to take a risk.

The inherit characteristic of a risk is that we might not succeed. And we should know from experience that we often fall short of success the very first time we try something unless we have some unusual advantage, skill or luck. So most of the time when attempting things, the first time we don't succeed. Yet, when those pursuits are really important to us the pain or disappointment can be pretty hard to accept. Once again this is what putting things in their proper perspective is all about.

Most things in life are a risk. Some things are greater risks than others. Yet when we get excited about something or it is really important to us and it is very high risk, then we are likely to be extremely disappointed if it doesn't work out. If this occurs and we expected our faith or religion to keep things from going poorly we will often blame God, religion, or the people associated with it. When we are hurt, it is hard to not take it personally and amongst our grief not put things in their proper perspective. So, we either blame or recoil and the net effect is we often stop practicing our faith instead of relying upon it. If we never make it back, then that experience of loss and disappointment is the last significant memory we have associated with our faith. After an experience like that it is easy to hold God at arm's length. We may be willing to believe still, but just not rely or depend upon our relationship with God to bring us peace.

Sometimes we are so interested in things working out the way we want, that when people try to tell us a fact-based or reasonable way to look at the risks we are taking, we may discount what they have to say or even turn on them. However, our friends typically have our best interests in mind. Here people are often trying to help you put things in their proper perspective up front, yet we have our idea of how we want things to turn out. And as if the power of concentration can make it happen, so we will sometimes focus hard repeating to ourselves how we want things to be. Yet not all things are influenced by positive or focused thinking.

The expectation that God is going to cure a sick parent every time is not realistic. God is not going to mend every marriage, even our parents' marriage. God is not going to keep horrible illnesses from killing and deforming innocent men, women and children. It is just not the way it works. The world is full of illness, poverty, and victims because there are always going to be people who choose to do careless, selfish, unkind and unspeakable things. As a result, many unfortunate things occur over time.

Western monotheistic religions all address God's desire to be worshiped. If we were not granted free will, then any regard would not be by choice but by compulsion. However, with the freedom to make many positive choices, man can also make many negative or destructive choices.

We have to stay engaged in our faith in times of great trouble and disappointment, if we want to be comforted. As things change in our lives we have to adjust to the differences in our surroundings. So, the practice of faith and the journey of leading a baggage shedding lifestyle is an ongoing journey. So, when we are hurt, disappointed, devastated we need to reach out, talk to others, a mentor, those who support us and do the other things that nurture and inspire us like read, pray and meditate on things that sooth our wounded soul.

Next, skip ahead to the chapter called, The Journey Begins.

For the Active Person of Faith

For those who are active in our faith we read about faith, we attend events that build our faith, we seek to be inspired and challenged and we will often be a part of being the hands and feet of God to others in service. We can do it all maybe even select ministry as a vocation and still not let go of some significant pieces of baggage we are carrying. We may be inspired and motivated and working with others, but unless we are able to put those remaining significant events in our lives into their proper perspective, we will carry that load till the day we die. So even having an active faith and great devotion in your world of faith, God rarely takes away our baggage without significant work upon our part.

As good as we can feel in the arms of faith there is still the work to be done. Our part includes being honest with ourselves and others, sharing and receiving feedback from a mentor, being engaged with a positive and nurturing support system, reading about the journeys of others and engaging in our faith with regular if not constant prayer and meditation. It is a lifestyle that puts us in the best posture to shed the baggage we have and to begin building strategies to not collect new baggage as we continue to live our lives.

Meditation has probably become more about being still, being present and being in the here and now. The more often we can clear our minds of all the future what ifs and the past would-a, could-a, should-a reviews, the better we can stay there for longer portions of our day. Our minds are like sophisticated video recorders, with one tuner for picking up the here and now signal. Whenever we are in the past or the future we are not able to record the events of the present, thus we record no memories when we are not living in the present. If we still have a significant amount of baggage weighing us down, we are often lured away from the healthier here and now. Sometimes guided meditation is very good for this, which can come in many forms; music, exercise (yoga), focusing on our breathing only, being among and observing nature, plus many others.

Regardless of the technique that is working for you now, the result you experience should be one of being refreshed and re-laxed and very aware of the current moment in your life.

If this is you, then you are already on a very productive path and probably already have a greater sense of hope. Things are improving and you should without much trouble be able to see and feel the difference most days with little effort. If this is not yet your experience, it will come with time. However, there is one additional thing I have found that really undermines my old baggage collecting behavior and that is focusing my prayers on the very things that tend to create the opportunities for new baggage.

Addressing Root Causes versus Symptoms

For believers it is often accepted as a concept that we should seek God's will for us rather than our own. However, the uncer-tainty of what is God's will for some often devolves to a return of what we prefer. On the contrary, when we have a problem it is easy for us to acknowledge that the symptoms are real, undesirable and we want it solved as soon as possible. That urgency often motivates us to address the symptom we are aware of rather than the cause. This approach leaves the cause free to create more and more problems for us again and again. The value in being able to identify root causes versus their symptoms can be very significant. If every problem we ever encountered had an identified root cause, then once addressed effectively the future problems would not occur. While this may sound great, in theory we deal with symptoms most of the time. Sometimes we eventually identify the root cause by the process of elimination. However, this is not a very effective approach and without a focused effort it is very common that root causes are never identified.

Much like the illness or disease that will not go away, in time, the causes for our reoccurring behaviors continue to motivate behaviors in a way that seems very natural to us. When these reoccurring behaviors are positive and constructive, such as maintaining our bank accounts and being on time, then it is a benefit. But when the behavior is destructive, such as being arrogant or critical of others, then it will continue to create havoc in our relationships and our lives.

The difference between root causes and symptoms can be difficult to identify for those without practice. Based upon the concept of cause and effect in its simplest form, there is one cause and one associated effect. However, it is very common for there to be many effects created by a single cause and there can be multiple causes to create a single identified effect. Most of what we identify easily as problems are symptoms. It is not that common to see the root cause of a problem without some analysis and often it is hard for us to make the identification objectively. This is why we need help. Even in business when the causes and the symptoms are not personal, it often takes a team of co-workers or outside consultants to accurately perform a root cause analysis.

Our baggage of our bad or poor lessons learned shape our character. As a result, our character can contain unhelpful characteristics. Common examples include fear, jealousy and pride. When present these unhelpful characteristics can be the root cause for our choices and our behavior. As we employ the tools (concepts and actions) of a baggage shedding lifestyle the problems in our lives begin to diminish. However, we can make significant progress if we can identify the root causes of our problems and apply these new tools to address them.

Taking the concept of addressing the root causes instead of the symptoms and using prayer together we can begin to undo problems before they have a chance to begin. A root cause focused prayer provides a means to employ your faith to laser focus you and God to address the areas of your character that result in your destructive behaviors.

If we continue on the path of dealing with symptoms we are putting ourselves in a posture to **react** to our problems at best. A root cause focused prayer takes a **proactive** posture towards the parts of our lives we want to change. It takes a step back and focuses on the underlying destructive characteristics of how we respond to everyday challenges. It uses that knowledge to ask God for assistance with those underlying characteristics to proactively stop our destructive and negative behavior from disrupting our lives. Even though the fire department is nearby to react if there is a fire in your home there is always unwanted and unnecessary damage. It helps to proactively practice fire safety every day to keep fires from occurring before they have a chance to do damage. A root cause focused prayer uses this same principle; eliminate as many things that we do that cause ourselves problems **before they occur**. With this in practice, over time less and less of the symptoms of destructive and/or negative behavior will be present in your life. More and more you will notice that your challenges will begin to change and less of them will be the old familiar problems. While this approach will not eliminate all reoccurring problems, it will go a long way to address the ones that are self-induced.

It is not always realistic to identify the past experience that lies at the root of a destructive behavior, but it is reasonable to get close by identifying the part of your character that is near the cause of the behavior. The level of your character that is practical at best to identify is at the characteristic level. What created this characteristic in you and getting it addressed is between you, God and the others you involve going forward.

Focusing on the characteristic level with God will direct your collective energy on addressing these areas of your character. God may choose to miraculously remove the destructive parts of your character in a short period of time or He may let you work on it a little at a time. You may need to reconnect with some memories and emotions from old experiences and consider if the perspectives and motivations you walked away with are worth keeping. Either way you will see improvement and gain the benefits in your improved behavior and results each day going forward.

Selecting Your Areas of Focus

Besides the objects of our own desire, there are many suggestions on things to pray for. My experience has been that praying about the removal and replacement of the destructive root cause characteristics in my character is one of the most productive practices I have adopted. Yet until I identified some of my root cause characteristics, I bounced around from the crisis of the day to any suggestion I had heard recently about what to pray about.

The practical starting point for most of us is to consider a list of candidates for our key characteristics. More than likely a few have already been mentioned to you before or you may recognize them in yourself. Try to resist deciding or editing out any possibilities right away. Make note of all possibilities and then set it down for a while. Below is a sample list of possible characteristics and their opposing asset. There are additional copies in the appendix.

For the flaw/asset pairs that neither are much like you, skip them and circle the flaw or asset that are significantly like you.

Flaw		Asset
Aggressive	vs.	Gentle
Angry	vs.	Calm
Arrogant	vs.	Humble
Conceited	vs.	Modest
Controlling	vs.	Accepting
Critical	vs.	Encouraging
Dishonest	vs.	Honest
Envious	vs.	Content
Fearful, Fear	vs.	Courage, Faith
Forgetful	vs.	Responsible
Gluttonous	vs.	Moderate
Greedy	vs.	Charitable

Hateful	vs.	Loving
Hypersensitive	vs.	Tolerant
Inconsiderate	vs.	Thoughtful
Intolerant	vs.	Understanding
Jealous	vs.	Trusting
Judgmental	vs.	Understanding
Lazy	vs.	Industrious
Lust	vs.	Chastity
Mean	vs.	Kind
Perfectionism	vs.	Realistic
Pessimistic	vs.	Optimistic
Prejudiced	vs.	Open-minded
Pride	vs.	Humility
Rash	vs.	Self-controlled
Resentful	vs.	Forgiving
Self-centered	vs.	God-centered
Self-hating	vs.	Self-accepting
Selfish	vs.	Generous
Stubborn	vs.	Willing
Suspicious	vs.	Trusting
Unrealistic	vs.	Realistic
Unreliable	vs.	Trustworthy
Vindictive	vs.	Forgiving
Violent	vs.	Gentle
Vulgar	vs.	Polite
Wasteful	vs.	Thrifty

It is helpful to know both your more significant flaws and assets to help know what can be focused on for improvement and what character strengths you already have. It may seem distasteful to you to appear to reduce your character to a few embarrassing characteristics. Becoming aware of our character flaws is often uncomfortable early on, but we have to become aware of them in order to improve upon them. As you consider your list of character flaws you will likely begin to identify that they are the likely cause of many bad outcomes in your life.

Now you can keep this list to yourself, but eventually it would be best to have a few trusted persons validate them for you.

If you don't have anyone you trust to validate this for you then just keep this information for your own benefit for now and skip to the next section called, Addressing Root Causes in Prayer.

Once you believe you have a fairly complete list then set it aside and consider who can best help you validate your list. Consider who are the individuals who have known you best over the years? It is best to stay away from family members since they often have various agendas for us that can cloud their judgment. These individuals can be anybody who has had a good opportunity to observe your behavior, in a variety of settings. It helps when these individuals are known to have journeyed through very tough times and they have emerged successfully. A person like this is usually in a better position of making a more accurate assessment of another person's behavior without significant bias.

If you are unsure how to make such a request you can simply tell them you are seeking to improve part of your character by minimizing the more destructive and/or negative characteristics. While you know they are not a professional they have had the opportunity to observe you and you would appreciate their observations in helping you to select the best characteristics to focus on. There are three copies of the Characteristic Observation Survey in the appendix that you can copy or remove to hand out.

The surveys provide a list of positive and negative characteristic pairs. Considering each pair, a continuum with the positive characteristic on one end and the negative characteristic on the other, the tool asks the participant to identify the more prominent of these characteristics. The more neutral or less significant evidence of either characteristic require no mark. For the ones where the negative characteristic is identified, these are your best candidates for root cause characteristics.

This exercise is best conducted with people you believe have your best interest as a priority. Before you ask anyone for feedback of this kind you need to prepare yourself to receive the feedback. One likely reaction to the feedback is you probably won't like it. It will probably be painful and maybe insulting to read. You might find yourself thinking, "Why I never knew they thought this way about me" and you may be tempted to argue or disagree with them about their feedback. Do not give in to the temptation to argue or disagree. Remember you asked them to be honest and give their observations, not to say nice things about you. Simply thank them for taking the time and assisting you. Actually, the best approach when receiving this written feedback is to not read it at all when you receive it until you are alone. This way you will have time to process whatever emotions arise from the information.

If you have feedback from multiple individuals, then look for the most common characteristics among them, including your own list. Since it is common to either tend to minimize our deficiencies or to hyper focus upon them, avoid the temptation to create a list of final characteristics that is amazingly short or long, somewhere between six and twelve is probably just about right. If you fall a little bit inside this range that is fine, but going beyond twelve is probably going to undermine the effectiveness of the prayer.

Addressing Root Causes in Prayer

Prayer is often as unique as the believer. It can be informal or formal, unspoken thought or spoken clearly where others can hear. It can be spontaneous or borrowed from prayer books. Literally, it can be anything from a brief utterance of a few words to a long confession or conversation since it really is a conversation with God. Depending upon the communities of faith you are a part of, if any, your method of prayer may be very different than the approach the Root Cause Prayer presents. This difference may be uncomfortable, yet I would encourage you to be open-minded.

We often pattern our approach to prayer based upon those we are exposed to and respect. You may have studied on the history of prayer or researched prayer practices as a means of improving your prayer life and relationship with God. If you are set about how you are supposed to pray then this approach to prayer may not seem appropriate to you, but I encourage you to be open minded. The Root Cause Prayer is not required to be a person's exclusive prayer, but it can be. It can be added to whatever prayer practices you have in place. However, there are key elements that are essential to include to get significant results.

If repeated on a continuous basis the Root Cause Prayer reinforces to you and God that these are the key things you want to address. If we create a prayer that says the same thing every day some may wonder if this will make it become meaningless. To some this statement may seem odd since some religions teach little else than standard prayers. It is true that the mindless reciting of memorized prayers may have a limited effect on the prayer experience, but the idea is to thoughtfully come up with a prayer that strategically focuses on the areas of our character that are root causes of our behavioral problems.

The Root Cause Prayer is structured to include gratitude, requests to have our negative characteristics removed, as well as requests for guidance into more positive actions and service to others. This way whenever we pray we are focusing on the things that are most impactful for us: Being grateful for the things in and about our lives, asking for help with the root cause areas that cause us the most trouble and heartache, asking for guidance into a more positive direction and asking for things for others. If done at the beginning of each day, you will start your day off with a powerful time with God expressing your gratitude, targeted requests and service to others. You may not feel great every day you do this, but you will likely feel much better the majority of the days you include this, approach. Let's take a more detailed look at the components of the root cause prayer.

Gratitude in General

Since I have found that an attitude of gratitude always enhances my day, I start all my prayers including this one with Thanking God for this Day. Yes, I may feel like it is a crummy day. I may not like the weather or what I have to do that day, but remember our feelings are not the best guide for our choices. I know I am very fortunate to have the life I am living and choosing to be glad about my circumstances is once again a choice I have independent of my current emotions. Whether I feel like it or not I start each prayer off with "Thank you God for this day." And by the time I have said it I have already logged a more positive view of my circumstances in my brain. After more than twenty years of adding this to the beginning of my prayers including my Root Cause Prayer I have little trouble being grateful. Yet, I do not always feel grateful and I suspect I never will. However, I rarely doubt how fortunate I am anymore and that is a great frame of mind to have the majority of the time. It certainly didn't start out that way.

Thank you, God, for this day.

Removal

Next, there is the request to remove the characteristics that I need to have addressed. "God, please remove from me the characteristics of (for example) lust, selfishness, self-centeredness, pride, jealousy and fear" Now if we stop here, God may or may not remove them per His will for us. God sometimes answers prayer requests with, "No" and "Wait" in addition to "Yes". God rarely removes something from us that took somewhere between a few years to a lifetime to create. Yet, continuing to petition Him with your desires keeps you focused on what is most getting in your way. But let's say for instance the best possible scenario occurs and this characteristic is removed. What is going to take its place? Remember we are creatures of habit.

If confronted with situations where you typically act out in a destructive way, it would be great if you no longer responded in the same old destructive or negative way, but what would be even better is if you responded the opposite constructive or positive way. This is where we are headed next.

So far, we have:

Thank you, God, for this day.

God, please remove from me the characteristics of lust, selfishness, self-centeredness, pride jealousy and fear.

Replacement

At the heart of the Root Cause Prayer are the requests for removal and replacement. Now that we have listed and requested for removal our list of undesirable characteristics, it is time to request replacements. This way when opportunities arise that we would have normally acted in an undesirable way, we will have God's assistance in becoming aware and carrying out the opposite, more constructive and/or positive actions. So, going with the above sample list, the opposites would be actions of chastity for lust, generosity for selfishness, God-centeredness for self-centeredness, humility for pride, trust for jealousy and faith for fear. So, the next line of our Root Cause Prayer would be, "God, please guide me into the actions of chastity, generosity, God-centeredness, humility, trust and faith. So, now I have expressed gratitude to God in general, asked Him to remove my key undesirable characteristics and to guide me into the opposite healthier actions.

So far, we have:

Thank you, God, for this day.

God, please remove from me the characteristics of lust, selfishness, self-centeredness, pride jealousy and fear.

God, please guide me into the actions of chastity, generosity, God-centeredness, humility, trust and faith.

Gratitude in Greater Detail

At this point, here is where we can express our gratitude in greater detail, once again thought out for the long term. This is not about how I feel or think today. This list should be about what specifically you are most grateful for in a little bit greater detail. For me it looks like this. God, thank you for my family, friends and co-workers, my opportunities and my experiences, my memories and my emotions and most of all, God my relationship with you. Now you may think this flows better with the two gratitude sections together and that is fine. It was more like me to talk in general first and then become more specific, but the order is not anywhere as important as the content being consistent and in your own voice. So now we have:

Thank you, God, for this day.

God, please remove from me the characteristics of lust, selfishness, self-centeredness, pride jealousy and fear.

God, please guide me into the actions of chastity, generosity, God-centeredness, humility, trust and faith.

God, thank you for my family, friends and co-workers, my opportunities and my experiences, my memories and my emotions and most of all, God my relationship with you.

Service to Others

Being of service to others has always been a great healing activity for me. Most of the miracles I had witnessed in my life up until this point were ones where I had gotten out of the way and let God guide me when working with someone else. Whether it was listening, serving food, repairing a home, sharing my experience or even confronting unacceptable behavior, it was like having a front row seat to the unbelievable healing that can occur if you let God work through you.

In my lowest points in life when I have been most tempted to isolate from others because of my feelings of brokenness, when I have worked with others even in the simplest of ways I began to heal. When we work with others we are hard pressed to continue to focus on ourselves. When we place the focus on someone else, we learn a great deal about not only them but ourselves and what God can do when we get out of the way and just make ourselves an instrument of His peace. This is why the Root Cause Prayer concludes with prayers for others.

You may have a much different way of thinking on this topic of what to pray for others. I travel in circles where there are regular requests for prayer from others. Prayers for healing and protection, prayers for opportunity and prayers for guidance and strength, but I figure ultimately people want to know God's Peace which can transcend all understanding.

The Root Cause Prayer concludes with prayers for God's Peace for all those we know who are in pain. Now you are probably thinking, "How do I know who is or is not in pain?" My conclusion based upon my knowledge of myself and others is that we all are experiencing pain to some degree each and every day. And just like a smile, a kind word, a warm meal, medicine, a coat, a hug or the knowledge we are loved, I figure we can all use God's Peace each and every day. So, I believe this is one of the greatest gifts we can give to others while in prayer. You may prefer to make this Intercessory part of the prayer more specific to each person or to limit it to only people you are close to, but it always makes it more likely to be implemented if we keep it simple. It makes more sense and I am much more likely to consistently pray daily for others if I keep it simple and I do not discriminate.

So therefore, I pray for God to grant His Peace upon every person in the world that is suffering in hunger, pain, illness, persecution, poverty, strife, prejudice, loss, violence and incarceration. Then I do the same for the groups of people meaningful to me. Then, I pray for God to grant His Peace upon every person from my old neighborhoods, schools and churches. Then, I pray for God to grant His Peace upon every person at my church, workplace and places I volunteer. Then, I pray for God to grant His Peace upon every person from my support groups. Then, I pray for God to grant His Peace upon every person in my family This includes first off, my immediate and complete family, my ex-wife and even my wife's ex-spouse. Why? We are all God's children and we all deserve God's Peace. I am already on my knees and it will do my character and me good to wish them the best gift I can when I pray with God regularly by asking that God grant them His peace as well. If you have another approach that will accomplish the same thing, Great! Then pray that, but it really needs to be in a similar spirit, not some back handed prayer like "God, I hope you give them what they deserve." That kind of prayer is already God's business, not ours, and also it does nothing constructive for our character or spiritual growth. So now we have:

Thank you, God, for this day.

God, please remove from me the characteristics of lust, selfishness, self-centeredness, pride jealousy and fear.

God, please guide me into the actions of chastity, generosity, God-centeredness, humility, trust and faith.

God, thank you for my family, friends and co-workers, my opportunities and my experiences, my memories and my emotions and my most of all, God my relationship with you.

God, please grant your Peace to All those in the world who are suffering with hunger, pain, illness, persecution, poverty, strife, prejudice, loss, violence and incarceration, God please grant them a little bit of your peace today. For my past neighborhood, school, church and recovery friends, God please grant them a little bit of your peace today.

For my current church family and staff, coworkers at His Story Coaching and Counseling and clients and my fellow Stephen Ministers and care receivers, God please grant them a little bit of your peace today. Support groups Stepping Stones, Grapevine Unity and Preston Men's Group. God please grant them a little bit of your peace today. Carla and I, David and Jonathan, Robert, Michelle and Kaylie, Mike, John, Lauren and Pete, Chad and Enid, Ella and Colin, Bubba, Pam and Brianna, Susan, Guy, Paige, Robert, Lola and Teddy, Scott and Lynette, Jeff and Cathy and Jane. Dylan, Jordan and Landon, Elizabeth, Jessica and Alex. Al and Kim, Sharon and Carman, Brandon and Colin. God please grant them all a little bit of your peace today.

I then proceed through a listing of specific friends and co-workers that I have interacted with lately that are on my mind.

Often, this last part of the prayer can vary significantly because of how many people come to mind. The point is to not exclude ones which are unpleasant. Just love them enough to wish them God's Peace. Imagine the effect upon your character just by being of service to others by praying for them.

Timing

Everybody has their approach to timing and anytime is a good time to pray. My best days are filled with prayer, but my busier and more distracted days may only have one or two prayers. What works best for me is to develop a routine that is independent of location, your schedule and even your preferences. For one, the Root Cause Prayer is fairly brief and typically takes at most five to ten minutes. Yet if I start my day with this prayer, then I have encouraged myself to consciously focus on being grateful, asked God for help with those issues most central to my poor behavior, taken positive action where I am typically motivated to do otherwise and prayed for others. Each day, even when I pray mindlessly, I am reminded of what is most important for me to keep in mind. Day-after-day, week-after-week, month-after-month and year after year this tradition of prayer in the morning has demonstrated to me that it is a practice with significant results. And absolutely no one I know has been hurt by it, so it is a pretty safe bet that it is a good idea to put into practice. The only catch is that if you do not keep it up, it cannot help you. Pick a point in your daily routine that will work for you and insert a targeted prayer.

The Results

What is amazing is the simplicity of the prayer in contrast to the overwhelming improvement it creates. In the business world this would be referred to as an off the chart return on investment. Just imagine if the problem areas of your character were all of the sudden becoming the positive opposites. Instead of being a pain for yourself and those around you, imagine what it would be like if you were all of the sudden being noticed for being the positive opposite. This is what happens when you consistently partner with God to do what you alone cannot.

When the idea to do this came about, I began writing out what the prayer might look like. At first, I was excited that I had a way to say all the things that I really wanted to say to God, but often would only touch on in bits and pieces in prayers. Now I was crisply and clearly expressing my appreciation fully and my requests in such a way that they were going to address the heartaches in my life in ways that I could not foresee.

After the first few days I could already tell things were improving. Week after week I was amazed how much more aware I was of the ways to act differently in situations where I typically had not been very nice. Slowly, I began to not only be aware of how I could act differently, but actually act differently as the opportunities would occur. First it would happen in one type of situation with a friend then with another and then at work, etc., Then the same improvement would show up in other aspects of my life. Pretty soon people started thanking me on a regular basis for helping them and being so understanding. The more I heard from others I couldn't help but be encouraged at the recognition, but what struck me more than anything else after a short period of time was that I noticed that I no longer was as burdened as much with the results of my own behavior.

The conflicts I used to have with family, friends and coworkers became significantly reduced. My tendency to have a negative attitude was becoming more and more scarce and my tendency to hold grudges and stay in conflict with others virtually disappeared. Over the years, I have had thousands of compliments from existing and new friends on my new positive characteristics. What used to be the norm, where my behavior was regularly creating problems for me and the people around me, now those same areas are working in a positive way in my life and the other lives I touch.

Even in the areas where God has not removed the negative characteristics from me, my behavior significantly masks my destructive tendencies. What really surprises me is that these areas also get frequent compliments from others.

Imagine the same areas of your character that have caused you so much pain over the years to be a source of appreciation by your family and friends because of God's handiwork. This is where the opportunity to minister to others actively comes in. When someone points out to me how they appreciate or ad-mire my behavior in some way, and it is one of my areas of focus with the Root Cause Prayer, I make a point to tell them it is not me. I tell them that I actually have a problem in this area and that it is God doing for me what I could not do for myself. It is a very strong testimony that often prompts them to inquire more about how this is possible and possibly work for them as well.

13. THE JOURNEY BEGINS

What does this new lifestyle look like? Who in the world lives like this and has time for work, family, friends, or fun?

Yes, I know it can seem daunting, but big pay offs almost always require a great deal of work. Our lives are no exceptions. Is it reasonable to expect someone to concentrate and implement all of the change agents at once? Absolutely not!

But as we begin to apply these concepts and baggage shedding actions in our lives, what begins to occur is a greater awareness of how we got here. Little-by-little we start seeing the dots connect. We can see how a diverse set of events, feelings, experiences and our choices brought us to the point we are today. The beauty of this awareness is that it brings even more hope that through this understanding more can be put into its proper perspective, more will be understood and eventually there will come a point when we realize that our best days of our lives are still ahead of us.

I have experienced this time and again despite the things that have occurred in between. As opposed to being defined by what happens to me, I am becoming defined by what I choose to do with what I have experienced and what I have at my disposal.

As a result of these practices, I am more mentally alert and aware than I have ever been. I tell myself things that are so skewed on the positive and gratitude side, I am constantly outnumbering the negative things I see on TV, hear from others and witness in this troubled world we live in.

Emotionally, I can still experience large swings, but now I rarely act on those emotions in ways I regret. If I am angry, I seek to understand why. If I am sad, I accept the things that are unfortunate and seek to let them go. If I feel joy, I relish it and know that it can't be sustained indefinitely. Instead of letting my emotions be the furnace that can rage out of control and burn for years, I rarely let them escalate for more than a few minutes rather than the hours, days, weeks and months that I allowed at one time. I now see my emotions as simply a barometer of what is going on in my mind.

Physically, I am no longer ashamed of my body. I am not the finest human specimen nor am I a real fan of exercise, but I am eating healthier, sleeping more, taking fewer risks with my body, getting regular checkups and in general taking much better care of myself than I ever have. It feels good to be healthier.

Socially, I have an amazing collection of circles of friends, family, acquaintances and co-workers. I work from home, so I have a limited amount of interaction with others face to face besides my wife unless I go out for lunch, dinner or attend an event during the course of the day. While I enjoy a great and diverse work environment, only so much connection can be made over the phone, so on busier days I eat breakfast down the street and talk to the servers behind the counter and the cashier. That and quietly eating my breakfast among the morning crowd satisfies my desire for face-to-face interaction. I would prefer more, but it is not always practical. However, on some nights my wife and I go dancing or out with friends, I attend support group meetings and occasionally meet with my mentor. I also attend church, participate in a small group of married couples, a group of men, and I volunteer to work with others who are hurting for various reasons.

Spiritually, I have developed a routine that is producing a conscious uplifting contact with God many times throughout the day. On great days this may count between ten and one hundred times in a day, On a rough day maybe just a few. Few days have zero moments any more. They do happen, but not that often. Usually they occur because I have become preoccupied and have squeezed out all good practices and healthy lessons I have collected over the years. It doesn't last long since I have developed a low tolerance for misery. I sing a short hymn to myself in the shower and that always softens my heart. My prayers are on my knees and targeted at my root causes.

All of these practices help me to navigate each day without as much burden of the baggage of my past. Likewise, I am not collecting new baggage and I am able to enjoy my days more and more. Also, this new lifestyle can prepare us to respond better when really bad things happen.

I once received a phone call that no one ever wants to receive that my son of thirty years was dead by his own hand. The call and how I felt about it was surreal. I immediately called my other children to let them know and to plan who was going to get to my ex-wife. Once I had those things done in react mode, I began the overwhelming search for why. He had called just the night before. It was such a good call. My mind raced, I was just recently trained to spot at risk people, where were those workbooks? In minutes, I found the section and risk checklist. Then it became apparent why I didn't notice. He had had a large number of those risk factors for fifteen years. We were all numb to his at-risk condition and behavior.

I called my mentor and he reassured me that he was there for me. I appreciated it, but I was now underwater and dulled to the overtures from others. I heard them, but they weren't very effective. Over the next few days I didn't sleep much and time just flew by as my mind raced. I gathered pictures for a memorial and one of my other sons helped me by putting it together for use at the service.

I ran some errands and ended up near where a support group I occasionally attended was meeting. I wandered in and when it came time for me to speak. I said the words aloud for the first time. My son Jerod died yesterday. That was all I could say without crying without control. Everyone was very kind, supportive and just loved on me. It helped. The next time I told someone I didn't cry as much, as hard or as long. I had initially started canceling everything I was involved in, but when the service was scheduled, so all key relatives could attend, I decided to reschedule and attend my regular activities anyway. I was a mess, people struggled with what to say to me, but it was helpful to be around others and be reminded that they were there.

This was the worst time in my life. Other tragic events came close, but this was the worst. Yet, there was still room to pray, read, reach out to a mentor and a support group and just let myself process the horrible things that had just occurred.

Two or three days later a guy I mentor called. Unaware of my troubles, he started to share with me his. I spent the next forty minutes listening to him and giving him some feedback. About thirty minutes into the call I realized that I felt great. I no longer felt under water. It hit me. I wasn't feeling bad since I was busy responding to and being there for someone else. As soon as I got off the phone I felt underwater and depressed again, but now I had a window into how I could break through the tremendous depressive feeling of being underwater. It was to be of service to others. While I worked with others on a regular basis, I started making a selfish point to do something for others a bit more so I could get a little relief.

I welcomed people who wanted to talk. As soon as I could get into what they were telling me I felt better. This was no way to deal with my grief, but it was a way to get a little bit of joy among my great pain from time to time. I attended meetings and events, services at church, and support groups and it was as if I was floating underwater, but I occasionally would get a break listening to others. But most importantly I didn't stop engaging. I prayed and felt bad, I read and felt bad, I attended meetings and felt bad, I would talk to family and feel bad, but occasionally I would work with others and I would feel normal, good, sometimes even great and that was a nice break.

None of it would have happened had I not engaged in this baggage shedding lifestyle. I knew better because this was not my first rodeo with great pain. It was just the worst one yet. I knew what to do and little by little I was able to grieve and put things in their proper perspective. It takes time, but it works and I am better for it.

It doesn't have to take a devastating tragedy to snap us into action, but no matter what the pain or experience faith can only help us if we engage and put it into practice. My distance from God is my choice. Pain and disappointment are a part of every relationship, even with God. And I am better off when I engage with God through prayer and meditation.

Eventually, the sensation of being underwater lifted and I continued to experience the pain of all the first times since Jerod had died. First look at his items in the attic, first time seeing his family, first time seeing each picture, first to hear records, etc. There were thousands of them, but most have now been experienced. And now I just miss him and carry mostly my fond memories of him by choice.

Putting Jerod's early death into its proper perspective for me means releasing myself from any responsibility for his death, forgiving him for no longer being around for me to enjoy him, and simply choosing to remember the pleasant memories among his often-troubled life. I no longer choose to torture myself for his early death and I choose to love him for the person he was and the joy he brought into my life while he was with us.

I am a blessed man that would not wish my life on you because it has been painful, but I would not trade it for the world because it is mine and God and I make one heck of a team. Each year I change things up just a little here and there, learn new things, go to different meetings, seminars or retreats, or do different types of service. Yet the path I have described is still the core of what I do and it has served me well. I hope it will serve you well too.

There is a famous comedian that used to say dieting is not necessary, just eat less and move around more. Keeping it simple is a great way to focus and stay on track.

In the case of our very complicated selves with our complicated pasts in our often very complicated lives this can be nearly impossible to do. The distractions are seemingly endless, but they are manageable. So, my version, might be do more good things and less bad things where the good things are change-creating actions of honest disclosure, having a mentor, having a support system, being of service to others, engaging in research, study, prayer and meditation. And the bad things are when I dwell on my baggage and negative characteristics. What used to be a life full of fear and pain is now a life full of laughter, faith and love. It is miraculous. I have not only experienced these results in myself, but I have seen them occur in thousands of others. Come on and join us and start leaving your baggage behind you.

P.S. Remember, nobody ever dies from being uncomfortable. So, let that be the first article of baggage you leave behind.

14. TWO LIVES RESTORED

As their lives progressed in their respective families, James and Jessica encountered more and more challenges. James experienced financial problems due to refusing promotions that would involve a good bit of walking and his son tragically sustained two head injuries during a high school football game. The result of the injuries was extensive, disrupting the rest of his high school years with intense rehabilitation. James and his wife after getting their son out of immediate danger found themselves racked with guilt over their love of sports and encouraging their son to play. Their son's doctor suggested they attend a brain injury support group. They were initially shocked there were others who were experiencing many of the same thoughts and feelings they were. They took comfort from the wisdom and support of the group (support system) and over time they found themselves being able to comfort newcomers to the group (service). Years later, after their son was able to complete high school and successfully attend college, James and his wife sought counseling since others in the group had mentioned benefiting from doing so.

Jessica's back pain increased and she began having more difficulty sewing with her declining eyesight and arthritis. She sought medical care for all three over the years, but the treatments were becoming less and less effective. Jessica's daughter suffered a miscarriage and called for help and support. Too consumed with her own pain and suffering Jessica offered only criticism. Her daughter lashed out and announced that her father was more of a mother than she was and she never wanted to talk to Jessica again. Jessica's husband insisted they seek counseling. The counselor helped them both make progress, but noticing Jessica was struggling the most he asked to meet individually (mentoring) with Jill. When they met she was very reluctant to offer much more than her usually blame and criticism of others, but did mention that, "kids nowadays sure seem to expect a lot. They don't realize that most people have very few things that they really enjoy in life."

James had not thought of Jessica consciously at all during his son's accident and rehabilitation, but he was carrying an overly ominous amount of guilt about it. James' counselor asked about his limp and he described the accident without thinking to mention Jessica. He described the impact the injury had on his ability to play at recess and sports and how he became such a big fan since he wasn't able to participate. It seemed like it became a blessing since that was what attracted him to his wife, but now it appeared to be the very thing that nearly killed their only son. The counselor helped Jack to see how he was drawing conclusions that were flawed and motivating him to undermined his relationship with his wife. From there he began to make progress and his marriage improved. It wasn't until James was describing a big argument he had with his wife over an upsetting exchange with their son, that he shouted, "I can't believe I let someone get hurt again!" The counselor asked James to identify the people he had hurt and Jessica's name came up. With more work James came to accept that the young boy playing with his friend was not responsible for the freak accident that broke his leg and rendered Jessica bedridden for rest of the school year.

Eventually, Jessica told her counselor that sewing was really the only thing that brought joy to her life. Initially, Jessica learned that following in her mother's footsteps may be natural and most comfortable, but they were not her only options. With encouragement, Jessica began to make some small changes and she did apologize to her husband and daughter for being so aloof and critical. However, when her daughter was over and joking loudly with her Dad, Jessica responded with another hatefully critical attack that seemed to set her back to where she started. Describing it to her counselor prompted more discussion about Jessica's past events and the accident shared with James was described (honesty/disclosure). She made it sound trivial until she mentioned that it rendered her bedridden for nearly 6 months. Before then Jessica described a little girl full of life that she soon turned into a much younger version of her mother.

James and Jessica with time began to see how they, as young children, concluded that a freak accident spawned misguided life lessons they both allowed to significantly impact their respective lives. When James saw physical movement and agility was involved, he naturally assumed he was not capable and would avoid them trying to avoid pain, disappointment and ridicule. When Jessica saw fun and playfulness, she saw imminent pain and isolation, thus enjoying entertainment with others was something she avoided with criticism and distain. James learned that physical movement and agility were triggers that unleashed a fearful wave of avoidance that kept him from many things, he was perfectly capable of doing. With his counselor's help (mentoring) he learned to pause when he felt that fear and would ask himself, "is there really anything to be afraid of here or am I or am I just re-feeling my emotions from past events?" The facts were that he was no longer on the school playground and no one was going to ridicule him if his leg limited his speed or agility. Eventually, he discovered that he was capable of walking great distances and playing golf and racquetball. Jessica's triggers were anything involving people having fun, so she avoided almost everyone including her own family in favor of sewing. Any fun opportunity rarely sounded interesting. Yet she learned that while laughing out loud and going out for entertainment was uncomfortable initially, it was certainly worth pushing through her reluctance to have more enjoyment and connection with others. Instead of saying no to invitations to have fun, at her counselor's suggestion (mentoring), she made a new habit of saying, "sure, it sounds like fun." Then if it turned out that it wasn't, she could always leave.

For a few years, it took conscious effort for both James and Jessica to not follow their default inclinations to avoid physical activity and fun with others, but eventually they began to naturally accept new opportunities that they routinely used to avoid. Eventually, the only time they would remember how they used to be gripped by fear and reluctance, was when they noticed it in others and would share their story (service) about overcoming the baggage of old unhelpful lessons learned. Eventually they both found themselves grateful for the new lessons they had learned.

APPENDIX

Character Observation Surveys

These surveys can help you identify the characteristics that are most likely undermining your relationships, your work performance, your ability to have fun and peace of mind. You will find four copies that you can replicate, copy or tear out of this book. Take the first one and rate yourself. If you have others you believe can give you unbiased feedback, give them each a copy, up to three people who observe you on a regular basis.

When you have your survey, plus one to three more from others, you can now create a combined version on your survey. For each characteristic on your version of the survey add a checkmark beside each asset or flaw that are circled on the other surveys. Some characteristics will have no checkmarks because these were not prominently noticed by a responder. When all responders agree on a characteristic that is marked then this is most likely an accurate assessment. When all responders agree on characteristics not marked, this is most likely accurate that neither characteristic is prominently displayed in your behavior. Make note of the assets and flaw characteristics that were identified the most. The list from the left side of the survey are the most prominent characteristics you have that get in your way of great relationships, great performance, great fun and peace of mind. The top characteristics from the right side of the surveys are the characteristics that are your strongest contributors towards great relationships, great performance, great fun and peace of mind. Anytime you are down and tending to think you do not have many things good in your life take a look at that list on the right.

The character traits listed on the left are highly likely to be the root causes behind many of the poor results you are getting as a result of your actions. Knowing the root causes you have is like knowing the problem and all you have to do is focus your journey to address them.

Character Observation Survey - Self

For the flaw/asset pairs that neither are much like you, skip them and circle the flaw or asset that are significantly like you.

Flaw		Asset
Aggressive	vs.	Gentle
Angry	vs.	Calm
Arrogant	vs.	Humble
Conceited	vs.	Modest
Controlling	vs.	Accepting
Critical	vs.	Encouraging
Dishonest	vs.	Honest
Envious	vs.	Content
Fearful, Fear	vs.	Courage, Faith
Forgetful	vs.	Responsible
Gluttonous	vs.	Moderate
Greedy	vs.	Charitable
Hateful	vs.	Loving
Hypersensitive	vs.	Tolerant
Inconsiderate	vs.	Thoughtful
Intolerant	vs.	Understanding
Jealous	vs.	Trusting
Judgmental	vs.	Understanding
Lazy	vs.	Industrious
Lust	vs.	Chastity
Mean	vs.	Kind
Perfectionism	vs.	Realistic
Pessimistic	vs.	Optimistic

Prejudiced	vs.	Open-minded
Pride	vs.	Humility
Rash	vs.	Self-controlled
Resentful	vs.	Forgiving
Self-centered	vs.	God-centered
Self-hating	vs.	Self-accepting
Selfish	vs.	Generous
Stubborn	vs.	Willing
Suspicious	vs.	Trusting
Unrealistic	vs.	Realistic
Unreliable	vs.	Trustworthy
Vindictive	vs.	Forgiving
Violent	vs.	Gentle
Vulgar	vs.	Polite
Wasteful	vs.	Thrifty

Character Observation Survey - 1

For the flaw/asset pairs that neither are much like your requester, skip them and circle the flaw or asset that are significantly like them.

Flaw		Asset
Aggressive	vs.	Gentle
Angry	vs.	Calm
Arrogant	vs.	Humble
Conceited	vs.	Modest
Controlling	vs.	Accepting
Critical	vs.	Encouraging
Dishonest	vs.	Honest
Envious	vs.	Content
Fearful, Fear	vs.	Courage, Faith
Forgetful	vs.	Responsible
Gluttonous	vs.	Moderate
Greedy	vs.	Charitable
Hateful	vs.	Loving
Hypersensitive	vs.	Tolerant
Inconsiderate	vs.	Thoughtful
Intolerant	vs.	Understanding
Jealous	vs.	Trusting
Judgmental	vs.	Understanding
Lazy	vs.	Industrious
Lust	vs.	Chastity
Mean	vs.	Kind
Perfectionism	vs.	Realistic

Pessimistic	vs.	Optimistic
Prejudiced	vs.	Open-minded
Pride	vs.	Humility
Rash	vs.	Self-controlled
Resentful	vs.	Forgiving
Self-centered	vs.	God-centered
Self-hating	vs.	Self-accepting
Selfish	vs.	Generous
Stubborn	vs.	Willing
Suspicious	vs.	Trusting
Unrealistic	vs.	Realistic
Unreliable	vs.	Trustworthy
Vindictive	vs.	Forgiving
Violent	vs.	Gentle
Vulgar	vs.	Polite
Wasteful	vs.	Thrifty

Character Observation Survey - 2

For the flaw/asset pairs that neither are much like your requester, skip them and circle the flaw or asset that are significantly like them.

Flaw		Asset
Aggressive	vs.	Gentle
Angry	vs.	Calm
Arrogant	vs.	Humble
Conceited	vs.	Modest
Controlling	vs.	Accepting
Critical	vs.	Encouraging
Dishonest	vs.	Honest
Envious	vs.	Content
Fearful, Fear	vs.	Courage, Faith
Forgetful	vs.	Responsible
Gluttonous	vs.	Moderate
Greedy	vs.	Charitable
Hateful	vs.	Loving
Hypersensitive	vs.	Tolerant
Inconsiderate	vs.	Thoughtful
Intolerant	vs.	Understanding
Jealous	vs.	Trusting
Judgmental	vs.	Understanding
Lazy	vs.	Industrious
Lust	vs.	Chastity
Mean	vs.	Kind
Perfectionism	vs.	Realistic

Pessimistic	vs.	Optimistic
Prejudiced	vs.	Open-minded
Pride	vs.	Humility
Rash	vs.	Self-controlled
Resentful	vs.	Forgiving
Self-centered	vs.	God-centered
Self-hating	vs.	Self-accepting
Selfish	vs.	Generous
Stubborn	vs.	Willing
Suspicious	vs.	Trusting
Unrealistic	vs.	Realistic
Unreliable	vs.	Trustworthy
Vindictive	vs.	Forgiving
Violent	vs.	Gentle
Vulgar	vs.	Polite
Wasteful	vs.	Thrifty

Character Observation Survey - 3

For the flaw/asset pairs that neither are much like your requester, skip them and circle the flaw or asset that are significantly like them.

Flaw		Asset
Aggressive	vs.	Gentle
Angry	vs.	Calm
Arrogant	vs.	Humble
Conceited	vs.	Modest
Controlling	vs.	Accepting
Critical	vs.	Encouraging
Dishonest	vs.	Honest
Envious	vs.	Content
Fearful, Fear	vs.	Courage, Faith
Forgetful	vs.	Responsible
Gluttonous	vs.	Moderate
Greedy	vs.	Charitable
Hateful	vs.	Loving
Hypersensitive	vs.	Tolerant
Inconsiderate	vs.	Thoughtful
Intolerant	vs.	Understanding
Jealous	vs.	Trusting
Judgmental	vs.	Understanding
Lazy	vs.	Industrious
Lust	vs.	Chastity
Mean	vs.	Kind
Perfectionism	vs.	Realistic

Pessimistic	vs.	Optimistic
Prejudiced	vs.	Open-minded
Pride	vs.	Humility
Rash	vs.	Self-controlled
Resentful	vs.	Forgiving
Self-centered	vs.	God-centered
Self-hating	vs.	Self-accepting
Selfish	vs.	Generous
Stubborn	vs.	Willing
Suspicious	vs.	Trusting
Unrealistic	vs.	Realistic
Unreliable	vs.	Trustworthy
Vindictive	vs.	Forgiving
Violent	vs.	Gentle
Vulgar	vs.	Polite
Wasteful	vs.	Thrifty

ABOUT THE AUTHOR

Mark Nixon

Mark Nixon has spent nearly 50 years un-
packing the things he had in an unhelpful
perspective. He is currently a Christian
Life Coach with His Story Coaching and
Counseling. Previously, Mark worked for
IBM and the Palmer Drug Abuse Program.
Mark and his wife Carla have four adult
children and four grandchildren.